PSYCHEDELICS

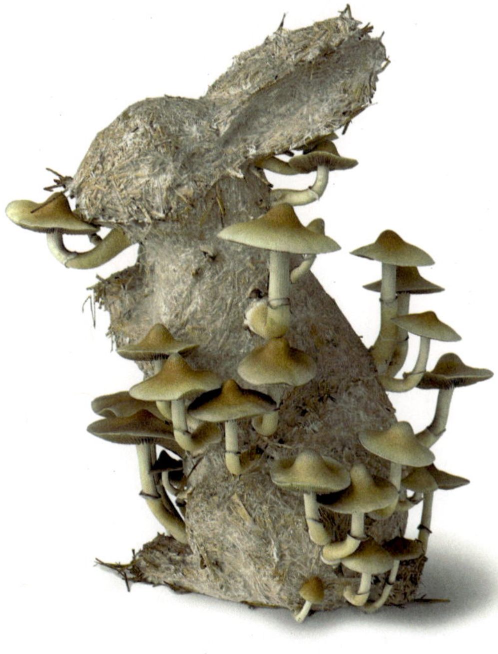

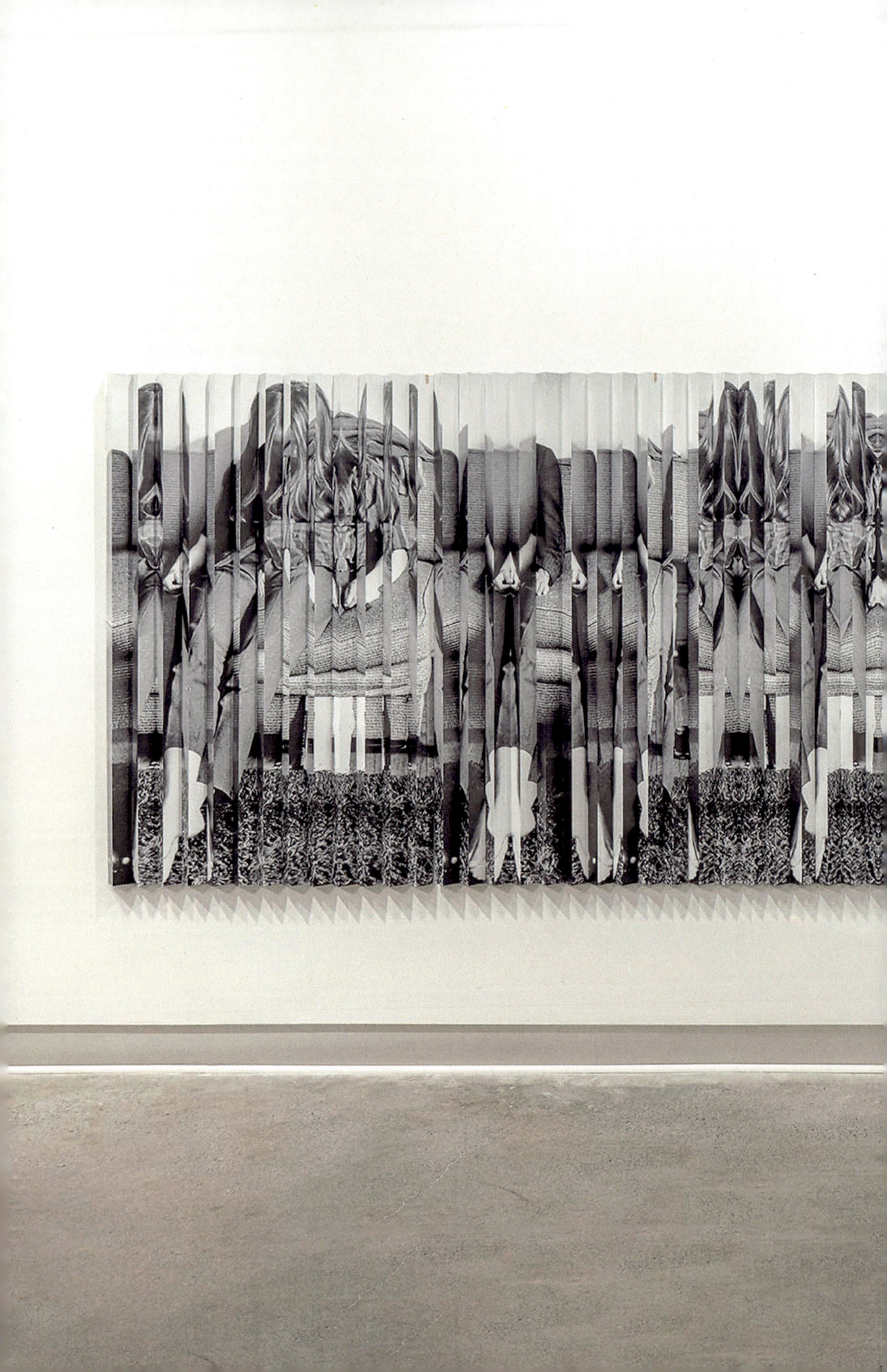

PSYCHEDELICS

culture. crime. cure.

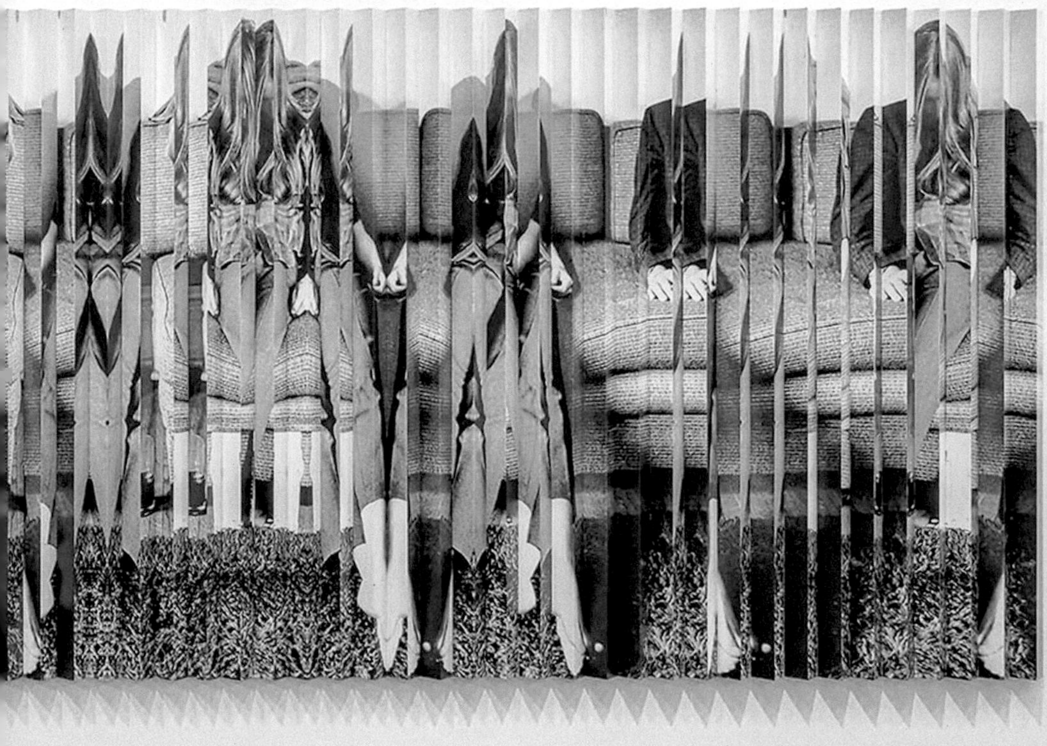

ROM

Edited by **Justin Jennings** and **Colin J. Fleming**

Contents

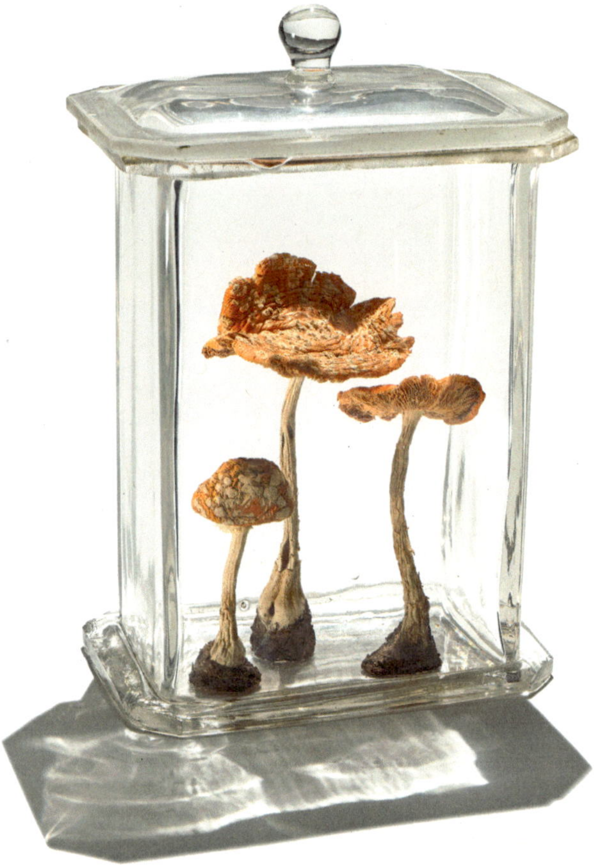

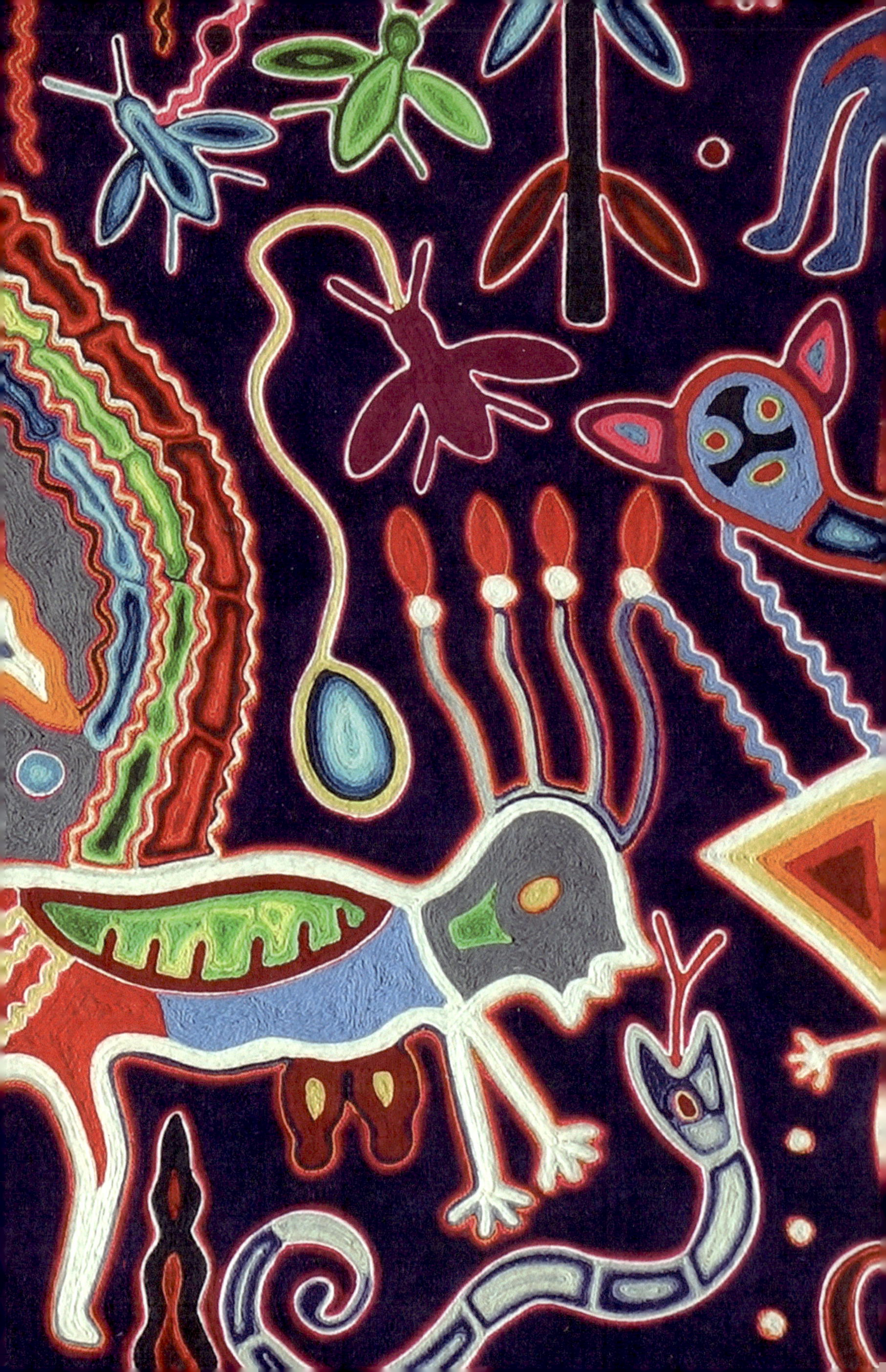

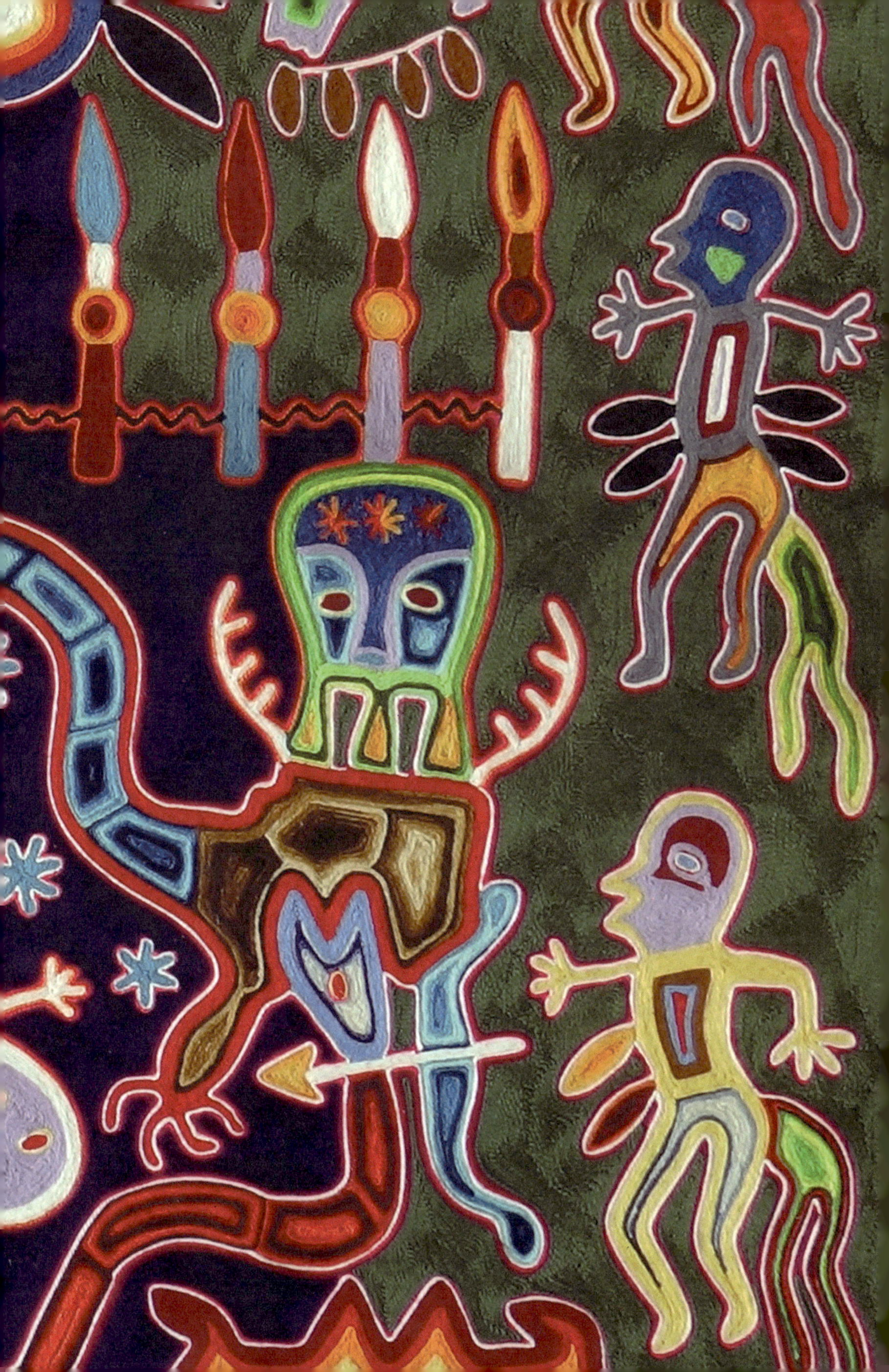

Foreword

While many of the objects in the collections at ROM are thousands, even millions of years old, the galleries and exhibitions speak not just to prehistoric ages and ancient civilizations, but to the present moment.

That is especially true of *Psychedelics*, an exhibition and book that arrive amid a resurgence of scientific and cultural interest in these powerful drugs. While the topic of psychedelics is undeniably of-the-moment, it is also complex, touching on everything from Indigenous rights and conservation efforts to brain science and mental health.

Fortunately, ROM is well-suited to address those complexities. Unlike most museums and galleries, the collections and expertise at ROM span art, culture, and nature, which allowed the exhibition team and the book's authors to take a holistic approach to the subject. The exhibition benefits from the contributions of the many community, Indigenous, and medical advisors who shared their experiences and knowledge with the exhibition team. Dr. Justin Jennings, the exhibition's curator and book's co-editor, leveraged his anthropological knowledge of the Americas to help us understand long-standing psychedelic practices around the world—and what they can teach us here. While fellow co-editor and ROM communications specialist, Colin Fleming, drew on his journalism expertise to map out the most pressing concerns around psychedelics today.

In cases where ROM did not have inhouse expertise for this complex topic, the editors sought it out, inviting experts to contribute essays on everything from psychedelic therapy to Canadian history.

The result of this collaboration is a timely, thought-provoking book full of big ideas—all grounded in research and informed by Indigenous ways of knowing. It is also an expression of what ROM does best: bringing together great minds from diverse fields to help make sense of our complex, ever-changing world.

Jennifer Wild
Interim Co-Director & CEO, ROM

Acknowledgements

Few institutions of ROM's size and stature would ever greenlight an exhibition on psychedelics. So first, we want to thank all the leaders at ROM who understood the importance of the exhibition and this book and believed in our vision for them: Jennifer Wild, Interim Co-Director & CEO and Deputy Director, Engagement; Josh Basseches, former Director & CEO; Valerie Huaco, Deputy Director, Collections & Research and Chief Innovation Officer; Chen Shen, Co-Chief Curator, Art & Culture; David Evans, Co-Chief Curator, Natural History; Sally Tindal, Chief Marketing & Communications Officer; Swarupa Anila, former Senior Vice President, Exhibition & Gallery Development; Maria Piacente, Chief, Exhibition & Gallery Planning; and Tamara Onyschuk, Assistant Vice President, Exhibition & Gallery Planning.

We are also indebted to the many cultural and scientific advisors who have steered the development of the exhibition and this catalogue, including our coauthors—Kelly Boutsalis, Alexandria Coles, Manoj Doss, Erika Dyck, and Ishrat Husain—most of whom have been working with us for years, as well as everyone whose name hasn't yet appeared in these pages: Kelly Daniels, former President of the Native American Church; Dr. Leah Mayo, Parker Psychedelic Research Chair, University of Calgary; Paul Armand Mombey Indaki, President, Néo-Bwiti; Francisco Carrillo Zamora, Huichol Elder; and all the folks at MAPS Canada.

We would also like to thank our exhibition colleagues Juline Chevalier, Assistant Vice President, Interpretation, and Brannavy Jeyasundaram, Interpretive Planner. Drawing on experts across vastly different fields, these two synthesized dizzyingly dense brain science, complex histories, and diverse voices into a compelling exhibition.

Finally, we would like to thank ROM's indefatigable publishing team: Tara Winterhalt, Senior Graphic Designer; Monika Tragarz, Communications Coordinator; and Sheeza Sarfraz, Assistant Vice President, Publishing & Editorial Content, for working with us on this complex, years-long process and turning our manuscript into a beautiful artwork. This book would not exist without them.

Justin Jennings and Colin J. Fleming

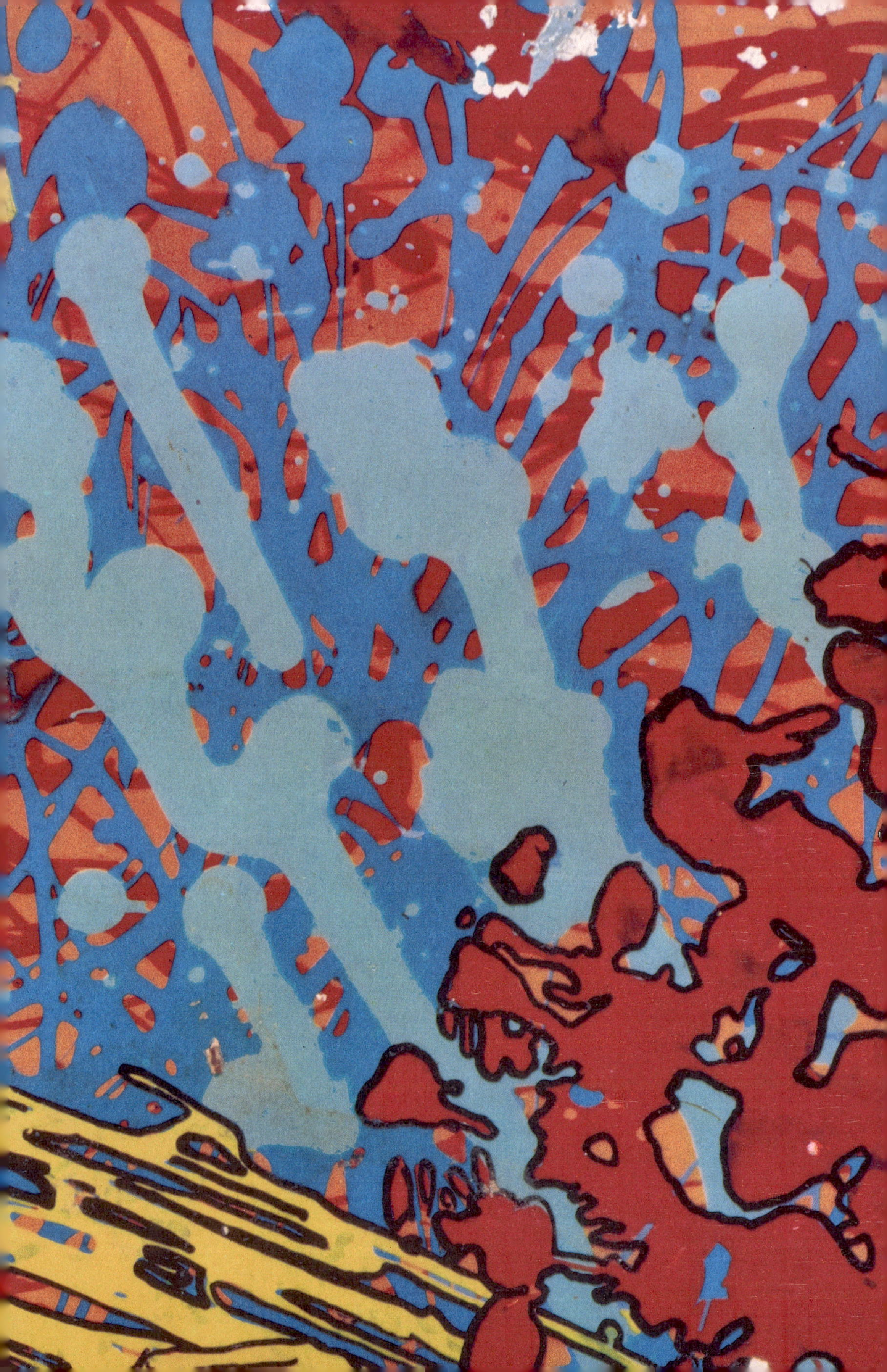

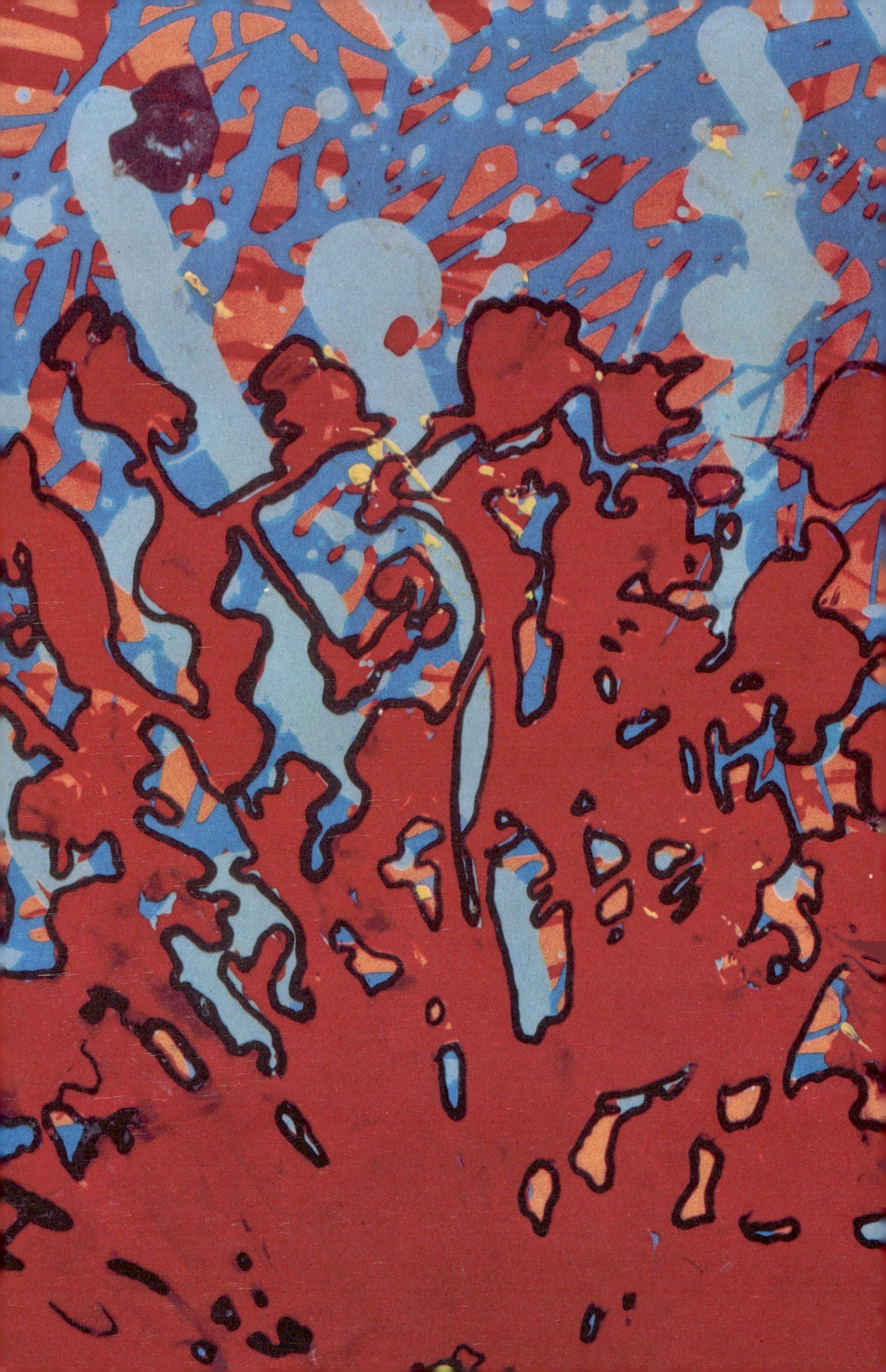

Introduction

COLIN J. FLEMING
JUSTIN JENNINGS

AT THE APEX OF THE PSYCHEDELIC RENAISSANCE in 2022, the hype was inescapable. Investors were pouring billions of dollars into psychedelic drug development. Talk show hosts were extolling the virtues of psychedelic-assisted therapy. Universities from Berkeley to Calgary were launching dedicated psychedelic research centres. And dispensaries with names like Shroomyz and Fun Guyz were popping up across North America like, well, mushrooms. To anyone paying even an iota of attention, the message was clear: after decades of prohibition, these once-taboo, mind-altering drugs were having their moment.

It didn't take long for the pendulum to swing back. Some psychedelic researchers, unnerved by their colleagues' near-religious zeal, urged caution.[1] Publicly traded companies, like Toronto-based Field Trip Health & Wellness, collapsed.[2] The U.S. Food and Drug Administration rejected the use of MDMA-assisted therapy for PTSD.[3] Matthew Perry, the actor famous for playing Chandler on *Friends*, died of a ketamine overdose after decades of struggling with addiction.[4] And the erratic behaviour of Elon Musk, the billionaire, psychedelics advocate, and erstwhile right-hand man to Donald Trump, was linked to the same drug.[5]

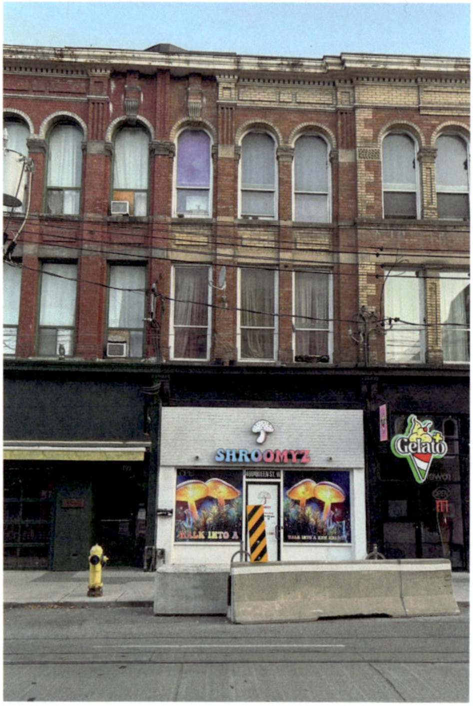

Figure 1
Shroomyz, one of many magic mushroom dispensaries in Toronto, on Queen Street West in 2023.

Photo: Colin J. Fleming.

Of course, Musk wasn't the only one in Trump's orbit extolling the virtues of psychedelics. "FDA's war on public health is about to end," Robert F. Kennedy Jr. posted on X days before the 2024 presidential election. "This includes its aggressive suppression of psychedelics, peptides, stem cells, raw milk ... and anything else that advances human health and can't be patented by Pharma."[6]

Long beloved by hippies and reviled by the right, psychedelics have now become a cause célèbre for many conservatives. While RFK Jr.'s brand of conspiracy-fuelled wellness is one reason, it's not the only one. Right-wing billionaire Peter Thiel, has poured millions into the psychedelic drug development company atai Life Sciences, for example.[7] Plus, many conservative politicians now support psychedelic therapy as a means of treating veterans' PTSD.

The right-wing push to fast-track psychedelics culminated on April 18, 2026, just days before this book went to press, when President Trump signed an executive order "seeking to hasten research into the therapeutic benefits of LSD, Ecstasy, psilocybin, and other mind-altering drugs by ordering federal agencies to ease restrictions that have long limited the ability of scientists to study them." The executive order also included "$50 million for state-level research into ibogaine"–a radical reversal on drug policy from the party of Richard Nixon.[8]

While this chaos around psychedelics may be disorienting, it's not unprecedented. Some psychedelic scientists have pointed to the Gartner Hype Cycle (see below), arguing that after plummeting from the "Peak of Inflated Expectations"—the apex of the psychedelic renaissance—we can now carefully ascend the "Slope of Enlightenment" until we reach the "Plateau of Productivity."[9] More simply, we are now primed for a more mature, thoughtful conversation about the role of psychedelics in society.

In that spirit, it needs to be said that there is substance behind the hype. Most psychedelics are non-toxic and non-addictive[10] and, in the right context, can offer therapeutic benefits. Plus, they have provided broad societal benefits in other cultures for millennia. Yet there are also considerable reasons for caution. Certain psychedelics can be lethal at high doses. Then, there's the risk of a psychotic break, which, while rare, is a particular concern for those with a family history of schizophrenia. Finally, very few studies on the long-term risks of regular psychedelic use exist, and scientists have only a partial understanding of how psychedelics work on the brain.[11]

As psychedelics move into mainstream society, this book can serve as a primer on the history, science, and cross-cultural uses of these compounds. Looming concerns must be addressed, ranging from the role of corporate interests in health care to public safety, conservation threats, and the appropriation of Indigenous knowledge. To chart a path forward, we need to understand where we are today.

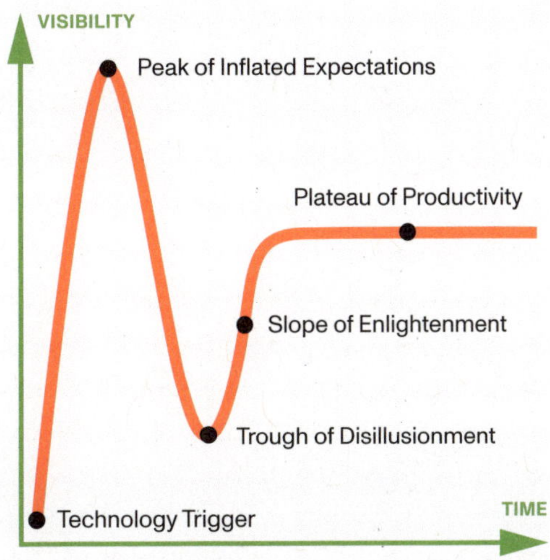

Figure 2
The Gartner Hype Cycle.
Many experts in the field argue that, after traversing the "Peak of Inflated Expectations" and "Trough of Disillusionment," we can now take a more mature and measured approach to integrating psychedelics into society.
Photo: © ROM.

Evolving Psychedelics

Translated as "mind manifesting" in Greek, psychedelics are a class of psychoactive substances that produce changes in perception, mood, and cognition.[12] The so-called classical psychedelics (LSD, dimethyltryptamine [DMT], mescaline, and psilocybin) affect serotonin 5-HT_{2A} receptors in the brain and central nervous system.[13] At moderate doses, psychedelics often heighten the senses–colours become more vibrant, sound and touch more intense–and higher doses can cause hallucinations.

These drugs are referred to by many terms. "Psychedelics" is a new word, coined in Canada in 1957.[14] In 1978, Albert Hofmann and Richard Evans Schultes famously named their ethnobotanical encyclopaedia on these substances "Plants of the Gods,"[15] an apt description for compounds that can launch you into the realm of the divine, sometimes in just minutes. Other cultures through the millennia have given other names like *vilca*,[16] teonanacatl,[17] and *iboga*[18] to their many mind-altering plants, fungi, and, to a lesser extent, animals. It is no surprise that many people, from ageing hippies to contemporary shamans, consider psychedelics a gift from the gods. That very well may be true. But the psychedelics found in nature did not emerge to serve human desires. They are a product of evolution.

Evolution, put simply, is descent with modification.[19] Every living organism on Earth today shares a common ancestor. Differences arise primarily through changes in the information encoded in genes. Over the course of millions of years, organisms have diversified through four basic mechanisms: mutation, migration, genetic drift, and natural selection. These processes change a population's genetic frequencies, producing birds, lizards, or lichen with slightly different properties. Mutation and migration introduce new genetic possibilities, while genetic drift and natural selection determine the changes in genetic frequencies over time.

Genetic drift and natural selection operate differently. Genetic drift is related to the vagaries of chance–the beetles in a population with smaller antennas just happen to have more offspring–and has the strongest impact in smaller populations. Natural selection, in contrast, is about an organism's "fit" within a particular environment. A beetle that is more difficult for a predator to see in the jungle will tend to have more offspring, over time increasing the frequency of the genes associated with this trait in a population.

Psychoactive compounds are products of evolutionary processes that began long before humans. As Noah Whiteman, an evolutionary biology and genetics professor at the University of California, Berkeley, told the *Microdose*, "Plants did not evolve with us in mind; they evolved to kill animals and pathogens that are attacking plants, not to help us. The fact that they do is just luck."[20] In other words,

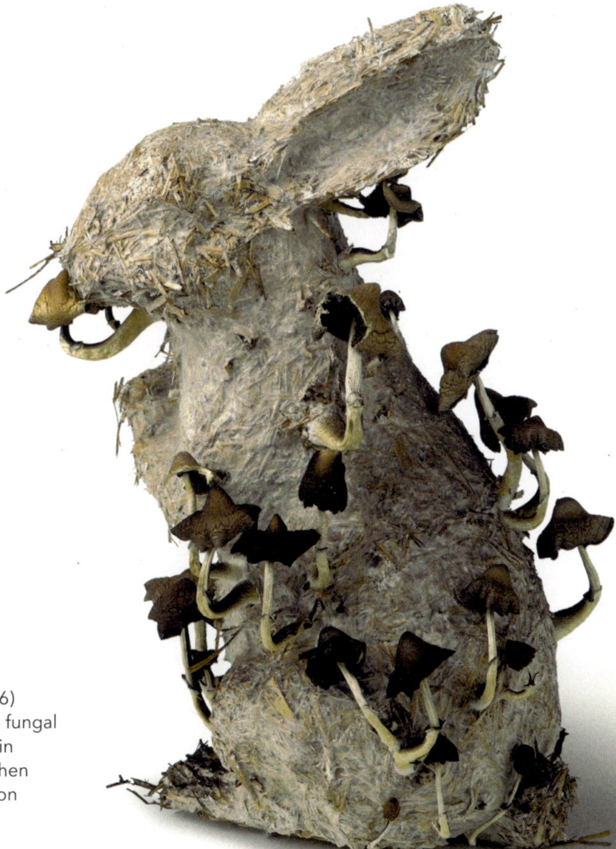

Figure 3
Xiaojing Yan's *Magic Rabbit* (2026) was made by filling a mould with fungal food, inoculating it with psilocybin (magic mushroom) spores, and then letting it grow—a true collaboration between the artist and fungi.

Photo: Courtesy of the artist.

compounds like psilocybin—the magic in magic mushrooms—probably evolved as insecticides.

Recent research backs this up. After studying psilocybin-producing mushrooms at the genetic level, researchers at Ohio State University theorized that the genes for psilocybin production spread to many species of mushrooms because the compound blunts the appetites of insects, including flies.[21] The evolutionary pathways for other psychedelics like mescaline and DMT are different, each a product of adaption to the nuances of their particular ecosystems.

Sacred Plants, LSD, and a War on Drugs

When humans spread out of Africa some 300,000 years ago, they encountered psychoactive compounds in Europe, Asia, Oceania, and eventually the Americas. Our species may have been aware of how the consumption of certain plants, fungi, and animals could instill other states of consciousness; some scholars speculate that psychedelic experiences were foundational to human cognition.[22] As humans settled down into various places, these compounds were sometimes integrated into cultural practices that continue to this day.

In many cases, psychoactive compounds are seen as gifts, enabling practitioners to see further, deeper, or in different ways.[23] The type of compound and its dose shape one's experiences, as do one's mindset and surroundings. A Tonkawa peyote ceremony may include a solitary contemplation of the sunrise,[24] while those who practise the Santo Daime religion consume ayahuasca together as a Eucharistic sacrament in a chapel.[25] The altered states achieved have as much to do with context as they do with chemistry.

Peyote and ayahuasca (a brew typically made from psychoactive *Banisteriopsis caapi* vines and *Psychotria viridis* leaves) have been used for millennia, but other psychedelics were born in a lab. In the 1930s, Swiss chemist Albert Hofmann was studying ergot, a fungus that can grow on rye (and other grains) and cause convulsions, hallucinations, gangrene, and even death. He synthesized one of ergot's active compounds and created lysergic acid diethylamide, or LSD. Hofmann first took the drug by accident in 1943, likely absorbed through his fingertips as he worked. The result was "an uninterrupted stream of fantastic pictures, extraordinary shapes with intense, kaleidoscopic play of colors."[26] For the remainder of the decade, Hofmann worked with LSD, gradually sending batches of the compound to scientists working in different parts of the world.

Psilocybin was shared with North American audiences by Western scientists who encountered the compound thanks to Indigenous peoples. In 1953, amateur mycologists Gordon Wasson and Valentina Pavlovna Wasson began taking yearly trips to Mexico in search of the hallucinogenic mushroom species described in 16th-century accounts by Spanish colonizers. In Huautla de Jiménez, they met Maria Sabina, a Mazatec Knowledge Keeper, who gave them psilocybin mushrooms to consume during a healing ceremony in 1955. Two years later in *Life Magazine*, Gordon Wasson published "Seeking the Magic Mushroom," a feature-length article about "strange and hitherto unstudied mushrooms with vision-giving powers."[27] In doing so, he revealed Mazatec sacred knowledge to the magazine's 5.7 million readers, catapulting psychedelics into the popular consciousness.[28]

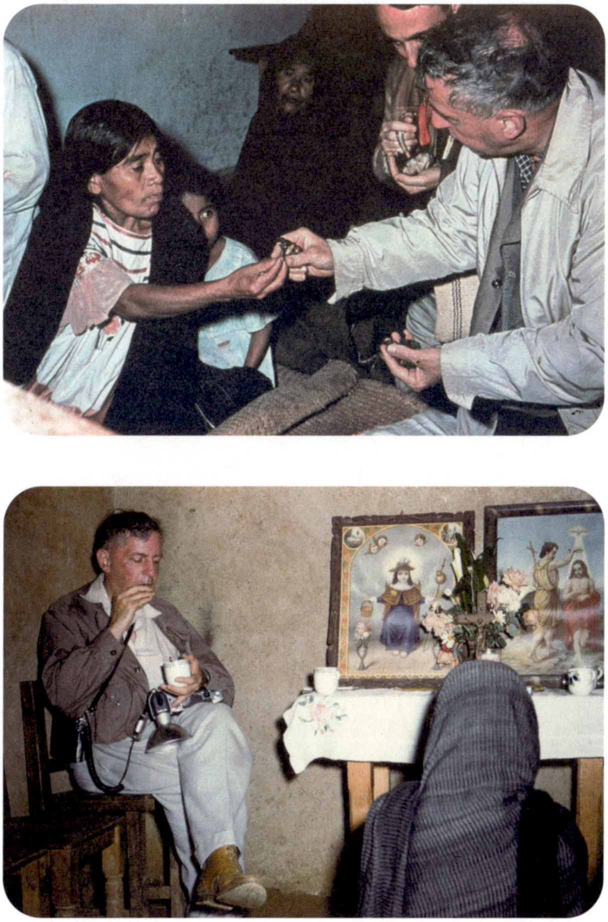

Figure 4
R. Gordon Wasson receiving and then ingesting *Psilocybe mexicana*, a psychedelic mushroom, from the Mazatec healer Maria Sabina in Huautla de Jiménez, Mexico, in 1955.

Photos: Courtesy of the Harvard Botanical Libraries and with permission of the Mary X. Britten and the R. G. Wasson estate.

The work of Hofmann and the Wassons was part of a broader engagement with psychedelics by North American and European scientists. As Michael Pollan noted in his book *How to Change Your Mind*, "For most of the 1950s and early 1960s, many in the psychiatric establishments regarded LSD and psilocybin as miracle drugs."[29] But by the 1960s, psychedelics could no longer be contained in the lab. Between dangerous CIA-funded psychedelic experiments and Timothy Leary's freewheeling antics, these compounds were loosed upon society like an agent of chaos, fuelling the nascent hippie movement and a powerful anti-psychedelic backlash.[30]

This chaos spilled over into Indigenous communities like Huautla de Jiménez. Gordon Wasson's popular writings turned Sabina into a celebrity, with pilgrims flocking to the town in the 1960s. Unwanted police attention followed—Sabina was briefly arrested as a drug dealer—and she was ostracized by many in the Mazatec community. People came to Huautla de Jiménez and other communities not to learn local practices but in search of Leary's promised transcendence.[31]

Thus, what began as a promising story ended in the rise of Richard Nixon—and the fall of psychedelic research, which came to a dead stop after Nixon signed the Controlled Substances Act in 1970.[32] Psychedelics were put on the same lists as opiates and cocaine, and billions of dollars were spent to eradicate their use. A war on drugs had begun that would criminalize psychedelic use into the present day.[33]

The Conversation

Fifty years ago, we made many mistakes. There were too few long-term studies and not enough guardrails to keep people safe on psychedelic trips. The drugs were touted as a quick-fix panacea, and associated Indigenous practices were either stolen or ignored. The results were disastrous.

Once again, we find ourselves at a critical juncture in history, with psychedelics being touted by some as a powerful tool for mental health and well-being. This time, we need to get it right. Exactly how we do that is the subject of heated debate everywhere from the pages of the *New York Times* to the Canadian House of Commons. While no clear consensus has emerged, almost everyone can agree that figuring out what role psychedelics play in our society—if any—begins with informed conversation.

Psychedelics is our contribution to this conversation.

In the first chapter, the "Past and Present Use of Psychedelics from around the World," Dr. Justin Jennings explores some of the ways in which psychedelics have been—and continue to be—used in different spiritual traditions around the world. These traditions demonstrate how psychedelics can be employed to address societal concerns.

Next, Dr. Erika Dyck, an expert on the history of medicine and a professor at the University of Saskatchewan, explores the origins of psychedelics in the West. Moving from the deserts of northern Mexico to the Canadian prairies, Dyck explains how drugs like mescaline and LSD sparked a new wave of psychiatric research.

In the third chapter, Dr. Manoj Doss, a cognitive neuropsychopharmacologist at the University of Texas at Austin, takes us into the human brain. He explains how psychedelics work at the level of neurons and guides us through the models of how they stimulate changes across the brain.

Dr. Ishrat Husain, the Department Head of the Centre for Mental Health, University Health Network, and Alexandria Coles, the Manager of Clinical Research at University Health Network, take the next step in their essay surveying the latest research on psychedelic therapy, which has the potential to treat everything from depression to PTSD.

Our fifth chapter, by Kelly Boutsalis, a Mohawk journalist from the Six Nations of the Grand River reserve, interrogates many of the foundational principles of the so-called psychedelic renaissance–including the word "psychedelic" itself.

The sixth and final chapter, by Colin Fleming, wrestles with the fundamental question at the heart of this book: How do we get psychedelics right this time?

The debate around these drugs doesn't lend itself to easy answers. Our contemporary psychedelic landscape is fraught with complex questions, from the harm caused by appropriating Indigenous traditions to the rise of private, high-priced psychedelic therapy clinics. But we don't have to repeat the mistakes of the past. We can create a better future, one informed by science, history, and Indigenous ways of knowing. That future begins now.

1 Yaden, D. B., Potash, J. B., & Griffiths, R. R. (2022). Preparing for the bursting of the psychedelic hype bubble. *JAMA Psychiatry, 79*(10), 943–944. https://doi.org/10.1001/jamapsychiatry.2022.2546.

2 Canadian Press. (2023, March 22). Field Trip Health & Wellness enters creditor protection, lays off staff. *Toronto Star*. https://www.thestar.com/business/field-trip-health-wellness-enters-creditor-protection-lays-off-staff/article_5e3c7afc-8fff-59c7-8ac2-dc0bd15d1ce9.html.

3 Jacobs, A. (2024, August 9). FDA declines to approve MDMA therapy, seeking more study. *The New York Times*. https://www.nytimes.com/2024/08/09/health/fda-mdma-ptsd-delay.html.

4 Stevens, M., & Taylor, D. B. (2023, December 15). Matthew Perry died of "acute effects of ketamine," autopsy says. *The New York Times*. https://www.nytimes.com/2023/12/15/arts/matthew-perry-cause-death-friends.html.

5 Grind, K., & Twohey, M. (2025, May 30). Elon Musk juggled drugs and family drama on Trump's campaign trail. *The New York Times*. https://www.nytimes.com/2025/05/30/us/elon-musk-drugs-children-trump.html.

6 Kennedy Jr., Robert F. [@RobertKennedyJr]. (2024, October 25). *FDA's war on public health is about to end. This includes its aggressive suppression of psychedelics, peptides, stem cells, raw milk, hyperbaric therapies...* [Post.] X. https://x.com/RobertKennedyJr/status/1849925311586238737.

7 Shead, S. (2020, November 23). *Peter Thiel backs Berlin start-up making psychedelics in $125 million round*. CNBC. https://www.cnbc.com/2020/11/23/peter-thiel-backs-psychedelics-startup-atai.html.

8 Jacobs, Andrew, and Noah Daly. (2026, April 18). Trump signs executive order to loosen restrictions on psychedelic drugs. *New York Times*. https://www.nytimes.com/2026/04/17/health/trump-psychedelics-ibogaine.html.

9 Yaden et al. Preparing for the bursting.

10 UC Berkeley Center for the Science of Psychedelics. (n.d.). *Substances*. https://psychedelics.berkeley.edu/substances/.

11 For more information about the potential benefits and risks of psychedelic use, please consult the Centre for Addiction and Mental Health's Frequently Asked Questions: https://www.camh.ca/en/camh-news-and-stories/psychedelics-faqs. You can also find information at the website for UC Berkeley's Center for the Science of Psychedelics: https://psychedelics.berkeley.edu.

12 UC Berkeley Center for the Science of Psychedelics. *Substances*.

13 UC Berkeley Center for the Science of Psychedelics. *Substances*.

14 Martin, D. (2004, February 22). Humphry Osmond, 86, who sought medicinal value in psychedelic drugs, dies. *The New York Times*. https://www.nytimes.com/2004/02/22/us/humphry-osmond-86-who-sought-medicinal-value-in-psychedelic-drugs-dies.html.

15 Schultes, R. E., & Hofmann, A. (2001). *Plants of the gods*. Healing Arts Press. (Original work published 1978)

16 Torres, C. M., & Repke, D. B. (2012). *Anadenanthera: Visionary plant of ancient South America*. Routledge. https://doi.org/10.4324/9781315864594.

17 Reko, B. P. (1940). Teonanacatl, the narcotic mushroom. *American Anthropologist, 42*(2), 368–369. https://doi.org/10.1525/aa.1940.42.2.02a00310.

18 Nyongo Ndoua, P. D., & Vaghar, K. (2018). Bwiti, iboga, trance and healing in Gabon. *Mental Health, Religion & Culture*, 21(8), 755–762. https://doi.org/10.1080/13674676.2018.1504012.

19 For the basics of evolution, see Futuyma, D. J., & Kirkpatrick, M. (2003). *Evolution* (5th ed.). Oxford University Press.

20 Hu, J. C. (2023, January 17). Why do plants and fungi produce psychedelics? 5 questions for evolutionary biology and genetics professor Noah Whiteman. *The Microdose*. https://themicrodose.substack.com/p/why-do-plants-and-fungi-produce-psychedelics.

21 Ohio State News. (2018, February 27). *Why are some mushrooms "magic?"* Ohio State News. https://news.osu.edu/why-are-some-mushrooms-magic/.

22 Rodríguez Arce, J. M., & Winkelman, M. J. (2021). Psychedelics, sociality, and human evolution. *Frontiers in Psychology, 12*, Article 729425. https://doi.org/10.3389/fpsyg.2021.729425.

23 Labate, B. C., & Cavnar, C. (2018). *Plant medicines, healing and psychedelic science: Cultural perspectives*. Springer International Publishing AG. https://doi.org/10.1007/978-3-319-76720-8; and Fitzpatrick, S. M. (Ed.). (2018). *Ancient psychoactive substances*. University Press of Florida.

24 Opler, M. E. (1939). A description of a Tonkawa peyote meeting held in 1902. *American Anthropologist, 41*(3), 433–439. https://doi.org/10.1525/aa.1939.41.3.02a00060.

25 Barnard, G. W. (2022). *Liquid light: Ayahuasca spirituality and the Santo Daime tradition*. Columbia University Press. https://doi.org/10.7312/barn18660.

26 Long, T. (2007, April 16). April 16, 1943: Setting the stage for the world's first acid trip. *Wired*. https://www.wired.com/2007/04/dayintech-0416-2/.

27 Wasson, R. G. (1957, May). Seeking the magic mushroom. *Life Magazine*.

28 Pollan, M. (2019). How to change your mind. Penguin.

29 Pollan. *How to change your mind*.

30 Cottrell, R. C. (2015). *Sex, drugs, and rock "n" roll: The rise of America's 1960s counterculture*. Rowman & Littlefield; and Minutaglio, B., & Davis, S. L. (2018). *The most dangerous man in America: Timothy Leary, Richard Nixon and the hunt for the fugitive king of LSD*. Twelve.

31 González Rubio, E., and Sabina, M. (2001). *La magia de los curanderos mazatecos: despues de María Sabina*. Publicaciones Cruz O., S. A.

32 Pollan, M. (2015, February 2). The trip treatment. *The New Yorker*. https://www.newyorker.com/magazine/2015/02/09/trip-treatment.

33 Farber, D. R. (2021). *The war on drugs: A history*. New York University Press.

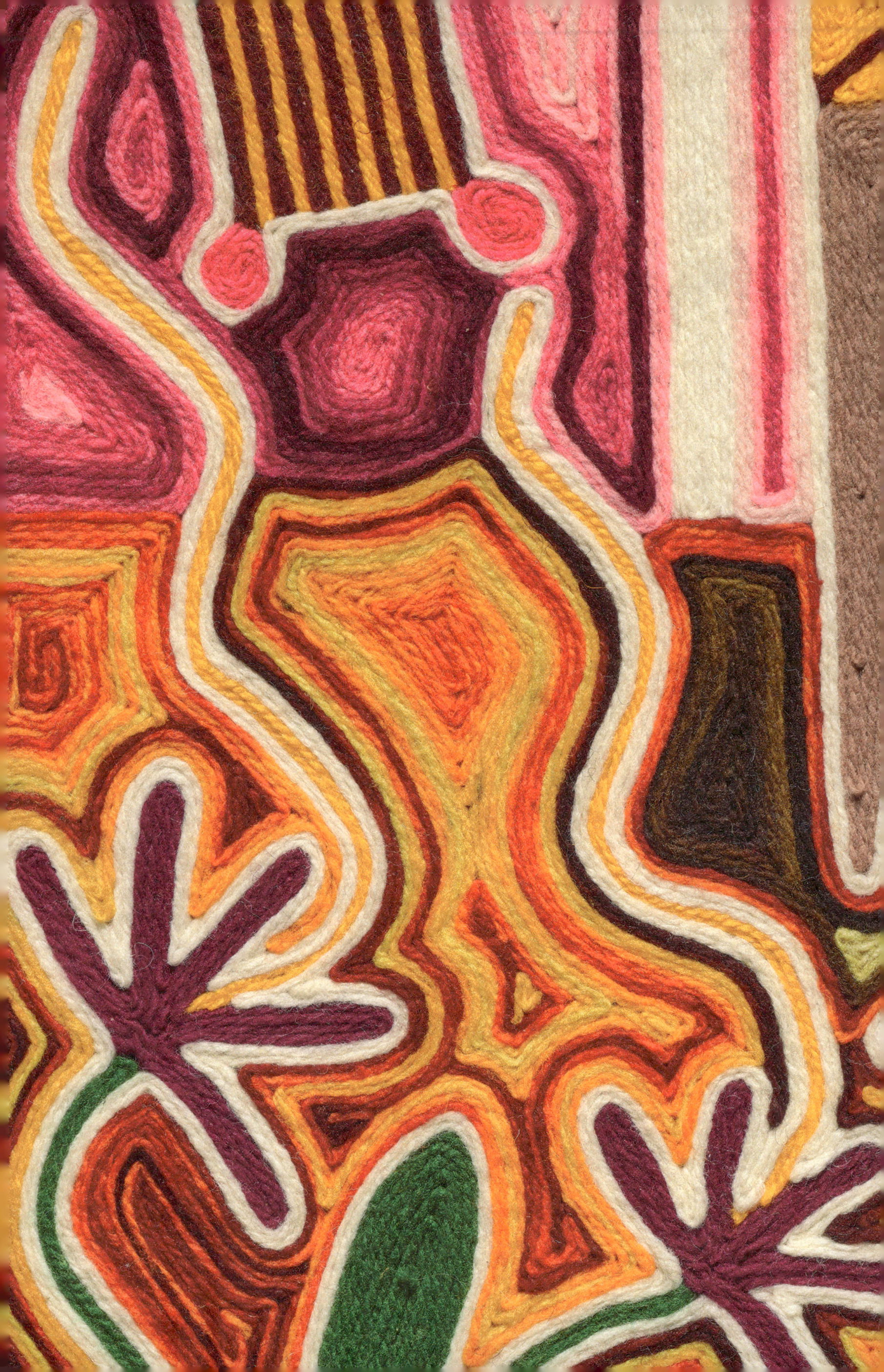

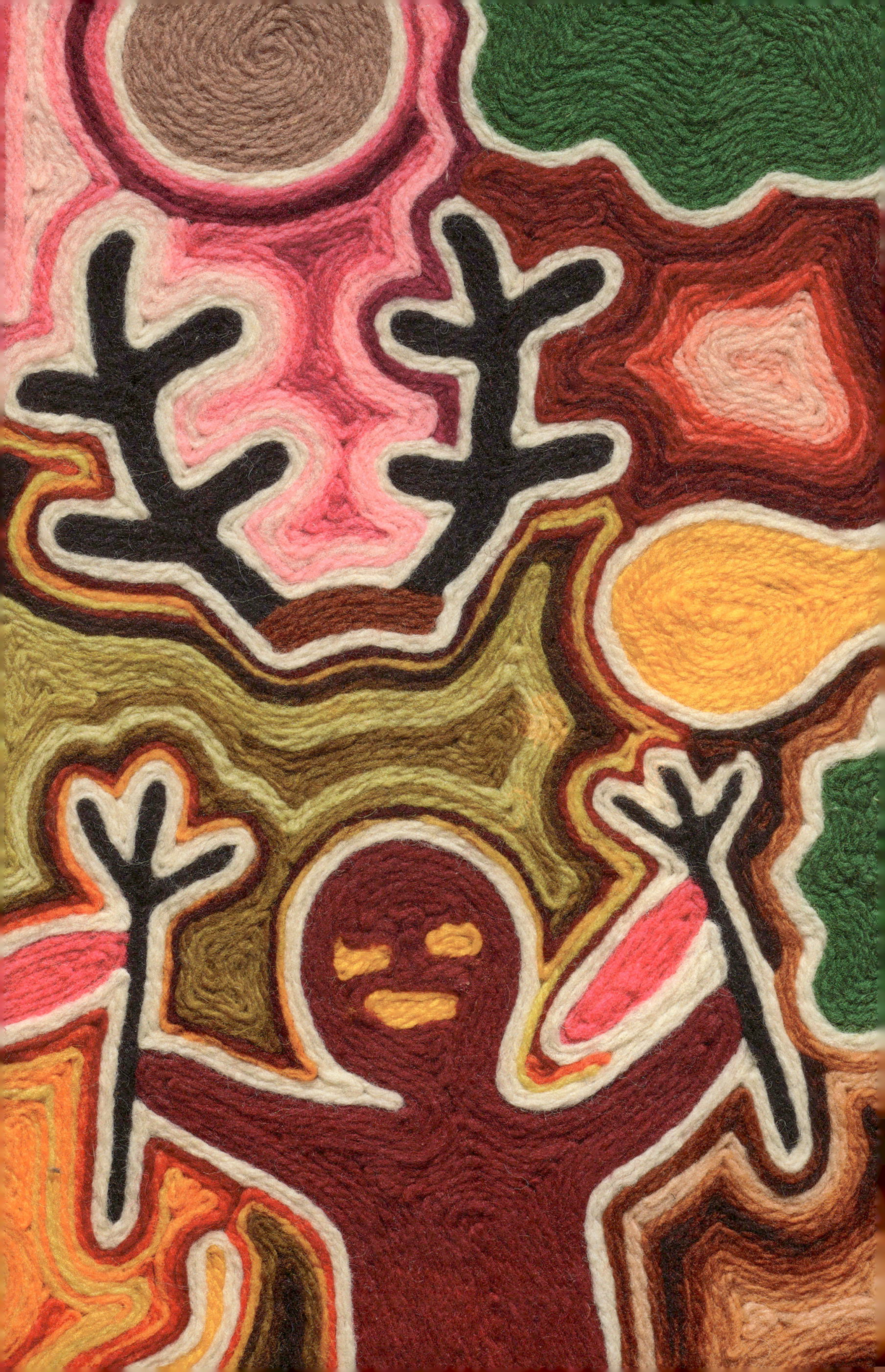

1

Past and Present Use of Psychedelics from around the World

JUSTIN JENNINGS

IN 2023, A PSYCHEDELICS STORY flashed across the Internet. Archaeologists digging in a Mediterranean island cave had chemically tested locks of human hair left by mourners 3,000 years earlier. The hair contained highly psychoactive tropane alkaloids that came from consuming such plants as thornapple (*Datura stramonium*) and henbane (*Hyoscyamus albus)*. The archaeologists suggested that this was the hair of a shaman, a highly trained practitioner who had harnessed the power of the plants to reach an altered state of consciousness.[1]

The 2023 findings were unsurprising to many scholars. There are thousands of psychoactive plants and fungi, with hundreds regularly consumed by humans (see the introduction).[2] We have centuries-old snuff tablets, powders, and depictions of human-animal transformation from around the world (Figure 1),[3] as well as vibrant contemporary traditions that incorporate psychedelic use.[4] Some psychedelic use was thus the norm rather than the exception in many societies—a bigger surprise might have been if the locks in the cave contained *no* psychoactive tropane alkaloids.

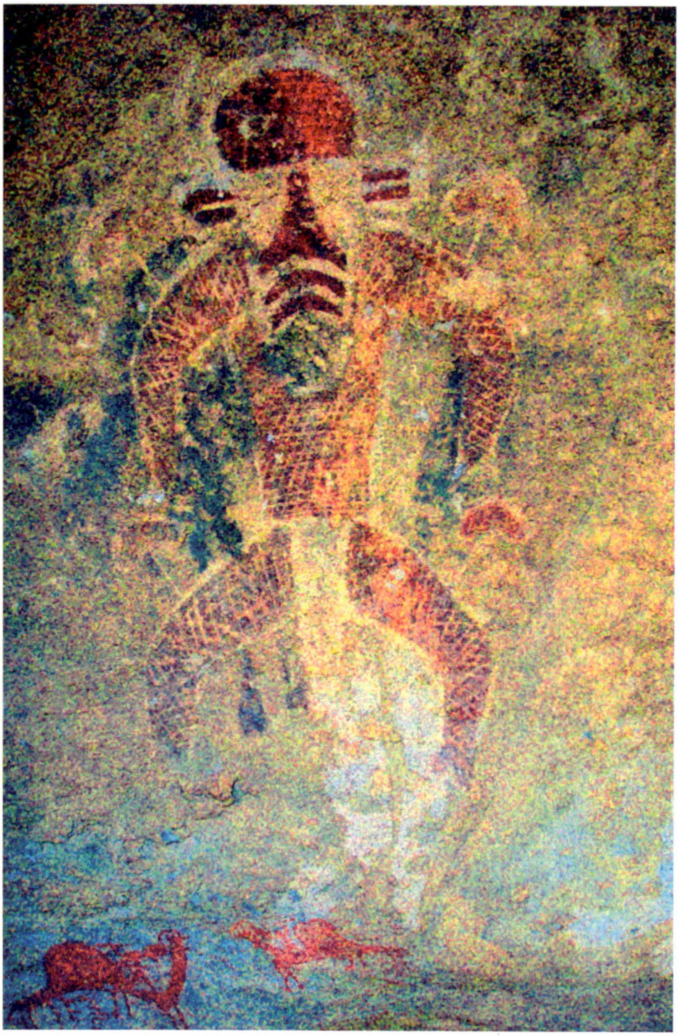

Figure 1
A pictograph from the site of Aouarnhat in the Tassili n'Ajjer plateau in Algeria and that may date to as early as 6000 BCE. The drawing is an example of a figure sometimes called the "bee-faced mushroom shaman," who holds what may be mushrooms in its hands, with mushrooms sometimes sprouting from the body. For some scholars, the figure represents an early depiction of an altered state of consciousness.

Photo: Courtesy of Jitka Soukopova, the image is processed through the DStretch program to make the pictograph more visible.

I begin this chapter with an example from Bronze Age Europe because this region would later engender many of the contemporary attitudes about psychedelics and their uses in the Western world. Shamans, magicians, druids, and wizards were powerful figures in Europe at the beginning of the second millennium CE, possessing special knowledge that allowed them to channel the power of nature, the gods, and ancestors.[5] Often, these practitioners consumed psychoactive plants and fungi in ceremonies to aid in their spiritual journey.[6] Although sometimes feared, these practitioners were crucial to a well-functioning society. A village's magician, for example, healed the sick, bestowed fertility, foretold the future, and brought the rain.

Europe's slow conversion to Christianity, however, would change attitudes about magic by the High Middle Ages (1000–1300 CE).[7] The Church would come to be seen as the only conduit to the divine—everything else was the Devil's work—and those that strayed from the path were unbelievers and heretics.[8] To achieve an altered state of consciousness through prayer, fasting, or even pain was praiseworthy, yet taking a drug to get oneself there was not.[9] The work of village magicians nonetheless continued, often conducted at night by marginalized women. These magicians were soon rebranded as malignant witches bent on destruction.[10]

The perceived threat of witchcraft and sorcery would remain omnipresent into the 20th century. Europeans would carry this fear with them during the Voyages of Discovery and throughout the era of colonization. Indigenous leaders who sought transcendence outside of the Church were demonized, as were the plants and fungi that they used to aid them on their journeys. The re-engagement with psychedelics in the West that began in the 1940s withered in part because it failed to overcome this millennium-long distrust of psychoactive plant and fungi use (see chapter 2). By 1970, psychedelics were placed in the same category as heroin, cocaine, and other highly addictive and destructive compounds, with the users of psychoactive drugs dismissed as crackpots and hippies.

Our current re-engagement with psychedelics remains hindered by an almost visceral distrust of the drugs by individuals and institutions steeped in Western traditions. For many, a major role of psychedelics in society does not *feel* right. One way to counterbalance these feelings is to look elsewhere in space and time to those cultures where psychedelics play a more central role. In the pages that follow, we will explore the role of psychoactive drugs in five important ceremonies on three continents. Understanding these ceremonies offers constructive frameworks for considering possible psychedelic futures that are not steeped in centuries of hysteria and recrimination.[11]

Teotihuacan's Butterflies

Psilocybe aztecorum is a species of mushrooms that grow in the mountains of central Mexico.[12] Small, with bell-shaped caps, the mushrooms are found in meadows and open forests. They get their unusual name from the 15th-century CE Aztec Empire. For the Aztecs, psychoactive mushrooms were *teonanacatl*, the "flesh of the god," that was lauded in poems and celebrated in art.[13] Teonanacatl was seen as a gift from the primordial past, and indeed, archaeologists have found "mushroom stones" that are from as early as the first millennium BCE in other parts of Mesoamerica. The stones feature the fungi transformed into humans and animals.[14]

One of the places where psychoactive mushrooms played a critical role is at Teotihuacan, a vast metropolis of more than 100,000 people in 500 CE.[15] The Aztecs thought that the universe was created at Teotihuacan and still visited its pyramids, buildings, and plazas a thousand years later. The city's core was bisected by the Avenue of the Dead, a road lined by mortuary temples and the homes of Teotihuacan's elites. Priests placed select dead inside these temples, honouring with feasts and other ceremonies those who had served the city.[16]

Teotihuacan's artists depicted ancestors on many of the incense burners used in these ceremonies.[17] The incense burner's central feature is typically a mummy bundle wearing a face mask, often set within elaborately decorated frames that evoke a temple and its surroundings. The depicted bundles are likely those of warriors killed in battle, the centrepiece of a cult to the dead central to the militarism that united the city. The warriors' souls, resurrected as butterflies in the flowery Otherworld (Figure 2),[18] were carried away by the smoke that billowed out of incense burners at funerals—a smoke that also purified the mourners who were left behind.

Psychoactive mushrooms provided a means for the living to interact with the dead. To consume these mushrooms, in the words of a later Aztec scribe, was to ignite "a red-hot blown fire inside,"[19] a fire that could take a person to other worlds. We don't yet know whether people consumed mushrooms during the warrior funerals at Teotihuacan, but we do have a depiction of a visit to the land of the dead from a mural at Tepantitla, one of the elite residential compounds at Teotihuacan.[20] The mural at Tepantitla has an upper and lower register.[21] The upper registrar shows two priests offering mushrooms to the Storm God in front of what might be the morning glory vine, *Ipomoea corymbosa*, a powerful psychoactive plant also central to Mesoamerican rituals.[22] The vine is a conduit into the lower register depicting the Otherworld.[23] Many of the people in the lower register are dying, sacrificed to ensure the flow of life-giving waters—many narratives are packed into the mural—but some are celebrating psychedelic rituals. One individual slumbers under a mushroom, for example, while another sprouts a double rainbow from their head.

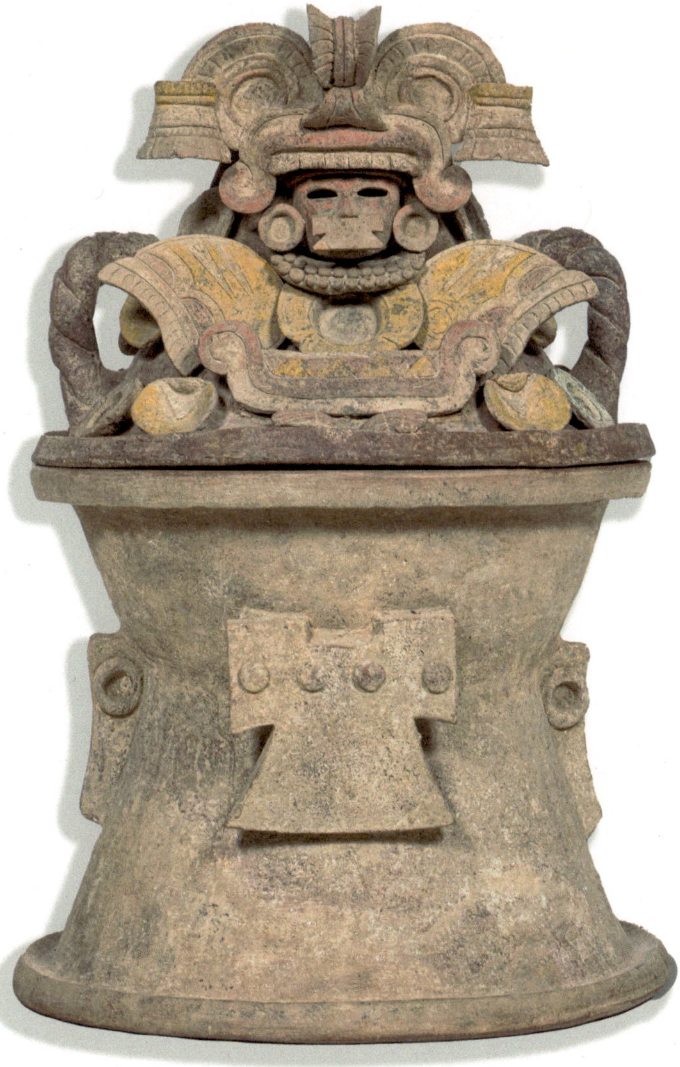

Figure 2
A Teotihuacan incense burner depicts an individual who is riding on a canoe and wearing a butterfly mask and a bird headdress. The individual may be the Butterfly Bird God himself or a deceased warrior honouring this powerful deity linked to rebirth. In either case, the individual is depicted mid-journey into the Otherworld.

Photo: The Gardiner Museum, G-83.1.19a–b.

Tiahuanaco Shamans

At around the same time, incense burners were also in use 5,000 kilometres to the south in Tiahuanaco, a city near Lake Titicaca in the Andes Mountains.[24] The incense burners often feature animals that are alluded to in the depiction of the culture's central deity, who sprouted snakes, felines, and birds from its flesh.[25] Rather than marking a death, Tiahuanaco's incense burners celebrated a more cyclical transformation: the ability of leaders to become powerful animals that could bring their community health and prosperity by engaging with destructive forces.

Tiahuanaco was organized around a series of platforms, waterworks, and plazas where large groups came together in ceremony.[26] In the shadows of great statues of gods clutching offerings of tablets used to prepare psychedelic snuff (Figure 3),[27] celebrants drank prodigious amounts of beer from vessels that often showcased the transformative capacities of their leaders.[28] Teotihuacan's mushrooms were available to many, but only a select few at Tiahuanaco could sustain the wallop of a psychoactive powder shot into their nose. These leaders worked for their followers, using snuff to take flight to places where others feared to go.

Chemical analyses of Tiahuanaco-era snuffs often reveal a cocktail of compounds.[29] A common ingredient was *vilca* (*Anadenanthera colubrina*).[30] Vilca trees grow best along the eastern slopes of the Andes. The seeds, dried and crushed to form a powder, were exchanged across hundreds of kilometres. Other psychoactive ingredients in these snuffs, such as yagé (*Banisteriopsis caapi)* vines,[31] came from deeper in the Amazon. The means of acquiring and preparing snuffs was likely secret knowledge at Tiahuanaco, and years of apprenticeship were needed to navigate the powerful psychedelic experiences.

Some objects related to the use of snuffs at Tiahuanaco still exist. Archaeologists recently found a complete snuff kit in the Cueva del Chileno in southern Bolivia, seemingly left behind as Tiahuanaco's influence waned.[32] Tubes, trays, and spatulas were also buried with individuals[33] or interred in ritual deposits. Snuffing equipment tends to be richly decorated, often with possible depictions of humans interacting with fierce animals.[34] Unfortunately, there was no writing at the time of Tiahuanaco to tell us more, and little was recorded when this region fell to the Spanish in the 1530s.

The echoes of these practices can nonetheless be seen in the actions of the *wayt'iri*, the contemporary shamans of Tiahuanaco's descendants.[35] They deduce why, for example, a woman cannot bear children or a farmer's crops are failing. By going into trance, the wayt'iri then transform into powerful beings that communicate with ancestors, spirits, and gods. Often, the shaman must go to multiple worlds, pleading, bribing, and even wrestling with different forces to solve the problem and restore proper order in the lives of their patients.

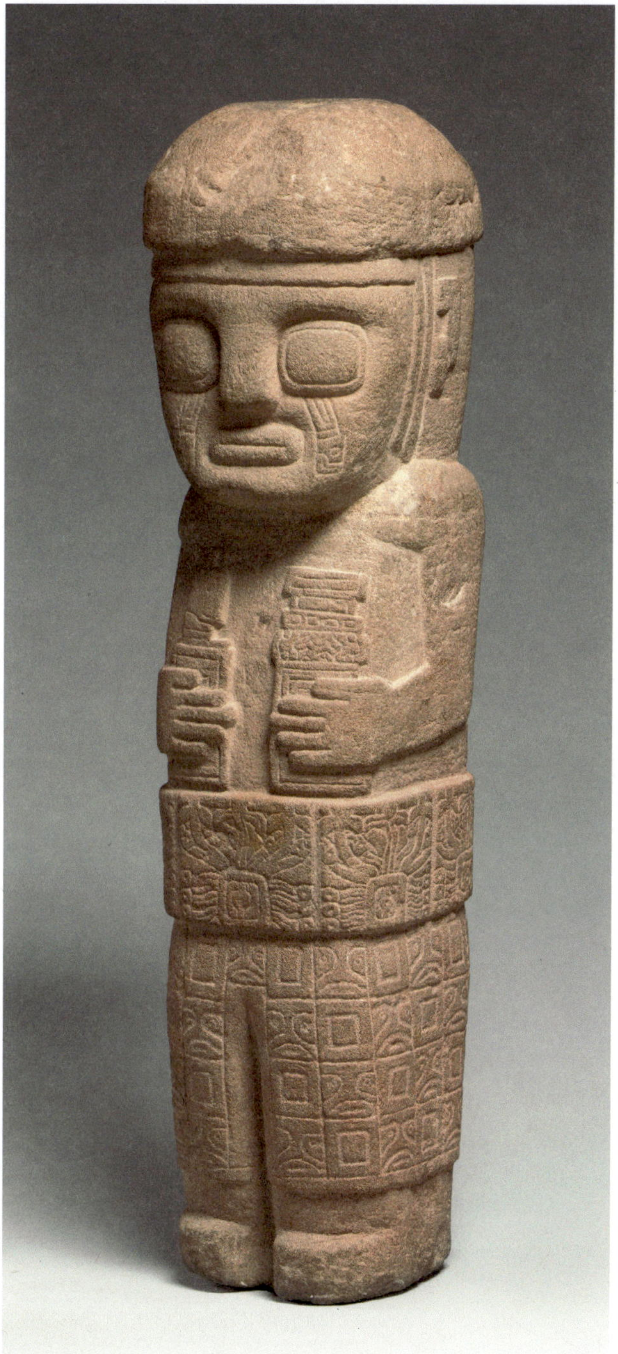

Figure 3
A statue of a Tiahuanaco god holding two trays for psychedelic snuff, 500-1000 CE. MET 1979.206.833

Photo: Courtesy of The Metropolitan Museum of Art.

Bwèté and Self-Realization

Bwèté (also known as "Bwiti") is one of the religions practised in Gabon today, a country in Central Africa that borders the Atlantic Ocean.[36] "Bwèté" can be translated as "emancipation," with the idea that Bwèté practitioners embark on a spiritual journey of purification and self-realization (Figure 4). Initiates are reborn in the faith and then grow throughout their lifetime at their own pace through a series of rites of passage that bring them closer to communion with their ancestors and other spirits.[37] Each person's journey is unique, but ceremonies are performed in a group and guided by a Bwèté master.

Self-realization is made possible by *eboghè* (also known as *iboga*). *Tabernanthe iboga* is an evergreen shrub that grows in the region.[38] Ibogaine, a psychoactive alkaloid, is concentrated in the bark of the roots. Bwèté practitioners peel, grate, and consume the bitter eboghè bark, inducing psychedelic experiences known for their colour vibrancy. Vomiting is also common at the beginning of one's journey, especially for initiates, as well as a loss of consciousness. Some practitioners suggest that this expulsion is necessary to leave the mundane world behind.[39]

Ceremonies involving eboghè follow a similar format. Most Bwèté rituals occur in or around a chapel, a rectangular structure that is open on one end. An orchestra typically sits in the back of the building, consisting of a harp (*ngombi*, Figure 5), mouth harp (*mougongo*), bell (*moukengué*), and rattle. Music and dance are critical for a ceremony's success, both in hastening the spiritual transition brought on by eboghè and engendering the ability to see one's self and surroundings in a new light. Rituals often occur at night and can last for several days, and a temple is packed with symbolism; it is therefore unsurprising that practitioners spend considerable time interpreting their eboghè visions in the days that follow.

Bwèté is a syncretic religion. Since Bwèté has neither an overarching leader nor agreed-upon scriptures, the experience at every temple is distinct.[40] A community's history, current concerns, and the interest of its leaders all shape how Bwèté is experienced from one village to another. Bwèté stories place the religion's origins in the ancestor worship of the hunter-gatherer Babongo, with elements incorporated from the beliefs of the Fang, Metsogo, Massango, and other more agriculturally orientated ethnic groups.[41] Contemporary Bwèté was further shaped by French colonization in the late 19th century and Catholic missionization efforts.[42]

Bwèté was, and remains, a countervailing tradition amidst rapid religious change—most Gabonese are now Christian—providing a sense of shared community amidst population dislocations, economic upheavals, and the erosion of local political autonomy that escalated after the First World War and continues to this day. Ancestor reliquaries, for example, have been reimagined in Bwèté

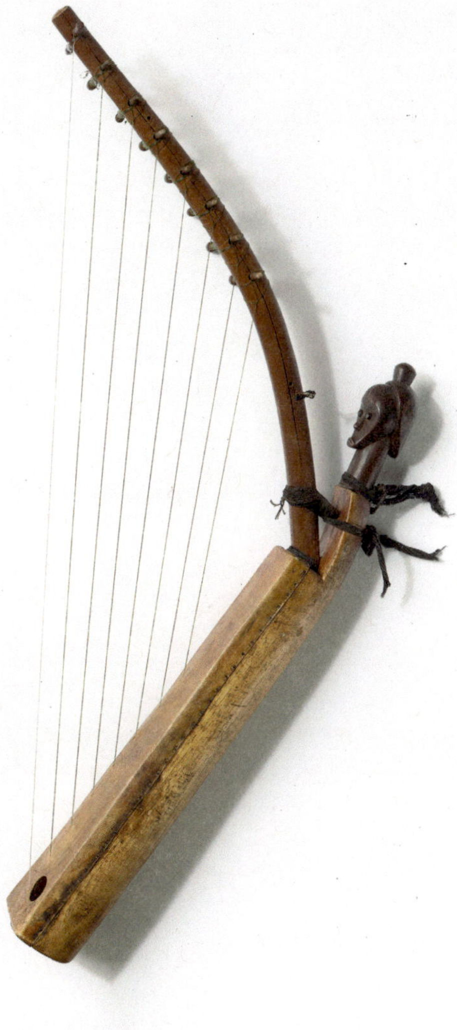

Figure 4
The ngombi is a harp used in Bwètè ceremonies that is crowned by a woman's head that symbolizes the links practitioners share to the First Ancestor, Disumba. The sounds of the harp are meant to return the listener to a powerful past that can help shape the future. Private Collection, Paul Mombey.
Photo: Paul Eekhoff © ROM.

to incorporate celestial bodies that can bridge across now-fractured kin groups, and Jesus, Mary, and the Holy Spirit have been absorbed into the Bwètè spiritual pantheon in some temples to incorporate their perceived power.[43] Bwètè flourishes in Gabon today *because* of its malleability, and it is now practised in many other parts of the world.

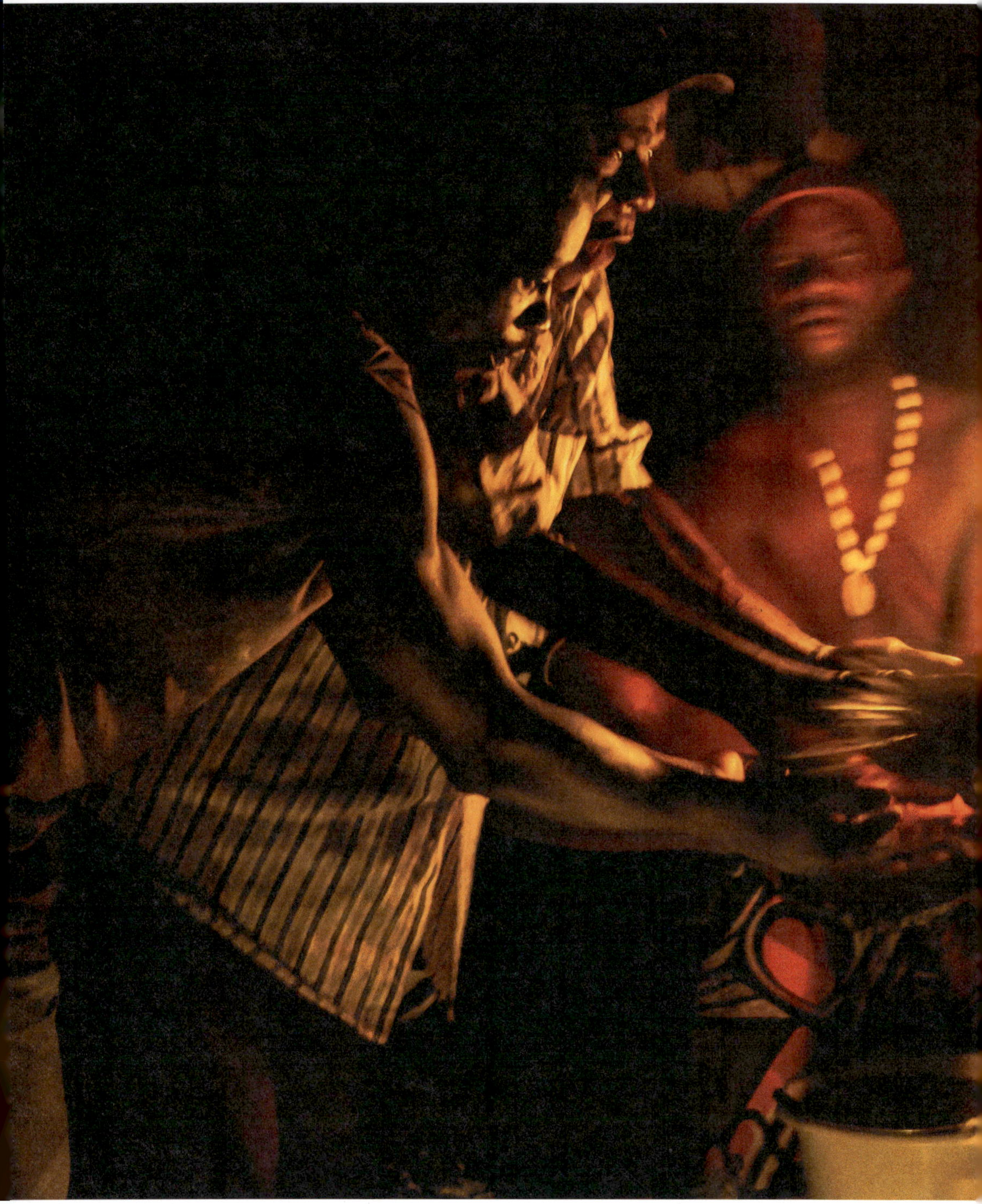

Figure 5 In a blessing ceremony in a Bwèté temple, an Elder offers words of good fortune to all participants.
Photo: Courtesy of Paul Mombey.

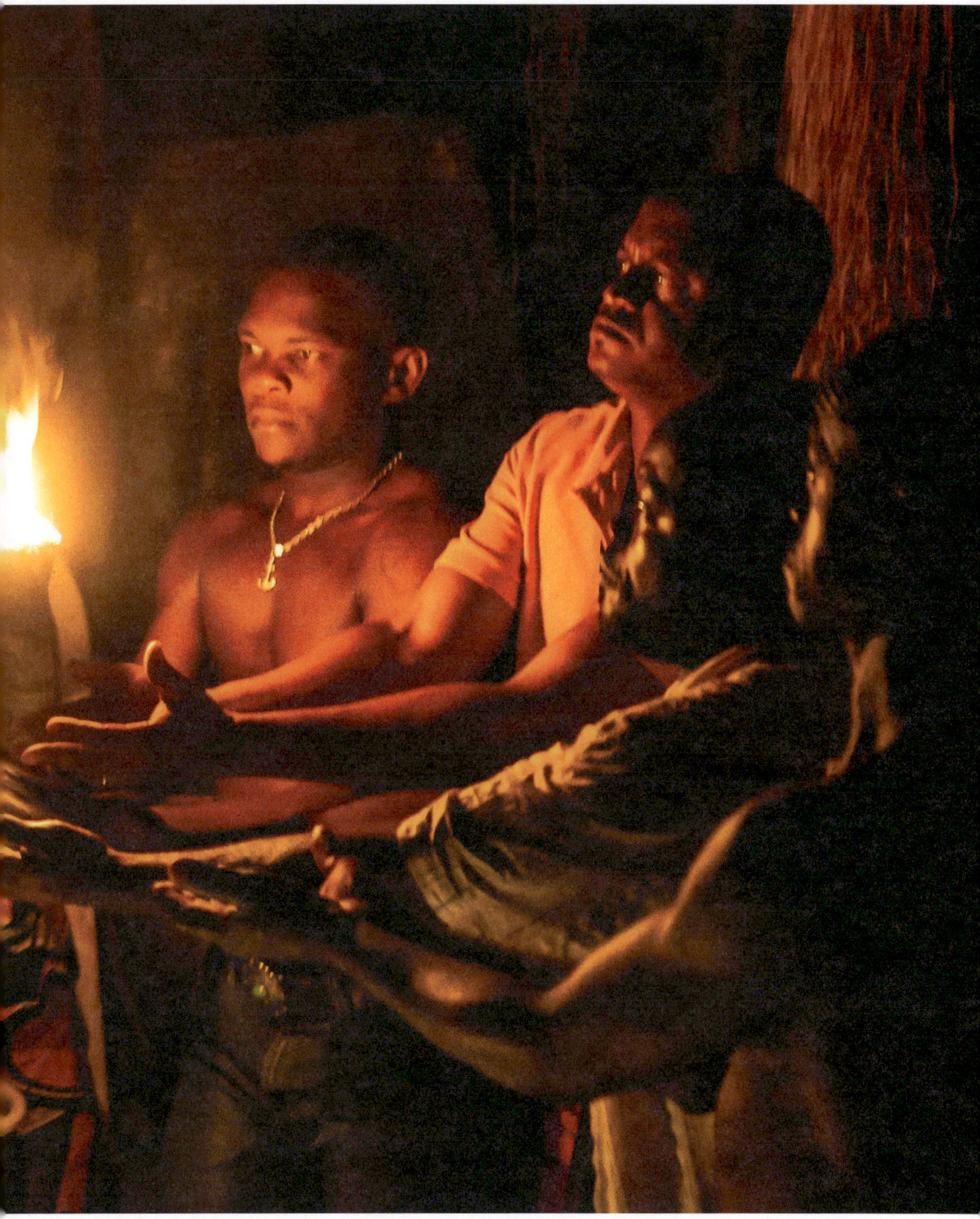

Huichol Pilgrimage

The homeland of the Huichol (or Wixárika)[44] is in the Sierra Madre Occidental Mountains of northwest Mexico. The rugged, isolated terrain served as a refuge during the Spanish Conquest–no roads led into the region until the 1970s–that then buffered the Huichol from the 500 years of cultural, economic, and political tumult that followed colonization.[45] The Huichol nonetheless trace their origins 450 kilometres east to a place in the desert of San Luis Potosí that they call "Wirikuta." Oral histories say that some of the earliest Huichol ancestors left the desert under duress, and small groups each year go on a pilgrimage to retrace the steps of the ancient ones.[46]

Pilgrims to Wirikuta now drive most of their journey, reducing a 40-day trek to less than a week (Figure 6). The journey from the mountains to the desert nonetheless remains a deeply spiritual experience that is fundamental to their identity as a people.[47] "To be Huichol," argued Barbara Myerhoff, "is to be sacred and this applies to all behaviours, objects, and ideas that make up the culture."[48] Understanding how to live a proper Huichol life requires a journey back to Wirikuta, a place that is the domain of gods and where the universe began. A *mara'akate* leads the group, as shaman, healer, and Knowledge Keeper.

The pilgrimage to Wirikuta is also a hunt for the Blue Deer, a deity transformed into peyote (*Lophophora williamsii*).[49] The harvesting of the small, spineless cacti is the culmination of a voyage that begins weeks earlier in the Sierra Madre with the preparation of offerings.[50] During these preparations, prayer arrows are made that will beseech the help of the gods (Figure 7), as are the decorated bowls made from gourds that will be used to hold peyote and maize. During their journey, the pilgrims confess their sins, fast, immerse in smoke, and avoid sleeping to purify themselves for their encounter with their gods. The mara'akate use landmarks along the way to speak about the ancestors and remind the group of the Huichol way of life.

Pilgrims consume peyote only after they arrive at Wirikuta. When they finally enter the domain of the gods on foot, the mara'akate stalks the cactus, bow in hand, shooting the peyote with an arrow. Often, this first cactus is dug up, with the resulting hole surrounded by some of the offerings that the pilgrims have carried on their journey. After more peyote is gathered, the group returns to a fire that embodies Tatewari, the first shaman among the ancestors. They ingest the peyote, with its mescaline soon creating a more vibrant and undulating landscape. Over time, visions arrive that reinforce the Huichol way.[51]

The Huichol were "discovered" in the 1970s by the tourism market.[52] Small paintings made by embedding coloured yarn in beeswax had long been used

Figure 6
Huichol prayer arrows are used to send messages to the gods. The arrows to the right are in the collection of the Royal Ontario Museum. ROM 961.163.18.B–D.

Photo: Paul Eekhoff © ROM.

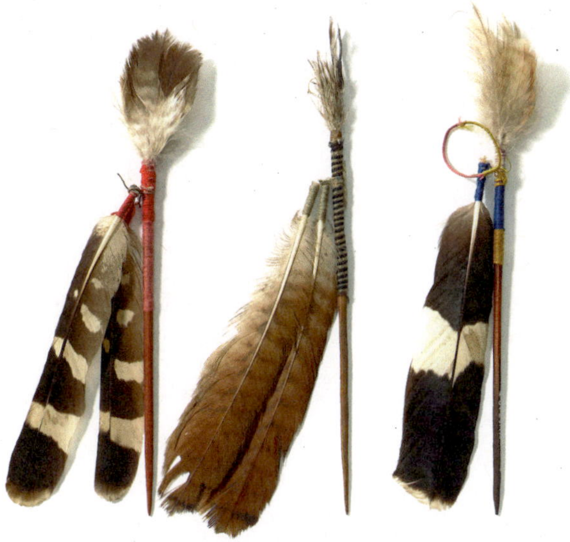

Figure 7
Francisco Carrillo Zamora preparing prayer arrows as part of an offering at a shrine on route to Wirikuta.

Photo: Coutesy of Francisco Carrillo Zamora.

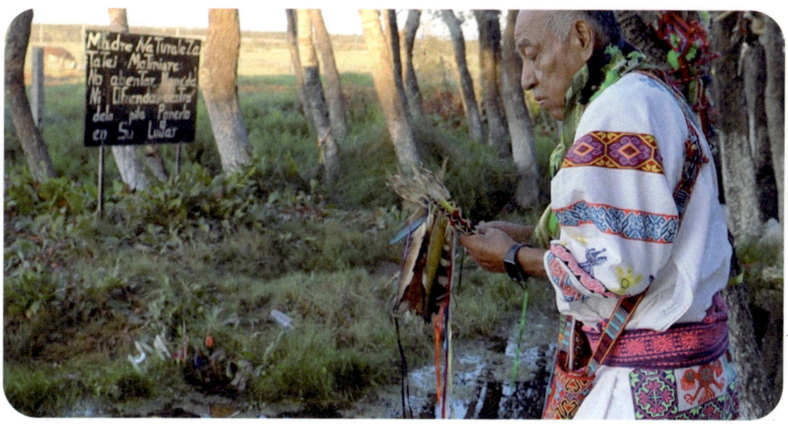

as offerings. Larger, more elaborate paintings were now created for sale, often featuring core aspects of Huichol cosmology (see Figure 10). At the same time, tourists went to Wirikuta to gather peyote.[53] Too many visitors were often too reckless; the Huichol are careful not to pull out a peyote's roots, so that the cactus can regenerate. The threat to Wirikuta galvanized political action, leading to Mexican legislation in 1975 that prohibited non-Huichol harvesting. The threats from tourists, as well as drug cartels and mining companies, nonetheless continue.[54]

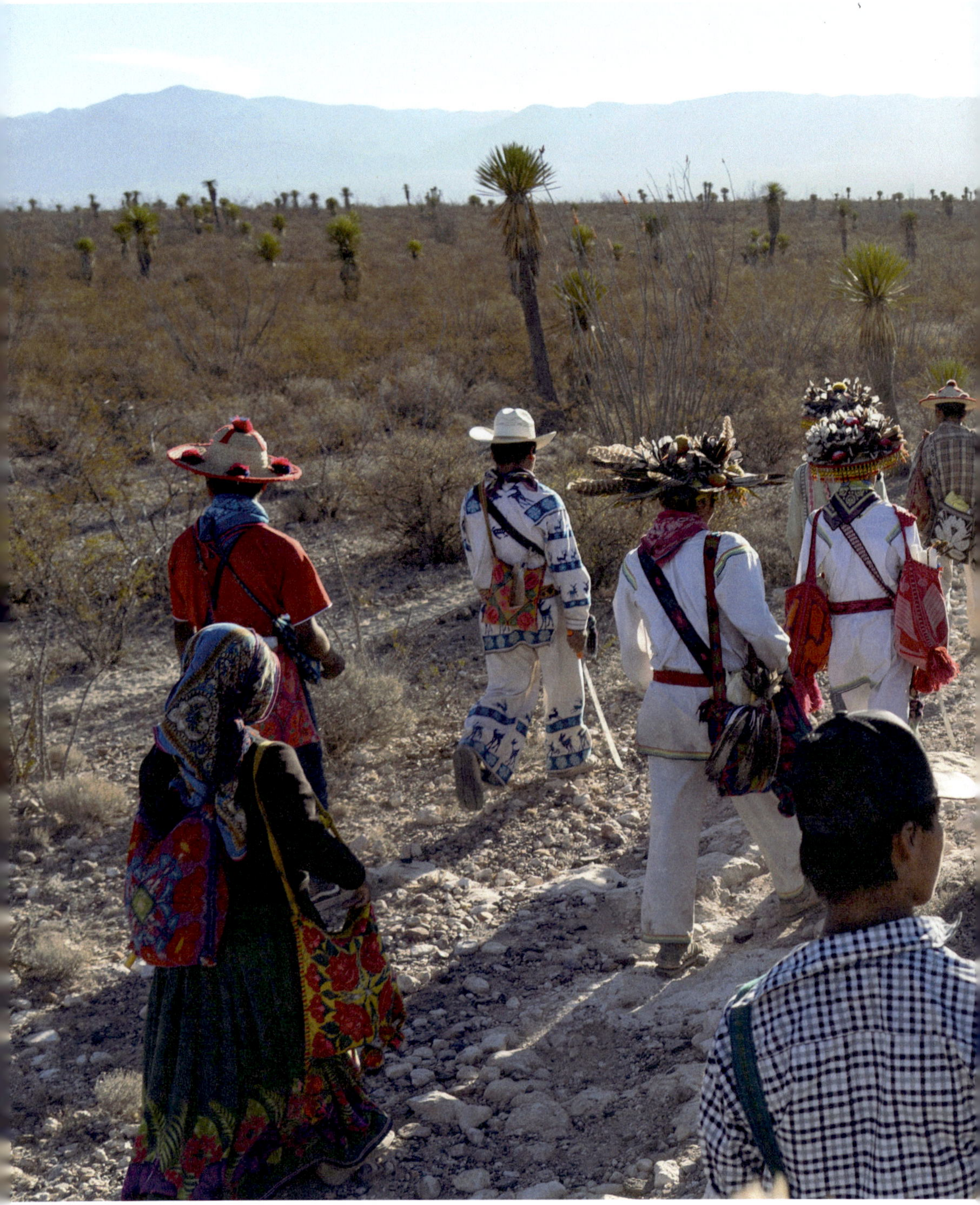

Figure 8 Huichol pilgrims arrive in Wirikuta to begin the peyote hunt.

Photo: Matt Reichel.

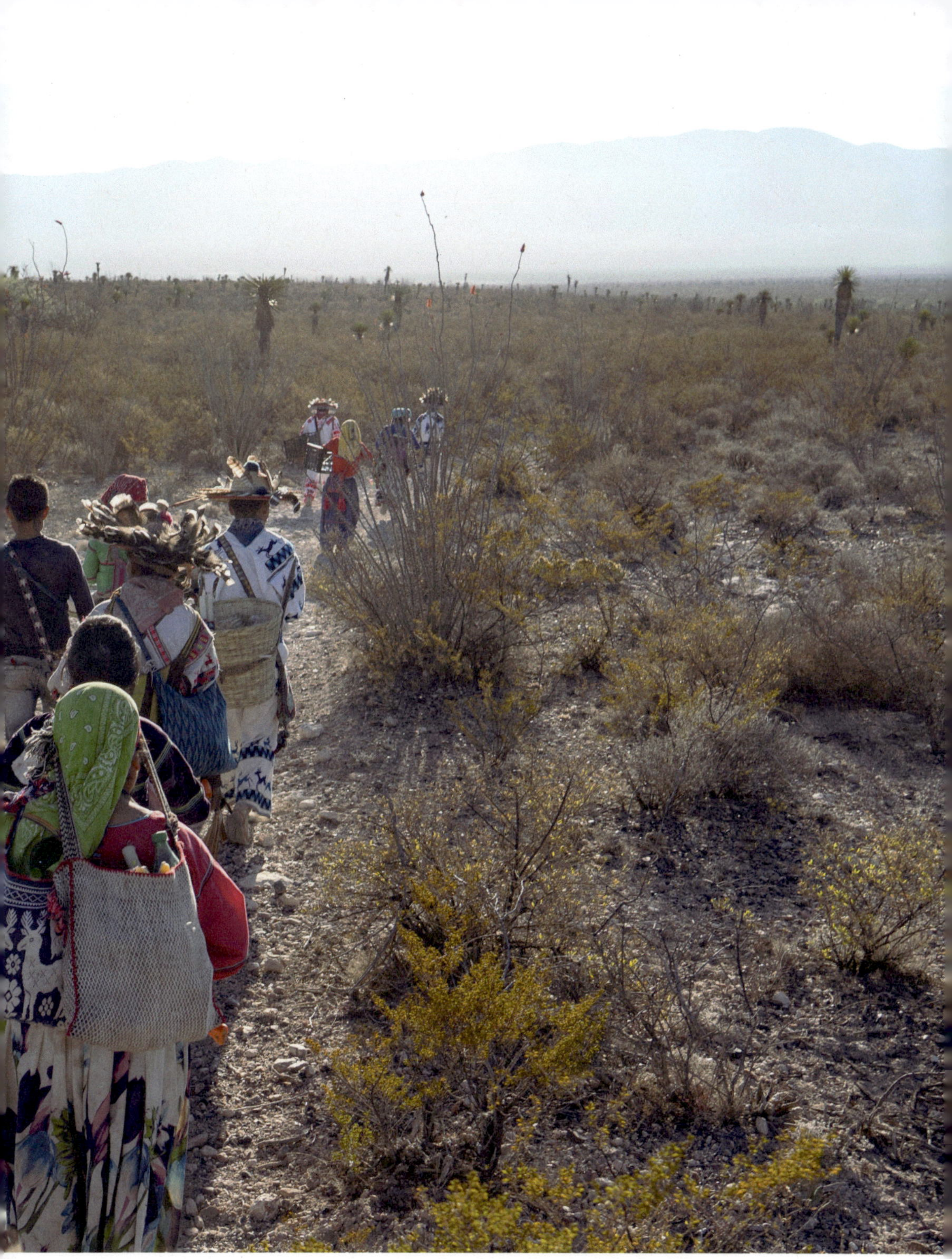

Shipibo-Konibo Art of Resistance

Olinda Reshinjabe Silvano paints what she sees (Figure 8).[55] The Shipibo-Konibo artist is a master of *kené*, the geometric lines that traditionally decorate the clothes, faces, and pottery of her community.[56] Kené come to Reshinjabe Silvano in visions induced from psychedelics. The lines are the embodiment of ancestral knowledge, given to her by the spirits of the forest for the benefit of her community. For Reshinjabe Silvano and other artists, kené have also become a symbol of resistance and survival in the face of the unrelenting forces of globalization that have impacted the Shipibo-Konibo in their homeland and across the diaspora.[57]

The Shipibo-Konibo, like the Huichol, believe that to be healthy in mind and spirit requires one to be in harmony with the world.[58] Kené designs, drawn largely by women, help to provide this harmony by materializing the positive energy, or *koshi*, that they encounter in psychedelic-induced visions.[59] The two plants said to induce these visions are *Banisteriopsis caapi*—the psychoactive ingredient in ayahuasca—and piripiri (*Cyperus sp.*).[60] As another Shipibo-Konibo artist noted (author's translation), "Everything seen in visions is covered with designs. Everything has its kené, it is its energy, it is medicine. Very beautiful, very bright. Everything is shiny."[61] Once the designs are received from the spirits, the artist's responsibility is to properly utilize them in her art, thus releasing their positive energy into the world.[62]

According to one of the Shipibo-Konibo's origin stories,[63] kené were first revealed to an ancient woman by Ronin, the primordial anaconda who is the mother of water and the source of all Amazonian people. Ronin gave the woman piripiri so that she could see the designs of all past, present, and future plants, animals, things, humans, and spirits on its skin. Over her lifetime, a Shipibo-Konibo woman learns to see the kené of the forest—male shamans also see these designs but tend not to draw them—with each design having a name that reflects its origins. One kené is the "spirit of the eye," while another is "spine of fish."[64] When properly combined, the designs produce a pathway, and an accompanying song, through which the koshi can flow from the forest into the community (Figure 9).

The homeland of the Shipibo-Konibo is the Ucayali River in the Peruvian Amazon.[65] Their roots in the region stretch back millennia,[66] but kené appear to be a product of the cultural tumult that followed Spanish colonization. Slavers, soldiers, and missionaries disrupted life throughout the western Amazon, and in 1698, the Shipibo, Konibo, and Shetebo Nations allied to repel a Spanish punitive force. Over time, these Nations came together to become the Shipibo-Konibo.[67] Kené, at least in part, emerged as a means of creating greater social cohesion in this group through shared ritual practices. A rubber boom began in 1884 that

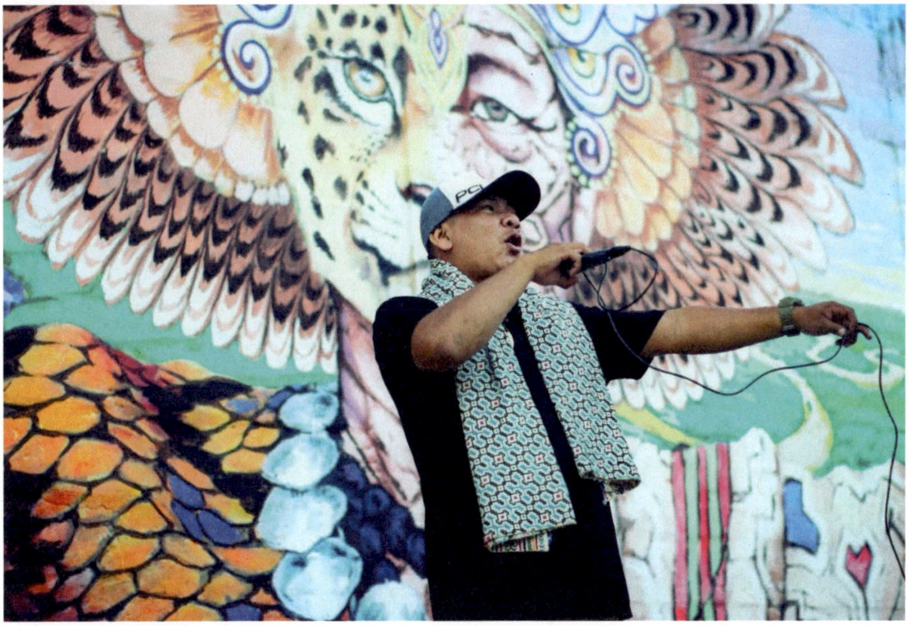

Figure 9
Shipibo-Konibo rap artist Wihtner FaGo sings in his native language as he wears a scarf decorated in kené patterns.
Photo: Courtesy of Erick Wihtner Fasabi Gonzales.

drew many Shipibo-Konibo men into the workforce, and then, the construction of a highway in 1945 brought more industrialization and a flood of cheap imports. This latest encroachment on their homeland has resulted in a wide diaspora, with families moving into cities and different parts of the Amazon.[68]

For the Shipibo-Konibo, kené have become both a potent symbol of their identity and an internationally acclaimed art form.[69] Creating the designs is seen as a mechanism to maintain connections to the forest and their ancestors: artists are meeting an existential need to retain the flow of koshi to their people and the world.[70] For women in particular, being Shipibo-Konibo and drawing kené are seen as inseparable.[71] To remain healthy, balanced, and whole, they draw the designs that they see in their visions onto their faces, weave them into their clothes, and paint them on their pottery.

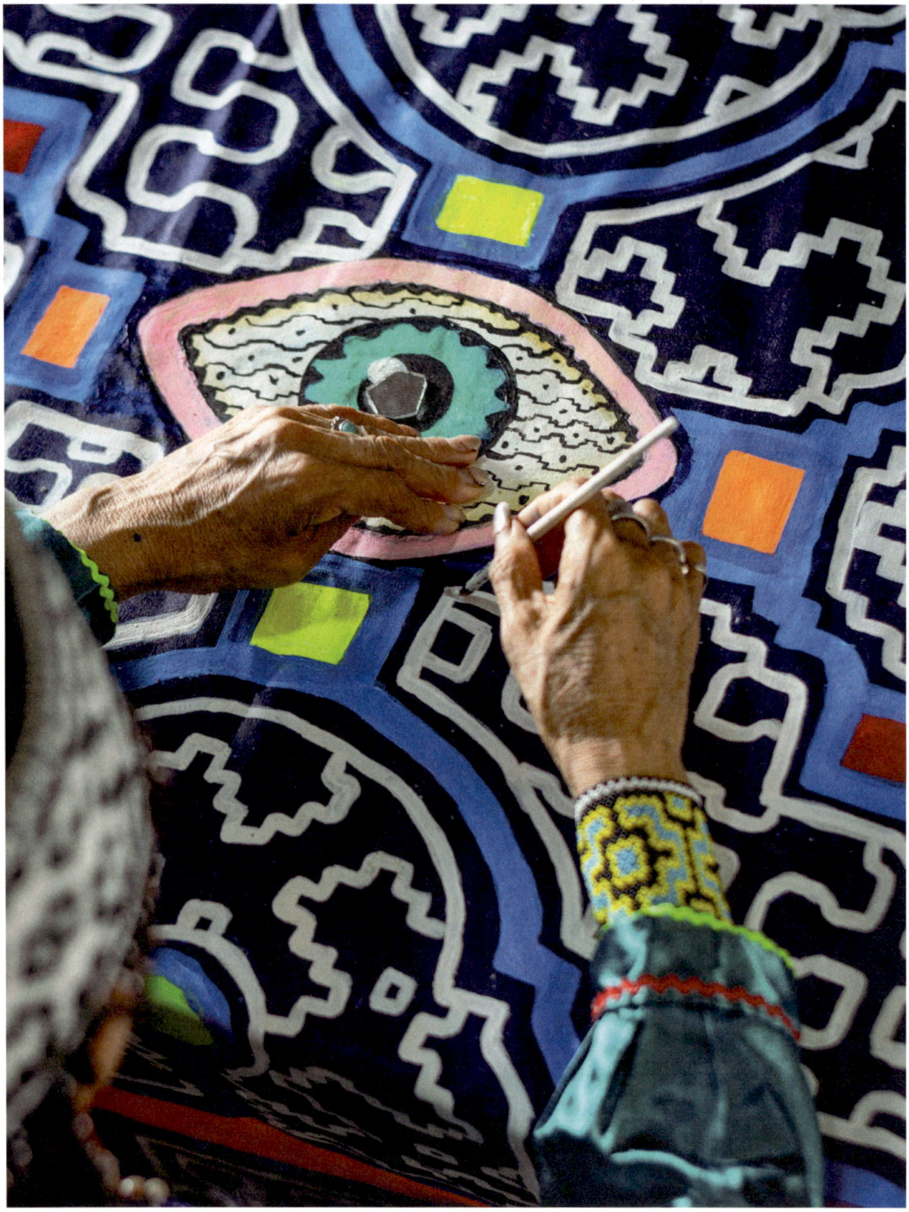

Figures 10-11
Shipibo-Konibo artist Olinda Reshinjabe Silvano touches up her painting *El ojo que ve todo* (*The All-Seeing Eye*), 2024. The painting celebrates the first time that Reshinjabe Silvano saw kené designs after consuming psychedelics.

Photos: Joao Sócola. Courtesy of Olinda Reshinjabe Silvano.

Figure 12 (pp. 34-35)
El ojo que ve todo (*The All-Seeing Eye*) by Olinda Reshinjabe Silvano.

Photo: Joao Sócola. Courtesy of Olinda Reshinjabe Silvano.

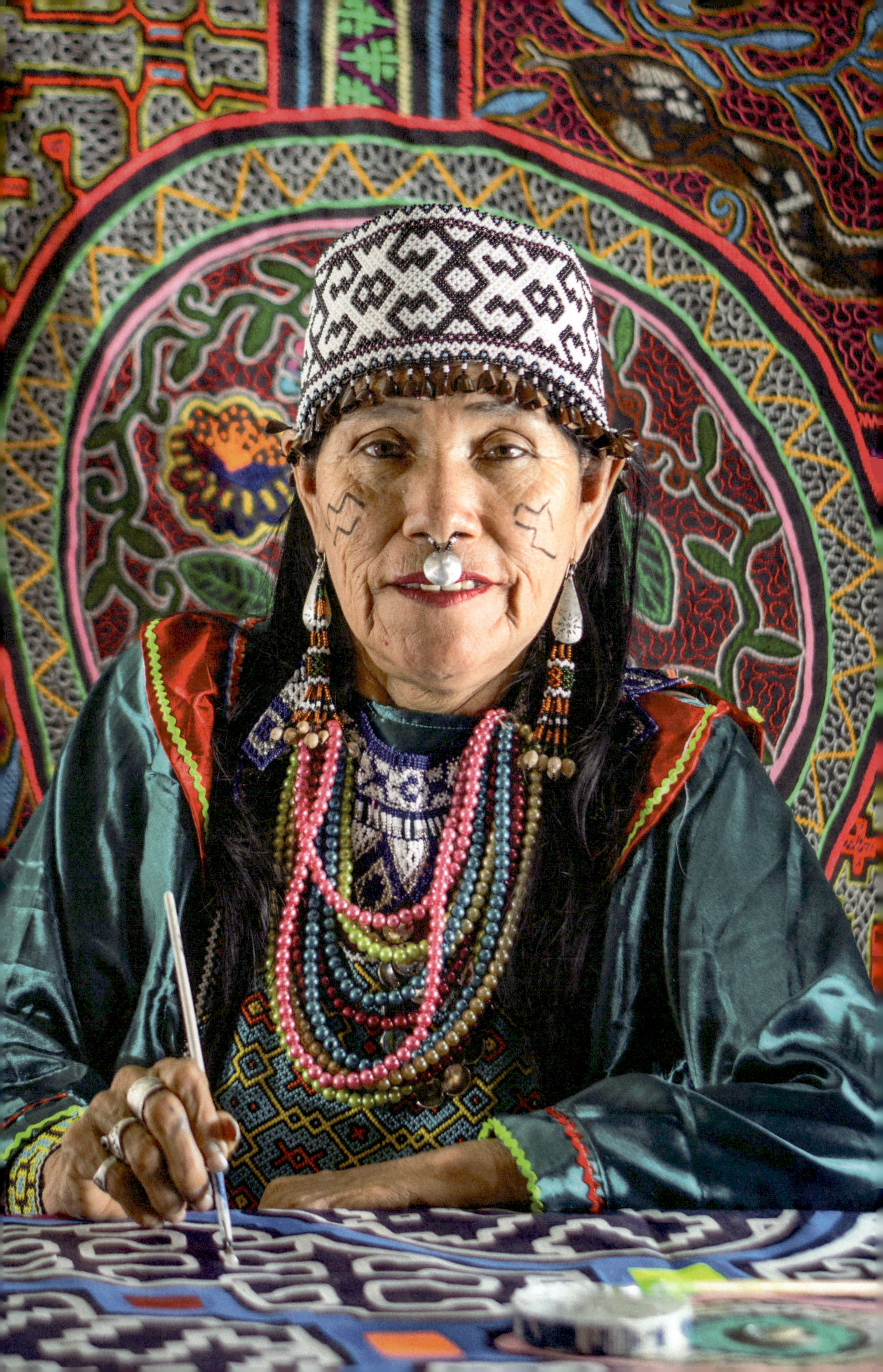

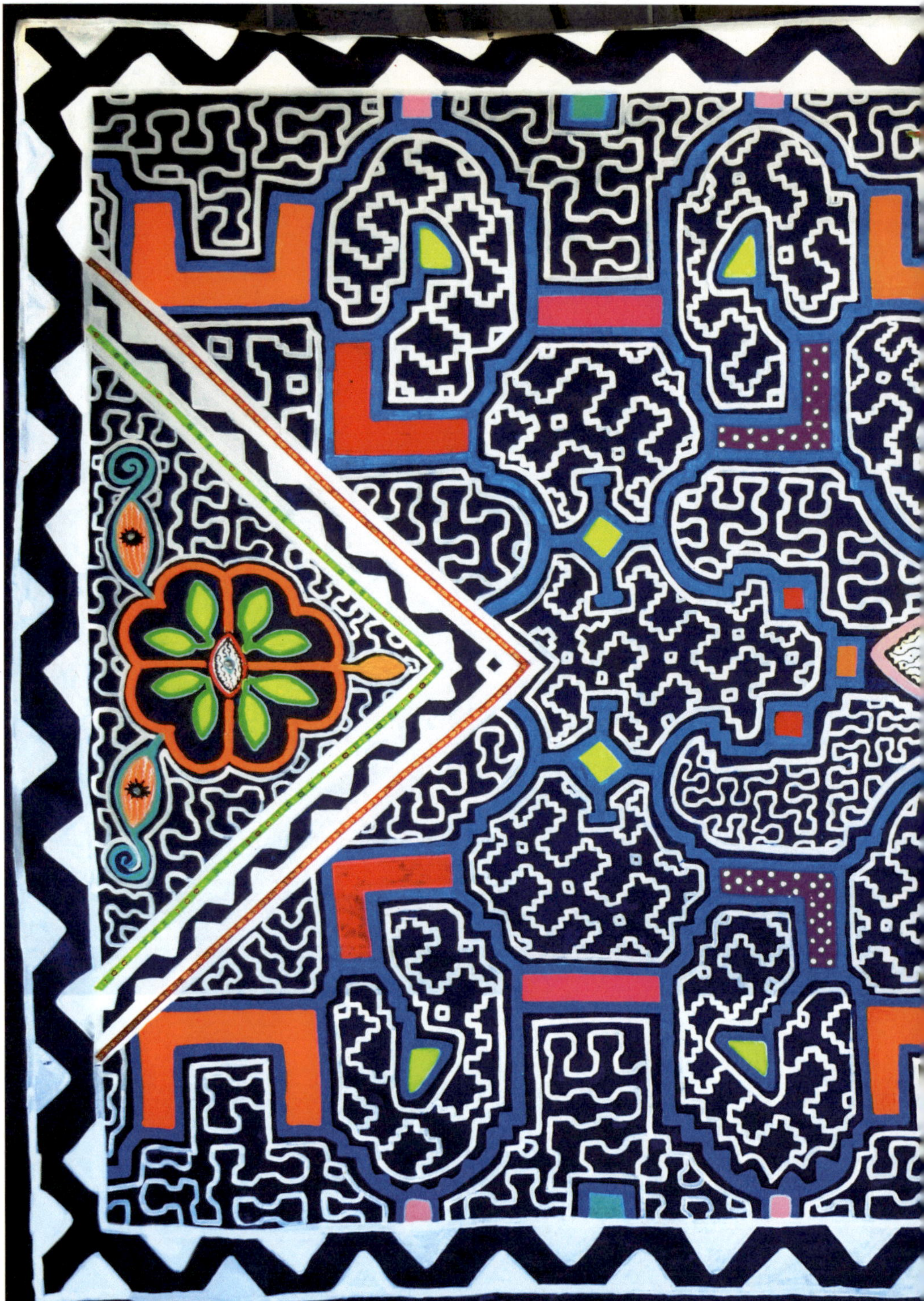

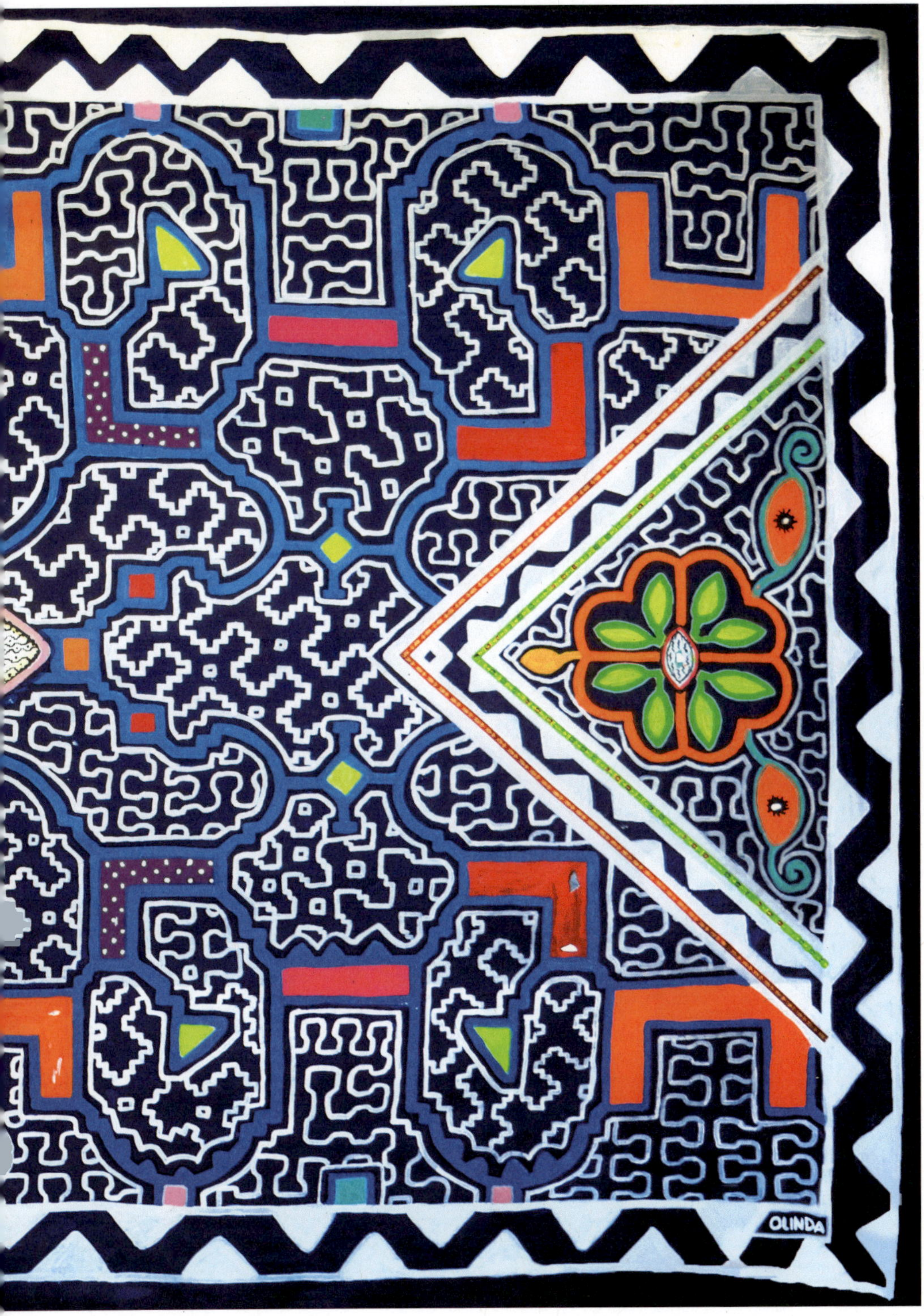
OLINDA

Learning from Other Cultures

Butterfly warriors and the Blue Deer may seem far removed from our lives. Yet as we debate the role that psychedelics can play in countries around the world, it is useful to turn to those societies that have effectively incorporated these drugs into everyday life. A better understanding of Bwètè rituals, for example, demonstrates the importance of guardrails in psychoactive experiences, such as attention to set and setting and the need for an experienced guide throughout the process. We are also reminded by Tiahuanaco's shamans that some drugs should be confined to well-trained professionals and by the Huichol of the necessity, on occasion, of letting go.

Perhaps, the greatest lesson from these case studies is about the value of visionary experiences for group cohesion and self-reflection. All lives are full of challenges, and psychedelics have been used in a variety of cultures to effectively help us navigate some of these difficulties. The drugs provide a means to communicate with lost loved ones, for instance, and allow us to recognize more fully the good in others. In enabling us to address these challenges together, psychedelic use helps to create a more unified "us" in relation to another world, forging a sense of community that could be invaluable in narrowing the fractures in our increasingly divided society.

Psychedelics are not a panacea (see chapter 4). This chapter's case studies nonetheless demonstrate some of the possibilities of more mainstream uses of the drugs and the essential work that would need to be done to make psychoactive substances beneficial for society.

As we look to the future, we must learn what we can from the hundreds of past and contemporary cultures that have used psychedelics for millennia—they have much to teach us.

Figure 13
Yarn paintings like these are made by the Huichol for the international art market. The top painting, by an unrecorded Huichol artist, is divided into two panels. The panel on the left celebrates a successful harvest, while the panel on the right shows a mara'akate going into a trance next to a fire. ROM 982.78.14.

Photo: Paul Eekhoff © ROM.

Figure 14
The bottom painting is by José Benítez Sánchez and entitled *The Deification of Tatéi Haitsi Kipiri, Our Mother Dew Soul* (1975). Benítez Sánchez illustrates part of the Huichol creation story, in which the divine life force emerges through the collective efforts of deities.

Photo: Courtesy of the Negrin Family and the Wixárika Research Center.

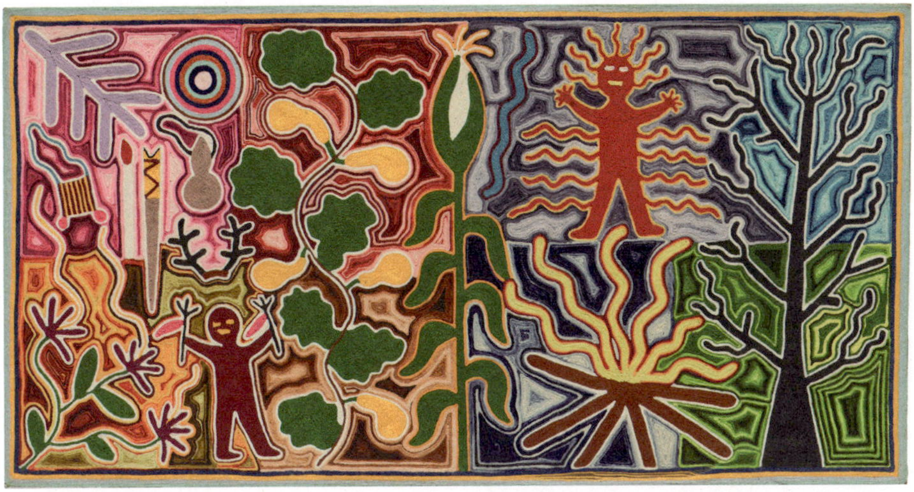

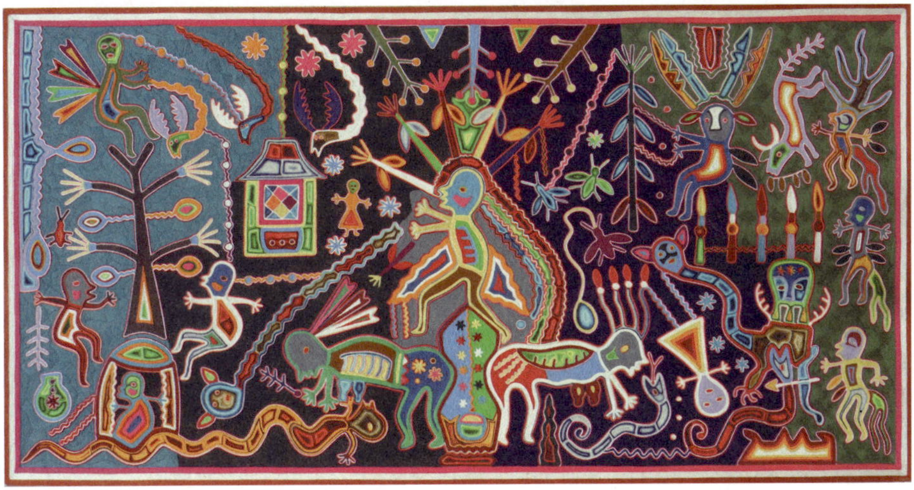

1 Guerra-Doce, E., Rihuete-Herrada, C., Micó, R., Lull, V., & Niemeyer, H. M. (2023). Direct evidence of the use of multiple drugs in Bronze Age Menorca (Western Mediterranean) from human hair analysis. *Scientific Reports, 13*(1), Article 4782.

2 Schultes, R. E. (1976). *Hallucinogenic plants*. Golden Press.

3 Fitzpatrick, S. M. (Ed.). (2018). *Ancient psychoactive substances*. University Press of Florida; Richert, L. (2021). Psychedelic pasts—and presents. *Journal of the History of Medicine and Allied Sciences, 76*(4), 462–468; and Samorini, G. (2019). The oldest archeological data evidencing the relationship of *Homo sapiens* with psychoactive plants: A worldwide overview. *Journal of Psychedelic Studies, 3*(2), 63–80.

4 De Rios, M. D. (1976). *The wilderness of mind: Sacred plants in crosscultural perspective*. Sage; Labate, B. C., & Cavnar, C. (2018). *Plant medicines, healing and psychedelic science: Cultural perspectives*. Springer International Publishing AG; and Millones, L., & Moisés, L. (2009). *Alucinógenos y Chamanismo: La Otra Curación*. SIDEA.

5 Bailey, M. D. (2007). *Magic and superstition in Europe: A concise history from antiquity to the present*. Rowman & Littlefield; Dukes, E. D. (1996). *Magic and witchcraft in the Dark Ages*. University Press of America; and Lawrence-Mathers, A., & Escobar-Vargas, C. (2014). *Magic and medieval society*. Routledge.

6 Harner, M. J. (1973). The role of hallucinogenic plants in European witchcraft. In M. J. Harner (Ed.), *Hallucinogens and shamanism* (pp. 125–150). Oxford University Press; and Hatsis, T. (2015). *The witches' ointment: The secret history of psychedelic magic*. Park Street Press.

7 Marrone, S. P. (2015). *A history of science, magic and belief: From medieval to early modern Europe*. Palgrave.

8 Brooke, R., & Brooke, C. (1984). *Popular religion in the middle age: Western Europe 1000–1300*. Thames and Hudson; and Collins, D. J. (Ed.). (2019). *The sacred and the sinister: Studies in medieval religion and magic*. Pennsylvania State University Press.

9 Beckman, P. Z., & Hollywood, A. M. (Eds.). (2012). *The Cambridge companion to Christian mysticism*. Cambridge University Press.

10 Ankarloo, B., Clark, S., & Monter, W. (Eds.). (2002). *The Athlone history of witchcraft and magic in Europe: Vol. 4. The period of the witch trials*. Athlone.

11 For example, see Celidwen, Y., Redvers, N., Githaiga, C., Calambás, J., Añaños, K., Evanjuanoy Chindoy, M., Vitale, R., Rojas, J. N., Mondragón, D., Vázquez Rosalío, Y., & Sacbajá, A. (2023). Ethical principles of traditional Indigenous medicine to guide western psychedelic research and practice. *Lancet Regional Health – Americas, 18*, Article 100410; and Williams, K., González Romero, O. S., Braunstein, M., & Brant, S. (2022). Indigenous philosophies and the "psychedelic renaissance." *Anthropology of Consciousness, 33*(2), 506–527.

12 Akers, B. P. (2007). *The sacred mushrooms of Mexico: Assorted texts*. University Press of America; and Guzmán, G. (1978). Variation, distribution, ethnomycological data and relationships of *Psilocybe aztecorum*, a Mexican hallucinogenic mushroom. *Mycologia, 70*(2), 385–396.

13 Carod-Artal, F. J. (2015). Hallucinogenic drugs in pre-Columbian Mesoamerican cultures. *Neurología, 30*(1), 42–49; and Schultes, R. E. (1940). Teonanacatl: The narcotic mushroom of the Aztecs. *American Anthropologist, 42*(3), 429–443.

14 de Borhegyi, S. F. (1961). Miniature mushroom stones from Guatemala. *American Antiquity, 26*(4), 498–504; and Mayer, K. H. (1997). *Mushroom stones of Mesoamerica*. Acoma Books.

15 Cowgill, G. L. (2015). *Ancient Teotihuacan: Early urbanism in central Mexico*. Cambridge University Press; and Robb, M. H. (Ed.). (2017). *Teotihuacan: City of water, city of fire*. Fine Arts Museums of San Francisco.

16 Headrick, A. (1999). The Street of the Dead … it really was: Mortuary bundles at Teotihuacan. *Ancient Mesoamerica, 10*(1), 69–85; and Solís Olguín, F. R., Castillo, G., & Alcántara, M. (Eds.). (2009). *Teotihuacan: Ciudad de los dioses*. Instituto Nacional de Antropología e Historia.

17 Berlo, J. C. (1984). *Teotihuacan art abroad: A study of metropolitan style and provincial transformation in incensario workshops*. British Archaeological Reports.

18 Headrick, A. (2003). Butterfly war at Teotihuacan. In K. Brown & T. W. Stanton (Eds.), *Ancient Mesoamerican warfare* (pp. 149–170). AltaMira Press; and Paulinyi, Z. (2022). The Lords of the

Butterfly Bird God: A new group of the Teotihuacan elite. *Boletín del Museo Chileno de Arte Precolombino, 27*(1), 151–166.

19 See page 269 of Knauth, L. (1962). The Teonanacatl–in pre-Conquest accounts and today. *Estudios De Cultura Náhuatl, 3*, 263–275.

20 Miller, A. G. (1973). *The mural painting of Teotihuacán*. Dumbarton Oaks; and Berrin, K. (Ed.). (1988). *Feathered serpents and flowering trees: Reconstructing the murals of Teotihuacan*. Fine Arts Museums of San Francisco.

21 Pasztory, E. (1976). *The murals of Tepantitla, Teotihuacan*. Garland.

22 Furst, P. T. (1974). Morning glory and mother goddess at Tepantitla, Teotihuacan: Iconography and analogy in pre-Columbian art. In N. Hammond (Ed.), *Mesoamerican archaeology: New approaches* (pp. 187–215). University of Texas Press.

23 Mathiowetz, M. D., & Turner, A. (Eds.). (2021). *Flower worlds: Religion, aesthetics, and ideology in Mesoamerica and the American Southwest*. University of Arizona Press.

24 Augustine, J. (2019). *Style, aesthetics, and politics: Polychrome ceramic iconography in the Tiwanaku Valley, AD 500-1100* [Unpublished doctoral dissertation]. University of Chicago.

25 Torres, C. (2018). Visionary plants and SAIS iconography in San Pedro de Atacama and Tiahuanaco. In W. Isabell, M. Uribe, A. Tiballi, & E. Zagarra (Eds.), *Images in action: The southern Andean iconographic sphere* (pp. 225–371). Cotsen Institute of Archaeology.

26 Janusek, J. W. (2008). *Ancient Tiwanaku*. Cambridge University Press.

27 Berenguer, J. R. (2001). Evidence for snuffing and shamanism in prehispanic Tiwanaku stone sculpture. *Eleusis: Journal of Psychoactive Plants & Compounds, 5*, 61–83.

28 Goldstein, P. S. (2003). From stew-eaters to maize-drinkers: The chicha economy and the Tiwanaku expansion. In T. Bray (Ed.)., *The archaeology and politics of food and feasting in early states and empires* (pp. 143–172). Springer.

29 Echeverría, J., & Niemeyer, H. M. (2013). Nicotine in the hair of mummies from San Pedro de Atacama (northern Chile). *Journal of Archaeological Science, 40*(10), 3561–3568; and Torres, C. M., Repke, D. B., Chan, K., McKenna, D., Llagostera, A., & Schultes, R. E. (1991). Snuff powders from pre-Hispanic San Pedro de Atacama: Chemical and contextual analysis. *Current Anthropology, 32*(5), 640–649.

30 Gili, F. (2022). Vilca, una semilla sagrada: De Sistemas terapéuticos y tecnologías de comunicación interespecie. *Cuadernos Médico Sociales, 62*(2), 65–76; and Torres, C. M., & Repke, D. B. (2012). *Anadenanthera: Visionary plant of ancient South America*. Routledge.

31 De Rios, M. D. (1972). *Visionary vine: Psychedelic healing in the Peruvian Amazon*. Chandler.

32 Albarracin-Jordan, J., Capriles, J. M., & Miller, M. J. (2014). Transformations in ritual practice and social interaction on the Tiwanaku periphery. *Antiquity, 88*(341), 851–862.

33 Horta Tricallotis, H. (2014). Lo propio y lo ajeno. Definicion del estilo San Pedro en la parafernalia alucinogena de los oasis del salar de atacama. *Chungará: Revista de Antropología Chilena, 46*(4), 559–583; and Llagostera Martínez, A., Torres, M., & Costa Junqueira, M. A. (1988). El complejo psicotrópico en Solcor 3 (San Pedro de Atacama). *Estudios Atacameños*, (9), 67–106.

34 Niemeyer, H. M., Salazar, D., Horta Tricallotis, H., & Peña-Gómez, F. T. (2015). New insights into the Tiwanaku style of snuff trays from San Pedro de Atacama, northern Chile. *Latin American Antiquity, 26*(1), 120–136; and Torres, C. M. (1987). *The iconography of South American snuff trays and related paraphernalia*. Göteborgs Etnografiska Museum.

35 Fernández Juárez, G. (2004). *Yatiris y chámakanis del altiplano aymara: Sueños, testimonios y prácticas ceremonials*. Ediciones Abya-Yala; Fernández Juárez, G. (2015). Diablo y Ch'amakani: Antropofagia simbólica y maleficio en el altiplano Aymara de Bolivia. *Chungara: Revista de Antropología Chilena, 47*(1), 157–165; and Bastian, J. W. (1989). A shamanistic curing ritual of the Bolivian Aymara. *Journal of Latin American Lore, 15*(1), 73–94.

36 Bonhomme, J. (2005). *Le miroir et le crane*. Éditions de la Maison des sciences de l'homme & CNRS Éditions; Bureau, R. (1996). *Bokayé! : Essai sur le Bwiti Fang du Gabon*. L'Harmattan; and Fernandez, J. W. (1982). *Bwiti: An ethnography of the religious imagination in Africa*. Princeton University Press.

37 My understanding of Bwètè is also informed by conversations with Paul Armand Mombey Indaki.

38 Iyer, R. N., Favela, D., Zhang, G., & Olson, D. E. (2021). The iboga enigma: The chemistry and neuropharmacology of iboga alkaloids and related analogs. *Natural Product Reports, 38*(2), 307–329.

39 Binet, J. (1974). Drugs and mysticism: The Bwiti cult of the Fang. *Diogenes, 86*, 31–54.

40 Bonhomme, J. (2018). Incident surrounding a post: Ritual, script and performance in the Bwiti of Gabon. *Homme, 3*(227–228), 153–178.

41 Fernandez. *Bwiti*, chapter 14.

42 Rich, J. (2021). Unsteady is the cross: Catholic missionaries, marriage, and Fang communities in the Gabon Estuary, ca. 1914–1945. *African Historical Review, 52*(2), 62–83; and Rich, J. (2007). *A workman is worthy of his meat: Food and colonialism in the Gabon Estuary*. University of Nebraska Press.

43 Havleka, O. (2022). The syncretism of the Gabonese Bwiti religion and Catholic Christianity from a theological and theological-ethical perspective. *Theologica, 12*(1), 145–159.

44 Guzmán Mejía, R., & del Carmen Anaya Corona, M. (2007). *Cultura de maíz-peyote-venado: sustentabilidad del pueblo wixarika*. Universidad de Guadalajara & Centro Universitario de Los Altos; and Pacheco, G. (2018). *Yuimákwaxa: ceremonia de los primeros frutos tiernos*. Universidad de Guadalajara.

45 Liffman, P. M. (2011). *Huichol territory and the Mexican nation: Indigenous ritual, land conflict, and sovereignty claims*. University of Arizona Press; Morris, N. (2017). "Civilising the savage": State-building, education and Huichol autonomy in revolutionary Mexico, 1920–40. *Journal of Latin American Studies, 49*(4), 739–769; and Stephens, M. M. (2015). "... As long as they have their land": The Huichol of western Mexico, 1850–1895. *Ethnohistory, 62*(1), 39–60.

46 Gutiérrez del Ángel, A. (2002). *La peregrinación a Wirikuta: el gran rito de paso de los huicholes*. Instituto Nacional de Antropología e Historia, Universidad de Guadalajara; and Medina Miranda, H. M. (2012). *Relatos de los caminos ancestrales: Mitología wixarika del sur de Durango*. Universidad Autonoma de San Luis Potosí.

47 My understanding of the pilgrimage is also informed by conversation with Francisco Carrillo Zamora.

48 Myerhoff, B. G. (1974). *Peyote hunt: The sacred journey of the Huichol Indians*. Cornell University Press, p. 74.

49 Lemaistre, D. (1996). The Deer that is peyote and the Deer that is maize: The hunt in the Huichol "trinity." In S. B. Schaefer & P. T. Furst (Eds.)., *People of the peyote: Huichol Indian history, religion, and survival* (pp. 306–329). University of New Mexico Press.

50 Benítez, F. (1968). *En la tierra mágica del peyote*. Ediciones Era; and Nahmad Sittón, S. (Ed.). (1972). *El Peyote y los huicholes*. Secretaría de Educación Pública.

51 Schaefer, S. B. The crossing of the souls: Peyote, perception, and meaning among the Huichol Indians. In Schaefer & Furst, *People of the peyote* (pp. 138–168).

52 MacLean, H. (2005). *Yarn paintings of the Huichol*. Singing Deer Press; and MacLean, H. (2012). *The shaman's mirror: Visionary art of the Huichol*. University of Texas Press.

53 Furst, P. T., & Schaefer. Peyote pilgrims and Don Juan seekers: Huichol Indians in a multicultural world. In Schaefer, S. B & Furst, *People of the peyote* (pp. 503–522).

54 For example, see Hollander, K. (2017, May 30). *Battle in the Mexican desert: Silver mining against peyote and Indigenous spirituality*. The Ecologist. https://theecologist.org/2017/may/30/battle-mexican-desert-silver-mining-against-peyote-and-indigenous-spirituality; and Tucker, D. (2017, June 16). An Indigenous Mexican people are battling cartels and peyote tourism. *Vice*. https://www.vice.com/en/article/a3jq5e/an-indigenous-mexican-people-are-battling-cartels-and-peyote-tourism.

55 Vidarte Basurco, G. (2025). Pintar un nuevo kené en territorios de migración y crisis. *América sin nombre*, 32, 179–197.

56 Belaunde, L. E. (2009). *Kené: arte, ciencia y tradición en diseño*. Instituto Nacional de Cultura del Perú; Gebhart-Sayer, A. (1985). The geometric designs of the Shipibo-Conibo in ritual context. *Journal of Latin American Lore, 11*(2), 143–175; and Gebhart-Sayer, A. (1986). Una terapia estética. Los diseños visionarios del ayahuasca entre los shipibo-conibo. *América Indígena, 46*(1), 189–218.

57 Gao, S. (2025). *El arte kené: expresión de resistencia del pueblo shipibo-konibo de la Amazonía peruana en la actualidad* [Unpublished master's thesis]. University of Barcelona; and Belaunde,

L. (2012). Diseños materiales y inmateriales: la patrimonializacion del kené Shipibo-Konibo y de la ayahuasca en el Perú. *Mundo Amazonico, 3*, 123–146.

58 Robinson, M. (2023). The curation of communities in Shipibo Onanyabo. *Journal of Arts and Communities, 14*(1), 125–139.

59 Belaunde, L. E., Colaianni, S. W., & Colaianni, S. W. (2016). Kené: Shipibo-Conibo design. In A. Wali & J. Odland (Eds.), *The Shipibo-Conibo: Cultures and collections in context* (pp. 81–92). Field Museum of Chicago; and Favaron, P. (2017). *Las visiones y los mundos: sendas visionarias de la Amazonía Occidental* (1st ed.). Centro Amazónico de Antropología y Aplicación Práctica.

60 *Banisteriopsis caapi*'s harmala alkaloids are pyscoactive, but there are no psychoactive properties to piripiri. Rather, these sedges are hosts to a fungus, *Balansia cyperi*, with ergot alkaloids. See Plowman, T., Leuchtmann, A., Blaney, C., & Clay, K. (1990). Significance of the fungus *Balansia cyperi* infecting medicinal species of *Cyperus* (Cyperaceae) from Amazonia. *Economic Botany, 44*(4), 452–462.

61 Belaunde, L. (2007). El brillo de los tintes de la selva: la pintura de Roldán Pinedo, maestro shipibo. *Gaceta Cultural del Perú*, 8, 24–25.

62 Favaron Peyón, P. (2025). Netebaon joi: La semiótica cósmica shipibo-konibo. *América sin nombre, 32*, 16–32.

63 Fundación Cultural Shipibo-Conibo. (1998). *Non requenboan shinan = El origen de la cultura Shipibo-Conibo: leyendas, historias, costumbres, cuentos* (1st ed.). Arteida Editores; and Ramírez Guimaraes, G., & Ramírez Cairuna, L. (1998). *Testimonio y cuentos Shipibos*. Universidad Nacional Mayor de San Marcos, Seminario de Historia Rural Andina.

64 Soria Casaverde, M. B. (2004). *Introducción al mundo semiótico de los diseños shipibo-conibo* (1st ed.). Universidad Nacional Mayor de San Marcos, Seminario de Historia Rural Andina.

65 Eakin, L., Lauriault, E., & Boonstra, H. (1986). *People of the Ucayali, the Shipibo and Conibo of Peru*. International Museum of Cultures.

66 Clasby, R., Yamamoto, A., & Olivera Nuñez, Q. (2024). The archaeology of Amazonian-Andean interactions. In *Oxford Research Encyclopedia of Anthropology*. Oxford University Press. https://oxfordre.com/anthropology/display/10.1093/acrefore/9780190854584.001.0001/acrefore-9780190854584-e-479?rskey=tinqYu&result=1; and Clasby, R., & Nesbitt, J. (Eds.). (2021). *The archaeology of the Upper Amazon: Complexity and interaction in the Andean tropical forest*. University Press of Florida.

67 Chocano, D. M., Baquerizo, A. M., Weber, R. L., & Colaianni, S. W. (2016). Continuity and change among the Shipibo-Conibo: Prehistory to modernity. In Wali & Odlund, *Shipibo-Conibo* (pp. 9–20).

68 Espinosa, O. (2012). To be Shipibo nowadays: The Shipibo-Konibo youth organizations as a strategy for dealing with culture change in the Peruvian Amazon region. *Journal of Latin American and Caribbean Anthropology, 17*(3), 451–471; and Górska, K. (2022). Shipibo-Konibo community in Lima and the right to the city. *Anuario Latinoamericano: Ciencias Políticas y Relaciones Internacionales, 13*, 113–135.

69 Granadino, C. (2003). *Artesanía Shipiba: gracia, utilidad, misterio y expresión de una visión del cosmos*. Ediciones Minka; Caruso, G. (2005). *Onaya Shipibo-Conibo: sistema médico tradicional y desafíos de la modernidad*. Ediciones Abya-Yala; and Favaron, P., & Chonon, B. (2020). Metsá kené: los diseños y la identidad del pueblo Shipibo-konibo. *Visitas al Patio, 14*(2), 100–114.

70 Canayo, L., & del Águila Rodríguez, C. (2019). *Magia y verdad del mundo shipibo* (1st ed.). Ikono Multimedia; and Tournon, J. (2002). *La merma mágica: vida e historia de los Shipibo-Conibo del Ucayali*. Centro Amazónico de Antropología y Aplicación Práctica.

71 Soria Gonzáles, M., & Carpo, A. (2006). *La ternura y el poder: voces de mujeres shipibo de las comunidades de Ucayali*. Ediciones Abya-Yala.

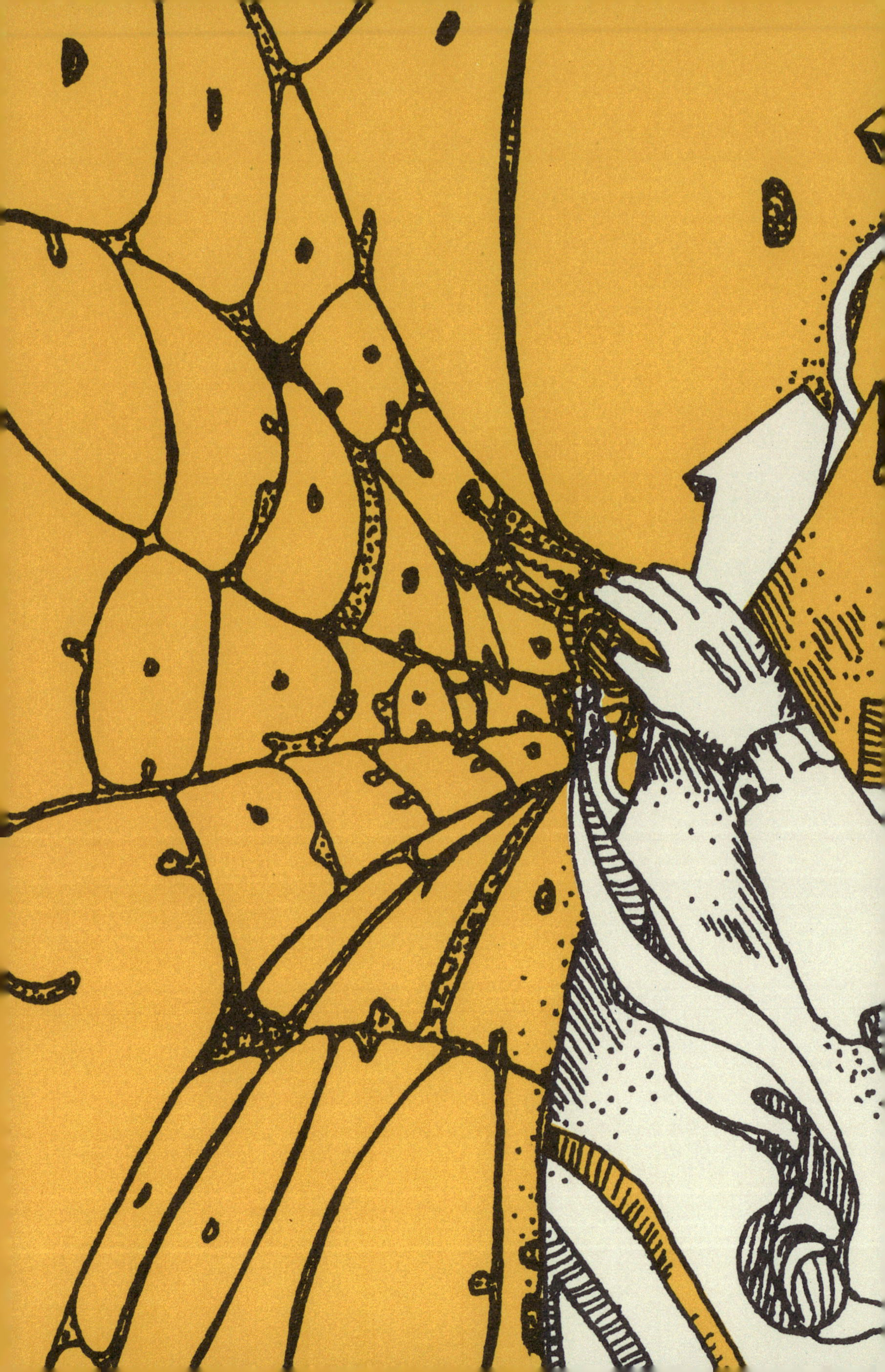

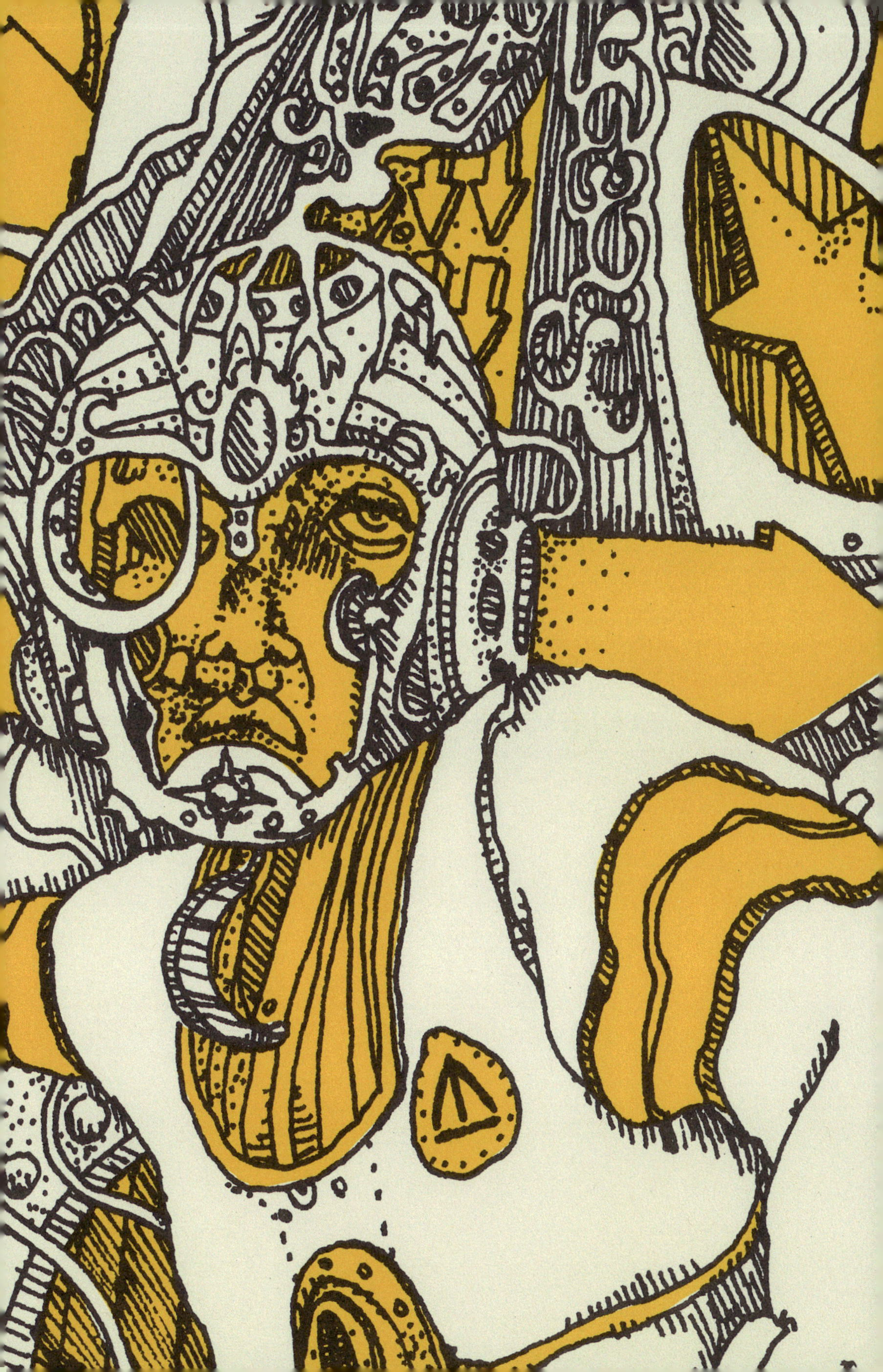

2

The First Big Trip: A Brief History of Psychedelics in the West

ERIKA DYCK

PLANTS, FUNGI, AND EVEN SOME ANIMALS with psychedelic properties have existed for millions of years. The first humans likely used some of these psychoactive plants and animals to achieve altered states of consciousness, and for millennia, psychedelic substances have been used in rituals, for healing, and just out of curiosity in many cultures around the world.[1] The term "psychedelic," however, is a Western neologism coined in 1957, during a period when a fascination with hallucination-causing agents met an expanding pharmaceutical industry.

The 1950s were a critical period of medical experimentation that generated new technologies, medicines, and even healthcare systems.[2] Research in this decade led to major breakthroughs in psychiatric medicine with the introduction of the first anti-psychotic and anti-depressant medications on the market. The birth control pill changed reproductive medicine and politicized women lobbying for their place in the workforce. Canadians began investing in publicly funded health-care programs in a series of policies that culminated in the national program of Medicare in 1966. The first generation of psychedelic experimentation unfolded in this period of reform and relative optimism for change. Psychedelics' rise and fall from the 1950s through 1970s was the West's First Big Trip, a story of discoveries, hype, and hysteria that holds important lessons for us as we navigate the current resurgence of interest in psychedelic use in North America.

Psychedelic Psychiatry

In 1953, British dystopian writer Aldous Huxley invited a young psychiatrist to Huxley's home in Los Angeles. Huxley had already earned a reputation as a compelling writer who was deeply interested in philosophy, biology, and politics. These themes had appeared in full force in his classic novel *Brave New World* (1932), a dark futuristic portrayal of civilization. He introduced readers to the idea of a drug–soma–that was available to all ages and numbed the human senses to produce a sense of satisfaction in a bleak world. But soma, and its ability to maintain states of pleasure and indifference to larger social forces, was not Huxley's fantasy drug of choice. He was curious about non-ordinary states of consciousness, and research taking place in Saskatchewan piqued his interest.

British-trained psychiatrist Humphry Osmond moved to Weyburn, Saskatchewan, in 1951 at the request of the premier, Tommy Douglas, who had been engaged in extensive reforms of the province's healthcare system.[3] Osmond arrived at a large provincial mental hospital that was overcrowded and in desperate need of improvement. His wife, Jane, was underwhelmed by the meagre amenities of the small prairie town, which paled in comparison with their more cosmopolitan life back in England, to say nothing of the bitterly cold and protracted winters. But Osmond relished the opportunity to flex his intellectual and administrative muscles as he faced the Herculean task of fixing an outmoded psychiatric system. Osmond had a novel idea: What if instead of merely warehousing people suffering from mental disorders, we tried to better understand them?

Osmond had 4,000 patients in his care, some of whom slept in shifts due to the extreme overcrowding, and he wondered how they experienced reality. At the time, a majority of the institutionalized patients throughout the Western world suffered from major psychiatric disorders. Some of these disorders were psychotic conditions like schizophrenia, which often featured extreme bouts of disorientation and even hallucinations and delusions. Osmond felt that he needed to understand what his patients–who were written off as sick members of society incapable of meaningful contributions–were going through. Perhaps, taking mescaline might help him empathize with this "sick society," as he put it.[4] One of the organic parts of the peyote cactus containing chemical components, the alkaloid mescaline is largely responsible for the psychoactive responses associated with consuming the peyote cactus.

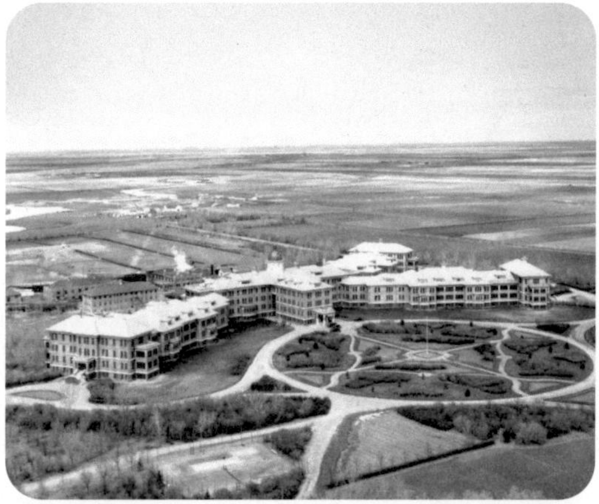

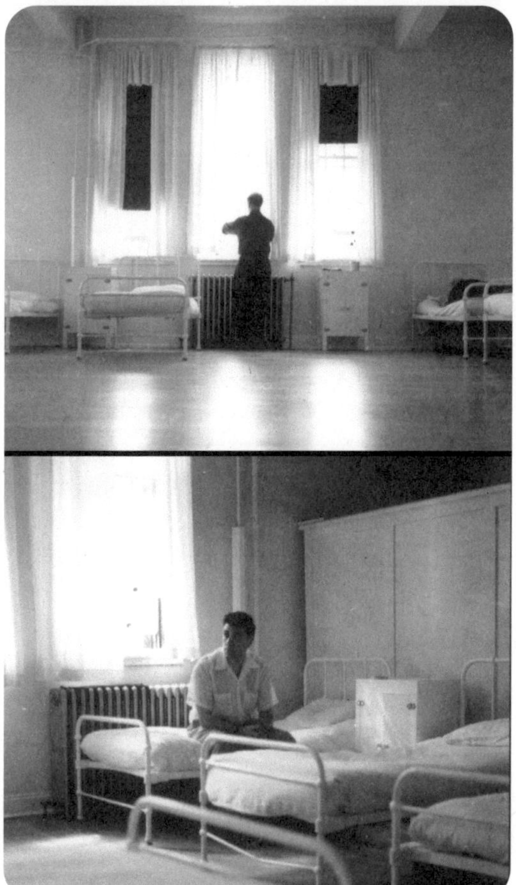

Figure 1
Weyburn Mental Hospital in Saskatchewan.

Photo: Courtesy of University of Saskatchewan Archives.

Figure 2
Reporter Sidney Katz pictured looking out a window (top) and sitting in an empty ward as he visits the Saskatchewan Hospital at Weyburn, to learn more about LSD experiments.

Photos: Mike Kesterton, courtesy University of Manitoba Archives & Special Collections, Mike Kesterton fonds, A2012-39, Box 1, Envelope #2, 12–13.

The Original Psychedelic

Alkaloids were pivotal to the development of the pharmaceutical industry. German chemists isolated and named the alkaloid (active principle) of the peyote cactus in 1897 as part of a larger process of harvesting plants for their potential medical applications. The first alkaloid was derived from opium in 1803 and named "morphine" after Morpheus, the Greek god of dreaming. Cocaine was isolated from the coca leaf in 1896. Both discoveries generated enthusiasm for finding chemicals that come from natural sources, especially plants, and could modernize pain relief, among other medical uses.[5]

Mescaline did not initially attract the same amount of attention as morphine and cocaine. In 1919, another German chemist artificially synthesized mescaline, demonstrating that you could produce this alkaloid without harvesting the rare cactus itself. Mescaline appeared to produce visions with fractal contents–lines and shapes that created mandalas and swirling visions. Not unlike the alcoholic drink absinthe, the intensely disorienting drug seemed to hold limited value for psychiatrists interested in treating disorders. Aside from a few published articles, mescaline, like numerous alkaloids of seemingly limited pharmacological use, appeared destined for a different historical legacy, perhaps one better left to the French salons where surrealist artists and intellectuals gathered to seek mind-exploring moments to inspire their work.

Osmond thought otherwise and began reading anthropological accounts of peyote ceremonies held by Indigenous groups in Central and North America. He reached out to chemists and botanists studying the cactus and then applied for his own supplies. In 1952, he and a colleague published their first paper on the topic, "Schizophrenia: A New Approach."[6] They began developing the idea that mescaline produced a model psychosis, a state of mind that mimicked symptoms of schizophrenia. The symptoms brought on were ones to learn from rather than fear. From this premise, Osmond felt they could better appreciate the patient's world and begin to imagine better ways of accommodating people suffering from psychotic disorders.

Osmond's paper came across Aldous Huxley's desk, and he immediately invited Osmond to visit him. Osmond arrived in Los Angeles with mescaline supplies to share with the famous author. Huxley was transfixed by his mescaline experience. He marvelled at the synesthetic qualities that distorted, and even seemed to combine, his senses, and he eagerly set about writing a new book describing his reaction. A month later, he had drafted *The Doors of Perception* (published in 1954), which became not only an early guide for medical researchers but a cult classic for psychedelic enthusiasts.[7]

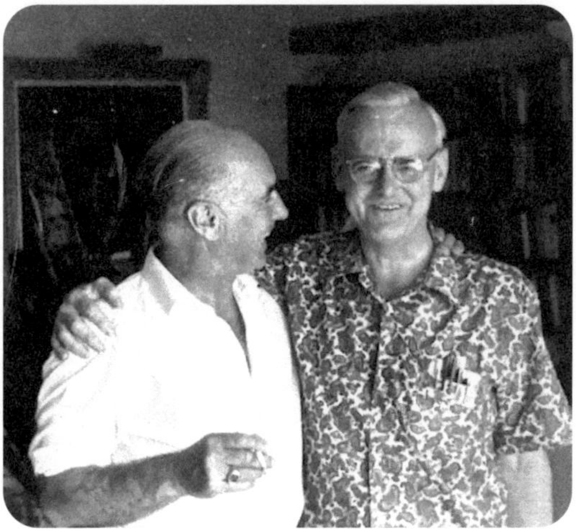

Figure 3
Albert Hofmann (left) and Humphry Osmond at Le Piol.

Photo: Courtesy of Euphemia Blackburn.

Huxley and Osmond became fast friends, writing to one another regularly and pondering the vast ways that these kinds of "mescalinized" experiences could improve humanity. They used similar substances as well, including lysergic acid diethylamide (LSD) and later alkaloids derived from mushrooms, especially psilocybin. By 1956, their regular conversations about these strange and powerful "psychosis-mimicking" drugs led them to propose a new word capturing the experience itself.

Huxley offered a word with Latin roots:
"to make this mundane world sublime
Just half a gramme of phanerothyme"

Osmond responded:
"to fall in hell or soar angelic
Just take a pinch of psychedelic."[8]

The word stuck. In 1957, Osmond introduced the word at a conference, and his published paper launched "psychedelic" into the English lexicon. The term continues to anchor the field today, but other psychedelics soon took the spotlight away from mescaline.

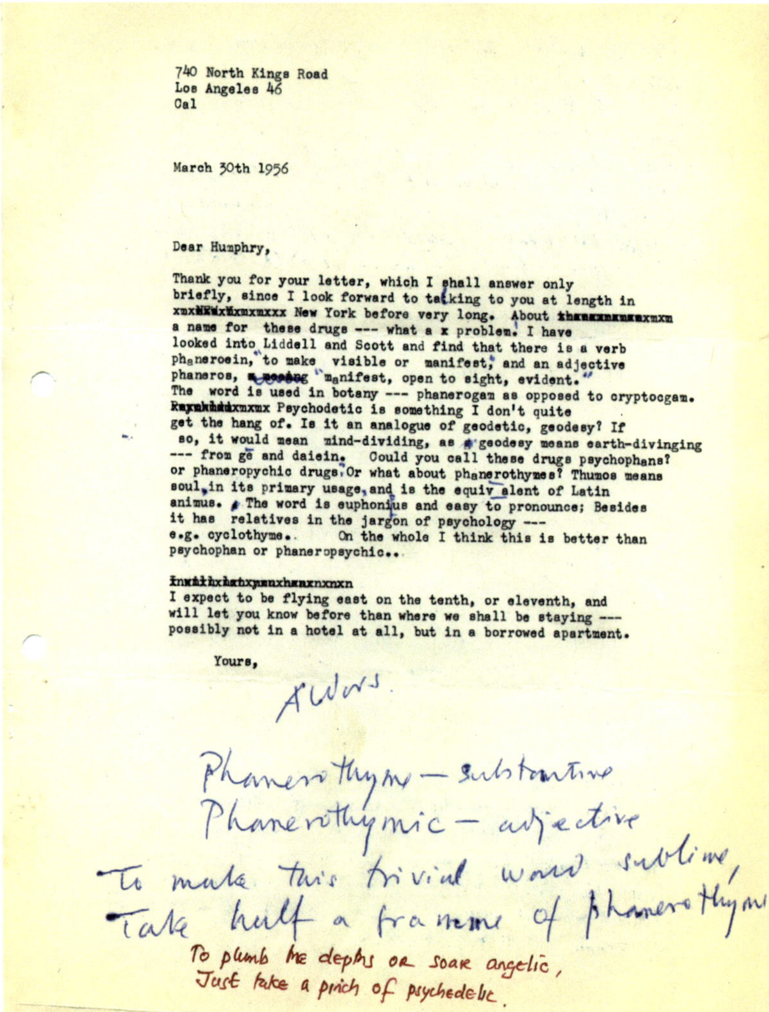

740 North Kings Road
Los Angeles 46
Cal

March 30th 1956

Dear Humphry,

Thank you for your letter, which I shall answer only briefly, since I look forward to talking to you at length in New York before very long. About a name for these drugs --- what a problem. I have looked into Liddell and Scott and find that there is a verb phaneroein, "to make visible or manifest," and an adjective phaneros, "manifest, open to sight, evident." The word is used in botany --- phanerogam as opposed to cryptocgam. Psychodetic is something I don't quite get the hang of. Is it an analogue of geodetic, geodesy? If so, it would mean mind-dividing, as geodesy means earth-divinging --- from gē and daiein. Could you call these drugs psychophans? or phaneropychic drugs. Or what about phanerothymes? Thumos means soul, in its primary usage, and is the equivalent of Latin animus. The word is euphonious and easy to pronounce; Besides it has relatives in the jargon of psychology --- e.g. cyclothyme.. On the whole I think this is better than psychophan or phaneropsychic..

I expect to be flying east on the tenth, or eleventh, and will let you know before than where we shall be staying --- possibly not in a hotel at all, but in a borrowed apartment.

Yours,

Aldous.

Phanerothyme — substantive
Phanerothymic — adjective
To make this trivial world sublime,
Take half a gramme of phanerothyme

To plumb the depths or soar angelic,
Just take a pinch of psychedelic.

Figure 4
A letter from Aldous Huxley to Humphry Osmond, on which Osmond penned a two-line poem showing his first use of the term "psychedelic," on March 30, 1956.

Photo: Courtesy of the Huxley Trust Foundation.

The Bicycle Trip That Turned on the World

In 1938, chemist Albert Hofmann first made LSD in Sandoz Laboratories in Basel, Switzerland. It remained untouched until April 16, 1943. That day, as Hofmann synthesized the drug, he got some on his fingertips. It was absorbed through his skin, and he took the first recorded LSD trip. Three days later, he tried it again, but deliberately this time, and rode his bicycle home with his lab assistant Susi Ramstein while experiencing the "terrifying" but also "dream-like" and "intoxicating" effects of LSD.[9]

LSD is an alkaloid derived from an ergot fungus, which grows on rye and other cultivated grains, and the drug has both benefits and drawbacks. Sandoz's chemists recognized that midwives had harvested ergot since at least the Middle Ages to affect blood flow and to trigger contractions in pregnant women. Longer term consumption of the fungus, however, can cause an infection, famously known in Europe as "St. Anthony's fire," that triggers delirium, convulsions, gangrene, and eventual death among many people in an affected area. In Basel, the local farmers were complaining that ergot in the food supplies was interfering with milk production in cattle. Sandoz assigned Hofmann the task of laying bare the chemistry behind these effects.

Although Hofmann had not anticipated hallucinogenic effects, the new drug eventually emerged as a psychedelic wonder drug. It did not require delicate harvesting techniques or careful cultivation practices from sacred plants, and in infinitesimal quantities, measured in the millionths of grams, it could launch subjects into a kaleidoscopic dreamscape that might even have therapeutic benefits.

Psychiatrists like Humphry Osmond were soon joined by hundreds of other scholars keen to study the psychological and pharmacological effects of this mind-manifesting drug. By the late 1950s, research units had appeared throughout Europe, the Americas, and, to a lesser extent, Africa and Asia. Beyond the drug's hallucinogenic novelty, the study of LSD defied simple categorization, demanding an interdisciplinary approach that saw medical researchers team up with anthropologists, linguists, artists, philosophers, and even unorthodox thinkers like those studying the paranormal, in an attempt to make sense of the psychedelic experience. Between 1950 and 1961, medical journals published over 1,000 scientific articles on LSD.[10] The studies ranged from animal experiments to clinical uses with humans, both those considered normal and those deemed mentally unwell.

By the end of the 1950s, LSD seemed to show real clinical promise. Major research publications claimed that a single dose of LSD, combined with a safe and supportive therapeutic environment, helped patients to fundamentally change their views of themselves. Most notably, LSD appeared to offer an effective treatment for alcoholism. Patients in research hospitals and other settings confirmed this claim, stating that under the influence of LSD they saw into themselves and recognized that they needed to change their behaviour, including their problematic drinking. For example, one woman treated with LSD in 1958 wrote about her experience, saying "I felt my old self having completely fallen away from me, with almost no recollection of what it was like before ... I felt totally loving, accepting, understanding, one with nature and the universe."[11] Another patient recalled that his LSD session produced a vision in which he was a piccolo in a great symphony, but he was out of tune. He came away from the session realizing that he needed to adjust his behaviour to tune himself. He credited Osmond's intervention into his problem drinking with saving his life.[12]

Osmond was also one of the pioneering researchers who collaborated with Alcoholics Anonymous (AA) co-founder Bill Wilson, as he sought his own LSD experience to test the theory that the drug could curb alcoholism. Wilson quietly agreed that the experience might help to simulate the idea of hitting rock bottom so that more people would seek help before it was too late. In 1961, Wilson wrote to Carl Jung, explaining that "lysergic acid (LSD) is very truly harmless and quite non addictive. Some of my AA friends and I have taken the material frequently - and with much benefit ... there is a great broadening and deepening and heightening of consciousness." Osmond, along with his colleague Abram Hoffer, continued to regularly communicate with Wilson about how the spiritual effects of LSD might help members of AA.[13]

Other clinics began testing the effects of LSD on a growing list of disorders, such as depression, trauma, and post-partum depression. Results varied, as did the methods and ethics–one of the treatments was for same-sex attraction (which was then considered a medical disorder according to the American Psychiatric Association).

Figure 5
A cartoon Albert Hofmann, the Swiss chemist and inventor of LSD, experiments in his lab at the pharmaceutical company Sandoz.

Illustration by Brian Blomerth from the graphic novel, Bicycle Day. Licensed courtesy of Anthology Editions, LLC.

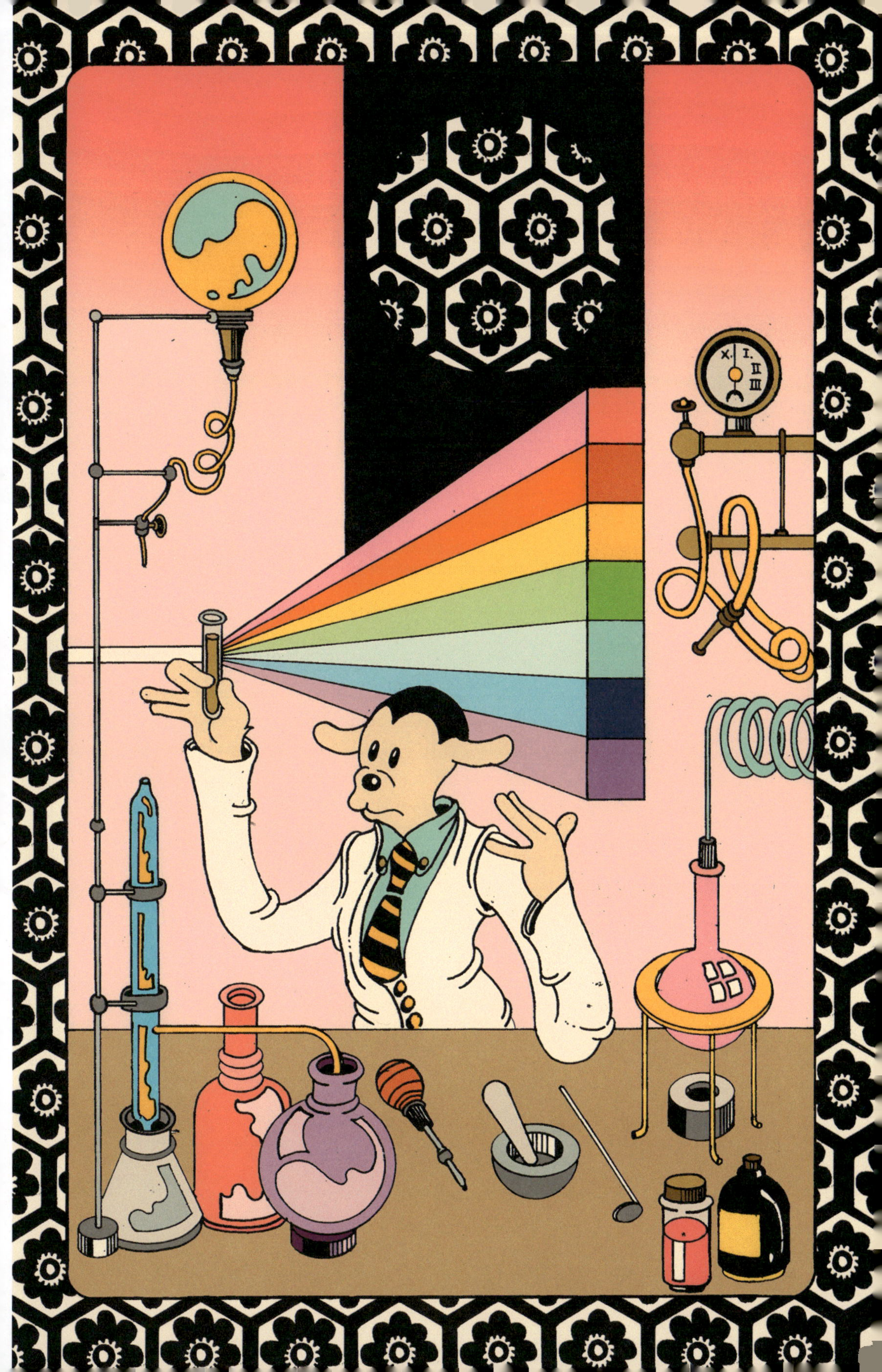

Miracle Chemicals?

Psychedelics were not the only game in town. In many of the same clinics, other pharmaceutical wonder drugs were gathering momentum. Daily-dose psychopharmaceuticals like chlorpromazine became blockbuster anti-psychotic medications, which some believed would revolutionize psychiatry by controlling unwanted symptoms and allowing people to live in communities instead of major psychiatric hospitals. These other pharmaceutical remedies operated on a different set of principles: daily usage, individual maintenance, and allegedly minimal side effects. Although the long-term side effects started mounting years later, this approach competed directly with a single-dose, therapeutic intervention that required a team of professionals to monitor and guide a patient through an active, consciousness-changing psychedelic experience.

Beyond medicine, the American Dow Chemical Company's slogan, "Better Living through Chemistry," for a moment seemed boundless. A chemical revolution appeared poised to fix the world's problems. Food shortages could be eradicated by investing in chemical fertilizers that reinvigorated tired, nutrient-depleted soils. The spectre of a ticking population bomb could be vanquished by the birth control pill, finally answering Thomas Malthus's intractable question about how to reduce the burden of fertility to balance the limits of the food supply. Investing in chemistry would make the world a better place, and LSD rode the chemical wave.

But cracks began to appear in this chemical facade. Some of the new fertilizers poisoned local water supplies, killing flora and fauna. Drugs like Chemie Gruënthal's thalidomide caused birth defects in children and sent shock waves through the European and Canadian marketplace, where the drug was stocked. The birth control pill caused fatal side effects, necessitating an American-based inquiry into the safety of these over-the-counter products.

Scientists were under political pressure to engage in more rigorous product safety testing before products could be sold publicly. The mounting pressure helped to usher in the randomized controlled trial (RCT), as a better way to evaluate the safety and efficacy of a potential drug. The RCT introduced new protocols, such as randomizing the selection process, using control groups to compare results between participants who received an active dose and those who received a placebo, and not telling participants which type of dose they received.

LSD did not perform well in RCTs. From its beginnings, whether with Indigenous peoples performing ceremonies, psychiatrists looking for models of psychosis, or alcoholics seeking self-insight, LSD worked best in an environment where those involved were aware of the drug *and* the environment. In fact, psychedelic researchers coined the concept of "set and setting" to suggest that both the mind

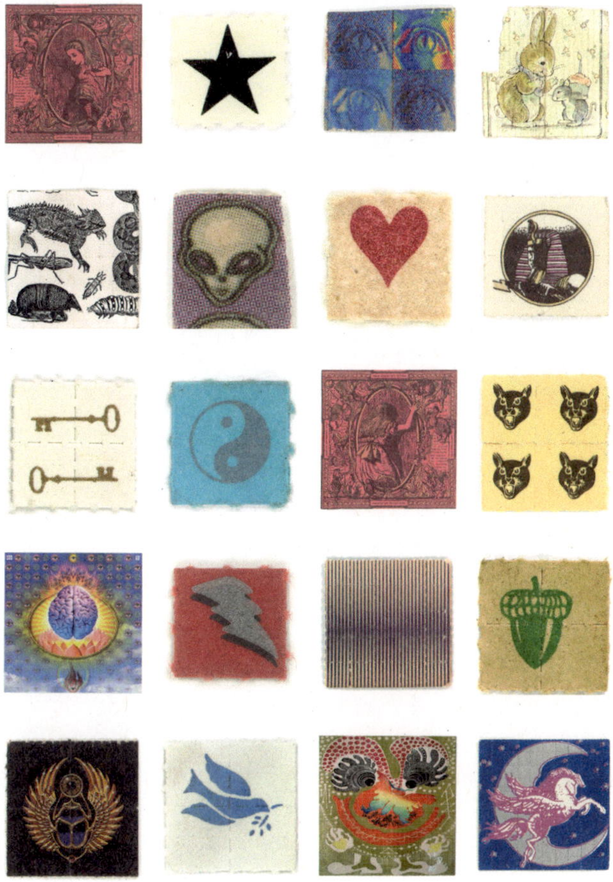

Figure 6
Blotter acid, tiny squares of paper dosed with LSD, evolved into its own art form.

Photos: Courtesy of Mark McCloud and the Institute of Illegal Images.

"set" and environmental "setting" were critical factors in optimizing the benefits of a psychedelic experience.[14] Many people argued that the best clinical results came from empathetic practitioners who had their own experiences with a psychedelic.

This approach did not suit the RCT, where neither the investigator nor the subject was supposed to know who had an active substance.[15] Imagining a psychedelic state without literally experiencing one is hard. Moreover, the environment itself was questioned as a distracting influence on one's subjective appraisal of the experience. Psychedelic researchers began to push back against the mantra of the RCT as the best arbiter of a drug's therapeutic value, but their attempts were soon overwhelmed by other concerns about psychedelics and safety.[16]

Who Spiked the Punch?

By the mid-1960s, the psychedelic genie was out of the bottle. Psychedelics had leaked out of the clinics and now flowed into an emerging drug scene that mixed cannabis, speed, and later heroin along with a cultural movement that seemed to embrace drugs as at least one's personal prerogative, if not a catalyst for cultural and political liberation.

Psychedelics seeped into the zeitgeist of a youth generation raised on post-war affluence and constrained by Cold War attitudes. Altered states of consciousness became the fuel for altered ways of thinking, living, and talking. Communal living arrangements, androgynous fashions and hairstyles, and a political alignment with civil rights, feminism, gay liberation, and environmentalism created the character of the hippie, and the hippie came to represent a challenge to Western, capitalist aspirations.

By the mid-1960s, a psychedelic aesthetic was in full bloom. Taking cues from the LSD experience itself, the arts played with a psychedelic signature: synesthesia. Posters, artwork, fashion, music, and even lifestyles began to express a psychedelic-*ness*. Folk and jazz influences colluded to produce new sounds. That same logic began to apply to psychedelics. You had to try them before you could talk about them. The Grateful Dead, a band that perhaps more than any other group in this period cultivated a psychedelic aesthetic, generated a concert experience that combined sounds and images in a festival-like atmosphere where people expressed themselves in dance, fashion, and, of course, the mind-blowing effects of "acid"—as LSD increasingly came to be called—and the pungent smell of marijuana.

Images and texts about the psychedelic 1960s suggest that acid was freely available, and some accounts blame clinical researchers for allowing their supplies to get into the wrong hands. Even the Swiss pharmaceutical company Sandoz, initially the sole legal distributor of LSD, worried that this might be the case. Albert Hofmann himself visited San Francisco and collected samples of acid tabs at a Grateful Dead concert to test these claims. To his surprise, Sandoz was not the problem. It turned out that Hofmann was not the only enterprising chemist out there.

Salacious and scandalous stories began to appear in the press about the dangers of psychedelics, and underground publications and films were making their way to conservative groups. The result was a growing backlash against these powerfully non-conformist drugs. In 1966, California authorities made LSD illegal in an effort to crack down on what appeared to be an epidemic in drug use. Authorities sought to disrupt the underground production of blotter acid—LSD distributed on blots of paper, often adorned with clever artwork—as politicians raged against the drug's harmful effects.

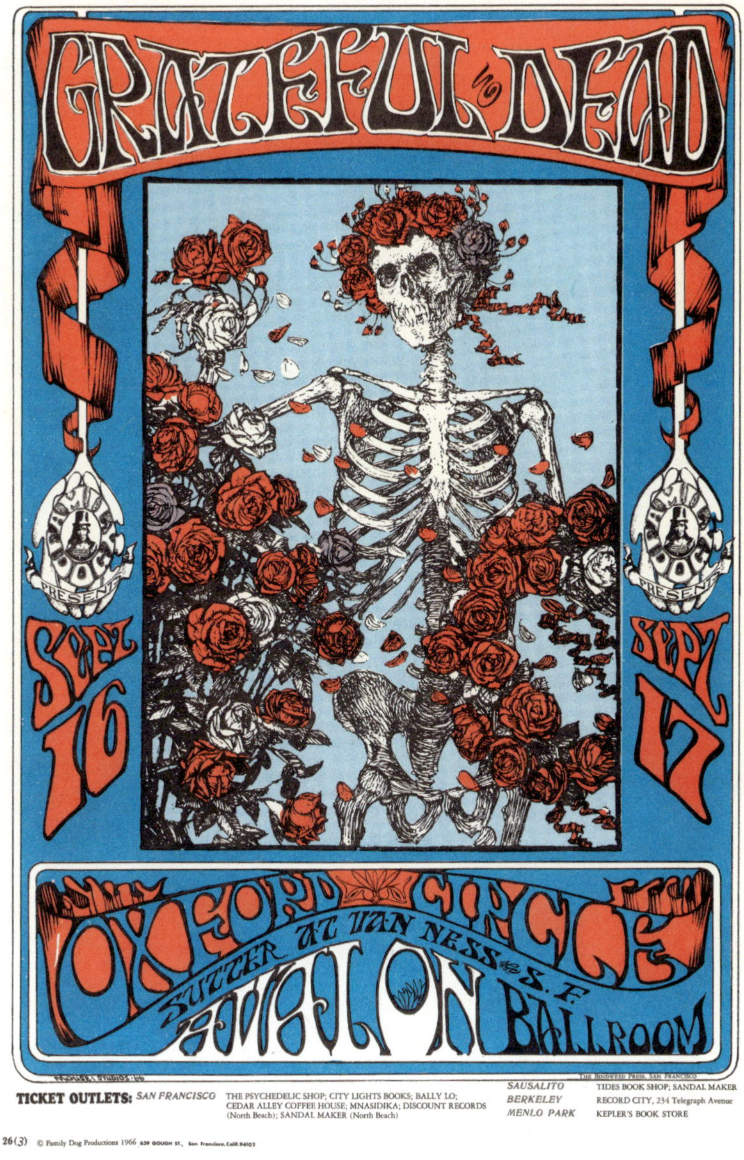

Figure 7
Skeleton and Roses, Grateful Dead,
Oxford Circle. Designed by Stanley Mouse
(American, b. 1940) and Alton Kelley
(American, 1940–2008), Mouse Studios, 1966.
Colour offset lithograph poster.
ROM 989.78.10.

Photo: © ROM.

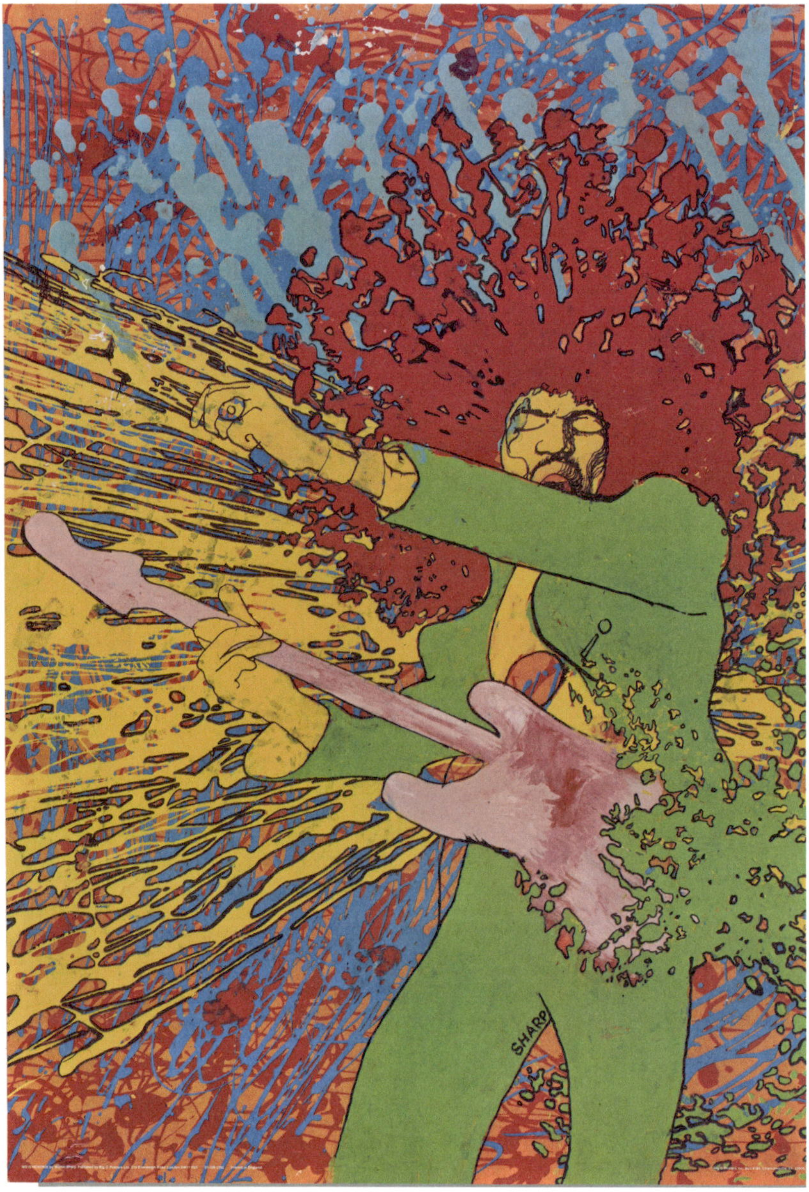

Figure 8
Explosion, Jimi Hendrix.
Martin Sharp (Australian, 1942–2013, active in London in the '60s), 1967.
Offset colour lithograph poster.
ROM 989.269.6.

Photo: Paul Eekhoff © ROM.

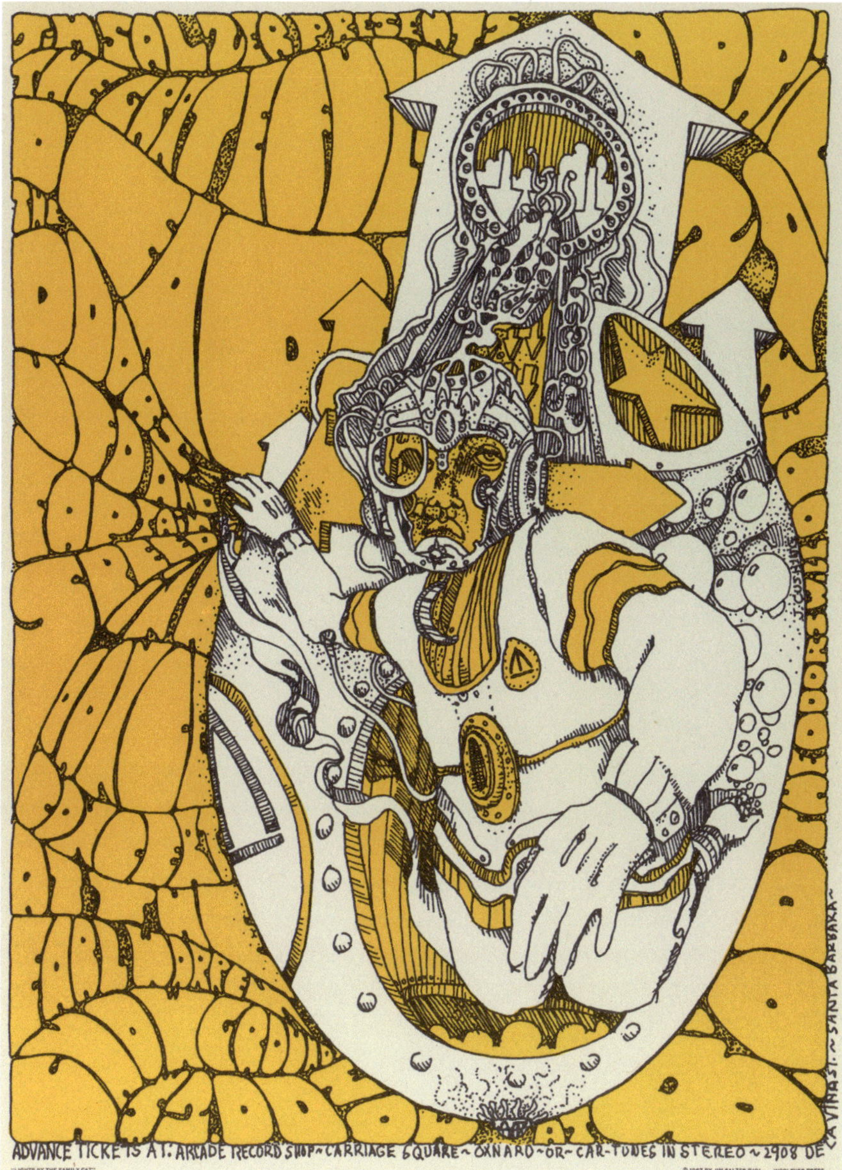

Figure 9
Grateful Dead, The Doors, U.F.O, Captain Speed.
J. Cushing, 1967.
Offset colour lithograph poster.
ROM 989.269.5.

Photo: Paul Eekhoff © ROM.

The backlash against psychedelics was just beginning. Newspaper reports ramped up efforts to associate psychedelics with brain damage rather than mind expansion. LSD was banned in the U.S. and Canada in 1968, with other psychedelics following in the next few years. And by the 1970s, an American journalist discovered that the CIA had been involved in unethical LSD experiments that amounted to brainwashing or torture. These kinds of stories decidedly shifted public attitudes against seeing psychedelics as either medicines or benign party drugs. They were dangerous and required prohibition and control.

Psychedelics and the War on Drugs

Historians typically describe the 1970s as the beginning of the war on drugs. American President Richard Nixon famously declared this moment in 1971, when a number of drugs, including psychedelics, moved into a new international designation as dangerous substances considered to have no medical value. Many institutional research labs shifted away from psychedelic studies due to the mounting political pressure, difficulties obtaining grants, and new rules about how to test psychedelics using RCTs.[17]

The war on drugs escalated over the next two decades. School programs warned about the dangers of drugs, and advertisements flooded the airwaves. This period also coincided with aggressive new government policies, including investments in foreign policing of the international drug trade, and the mass incarceration of people involved in domestic drug crimes; in the U.S. and Canada, the majority of those people jailed for drug possession were people of colour.[18]

Psychedelics users, and some chemists, moved underground.[19] Throughout the 1980s and 1990s, while psychedelics remained illegal, underground publications circulated with information about how to find or even grow your own psychedelics. Cultural gatherings and music festivals continued to provide health support for people attending these events who might have come with their own psychedelics, like the MDMA, or ecstasy, that became increasingly popular at raves.

The resurgence of psychedelics in medicine in the 21st century brings together some of the same historical threads as Western medicine once again faces an overburdened healthcare system struggling to accommodate the growing mental health demands. Revisiting the first generation of psychedelic science from the 1950s, some investigators today are careful to avoid the mistakes of the past, seeing individuals like Osmond as cautionary tales. Others are keen to learn more about those earlier trials, buoyed by the kind of optimism that psychedelics might

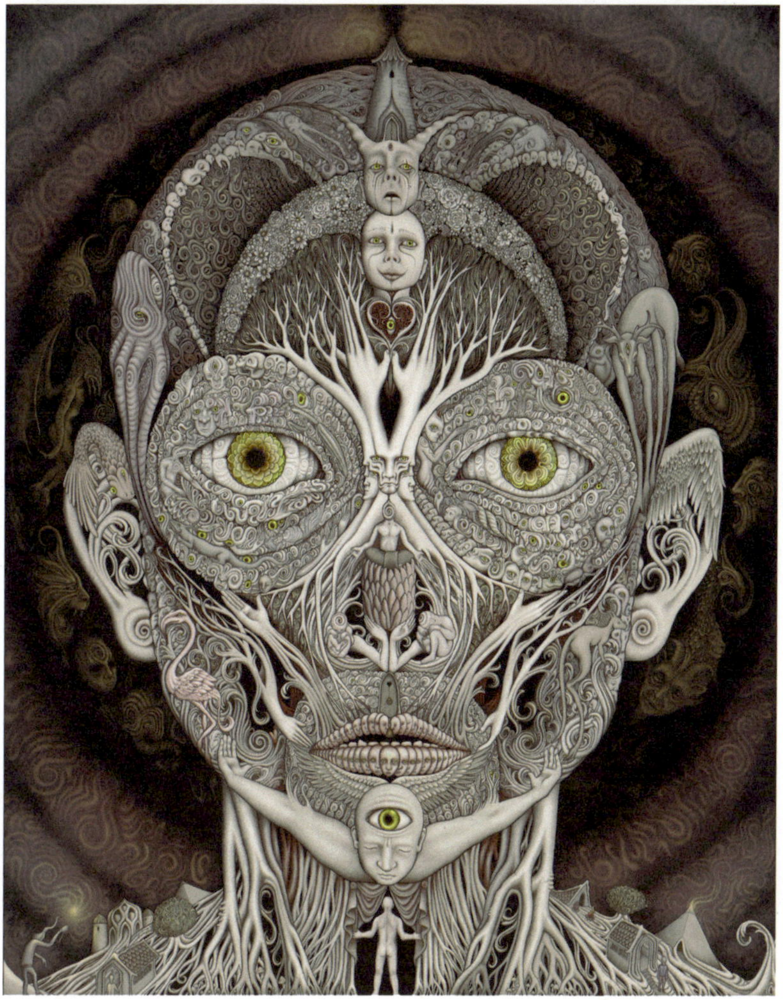

Figure 10
Face the Abyss by Mr Crystalface.
Photo: Courtesy of the artist.

help us think differently about psychological distress, suffering, and the growing global burden of mental illness.

As the war on drugs fades away and several jurisdictions begin to relax prohibitions on substances like cannabis, the regulatory fate of psychedelics has re-emerged as a genuine topic of interest in an era when mental illness continues to demand bold new solutions. The 1950s is here again, and we have a chance to reconsider the possibilities of psychedelics.

1 Osmond, H. (1957). A review of the clinical effects of psychotomimetic agents. *Annals of the New York Academy of Sciences, 66*(3), 418–434.

2 Healy, D. (2002). *The creation of psychopharmacology*. Harvard University Press; and Herzberg, D. (2020). *White market drugs: Big pharma and the hidden history of addiction in America*. University of Chicago Press.

3 Dyck, E. (2008). *Psychedelic psychiatry: LSD from clinic to campus*. JHU Press.

4 Osmond wrote extensively on this idea of a "sick society" or rethinking the "sick role." For example, see Siegler, M., & Osmond, H. (1973). The "sick role" revisited. *The Hastings Center Studies, 1*(3), 41–58. https://doi.org/10.2307/3527465.

5 Jay, M. (2019). *Mescaline: A global history of the first psychedelic*. Yale University Press.

6 Osmond, H., & Smythies, J. (1952). Schizophrenia: A new approach. *Journal of Mental Science, 98*(411), 309–315.

7 Huxley, A. (1954). *Doors of perception*. Chatto & Windus.

8 Bisbee, C. C., Bisbee, P., Dyck, E., Farrell, P., Sexton, J., & Spisak, J. (Eds.). (2018). *Psychedelic prophets: The letters of Aldous Huxley and Humphry Osmond: Vol. 48*. McGill-Queen's University Press.

9 Hofmann, A. (1980). *LSD: My problem child*. McGraw-Hill.

10 Osmond makes this claim in Hoffer, A., & Osmond, H. (1967). *The hallucinogens*. Academic Press.

11 Hollywood Hospital patient (anonymized), 1958. Cited in Dyck, E., & Donaldson, J. (2022). *The acid room: The psychedelic trials and tribulations of Hollywood Hospital*. Anvil Press, p. 41.

12 Patient (anonymous) interview with E. Dyck, 2002. For more on the concept of "problem drinking," see Dyck, E. (2006). "Hitting highs at rock bottom": LSD treatment for alcoholism, 1950-1970. *Social History of Medicine, 19*(2), 313-329.

13 McCabe, I. (2015). *Carl Jung and Alcoholics Anonymous: The twelve steps as a spiritual journey of individuation*. Routledge, p. 149.

14 Hartogsohn, I. (2016). Set and setting, psychedelics and the placebo response: An extra-pharmacological perspective on psychopharmacology. *Journal of Psychopharmacology, 30*(12), 1259–1267.

15 Shorter, E. (2011). A brief history of placebos and clinical trials in psychiatry. *Canadian Journal of Psychiatry, 56*(4), 193–197; and Dyck, E., & Delille, E. (2022). Human experimentation and clinical trials in psychiatry. In D. McCallum (Ed.),*The Palgrave handbook of the history of human sciences* (pp. 1357–1378). Springer Nature Singapore.

16 For example, see Hoffer, A. (1967). A theoretical examination of double-blind design. *Canadian Medical Association Journal, 97*(3), 123–127.

17 Oram, M. (2018). *The trials of psychedelic therapy: LSD psychotherapy in America*. JHU Press.

18 Farber, D. (Ed.). (2021). *The war on drugs: A history*. NYU Press; and Sangster, J. (1999). Criminalizing the colonized: Ontario Native women confront the criminal justice system, 1920-60. *Canadian Historical Review, 80*(1), 32–60.

19 Shulgin, A. T., & Shulgin, A. (1991). *PIHKAL: A chemical love story*. Transform Press.

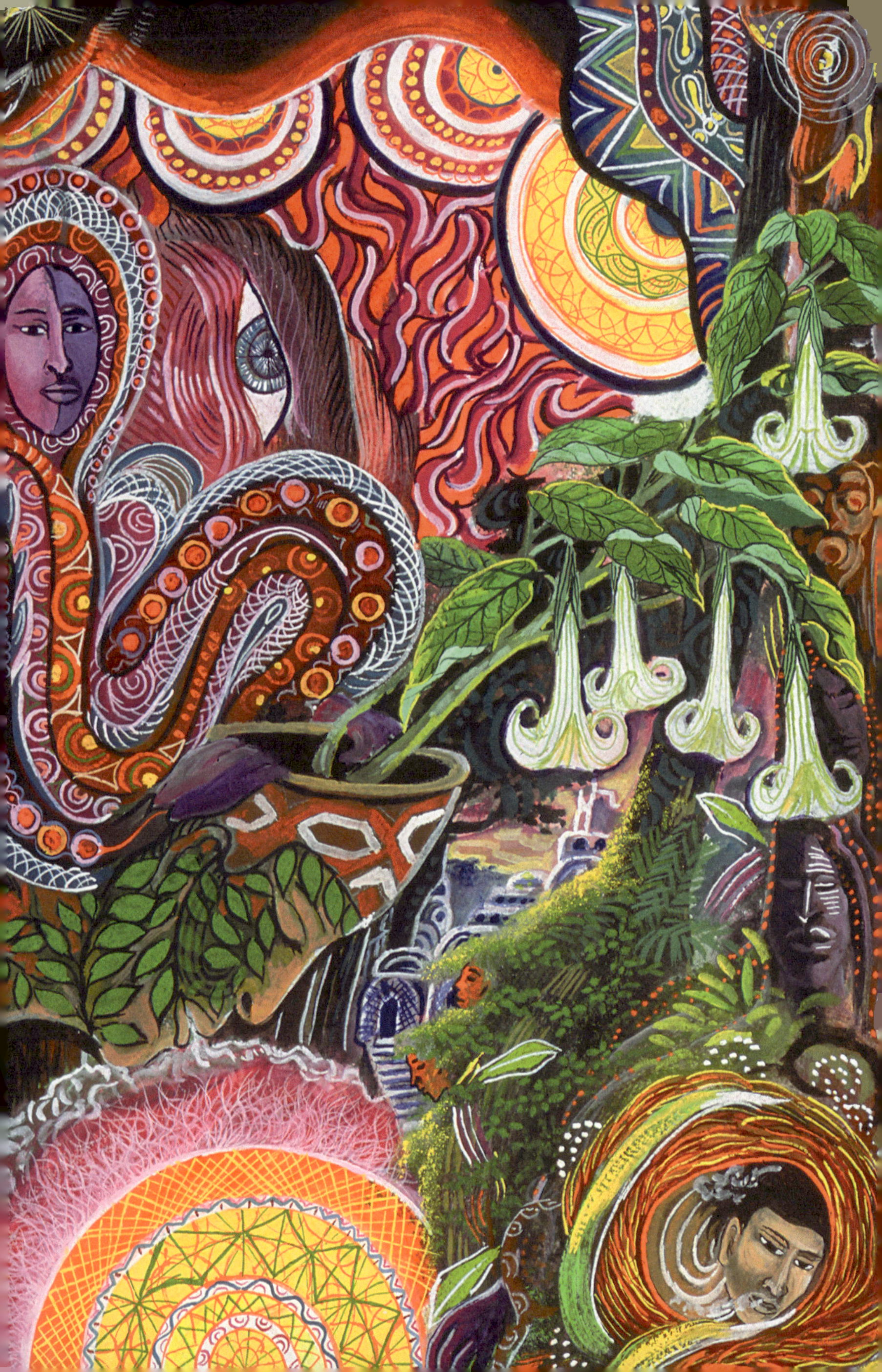

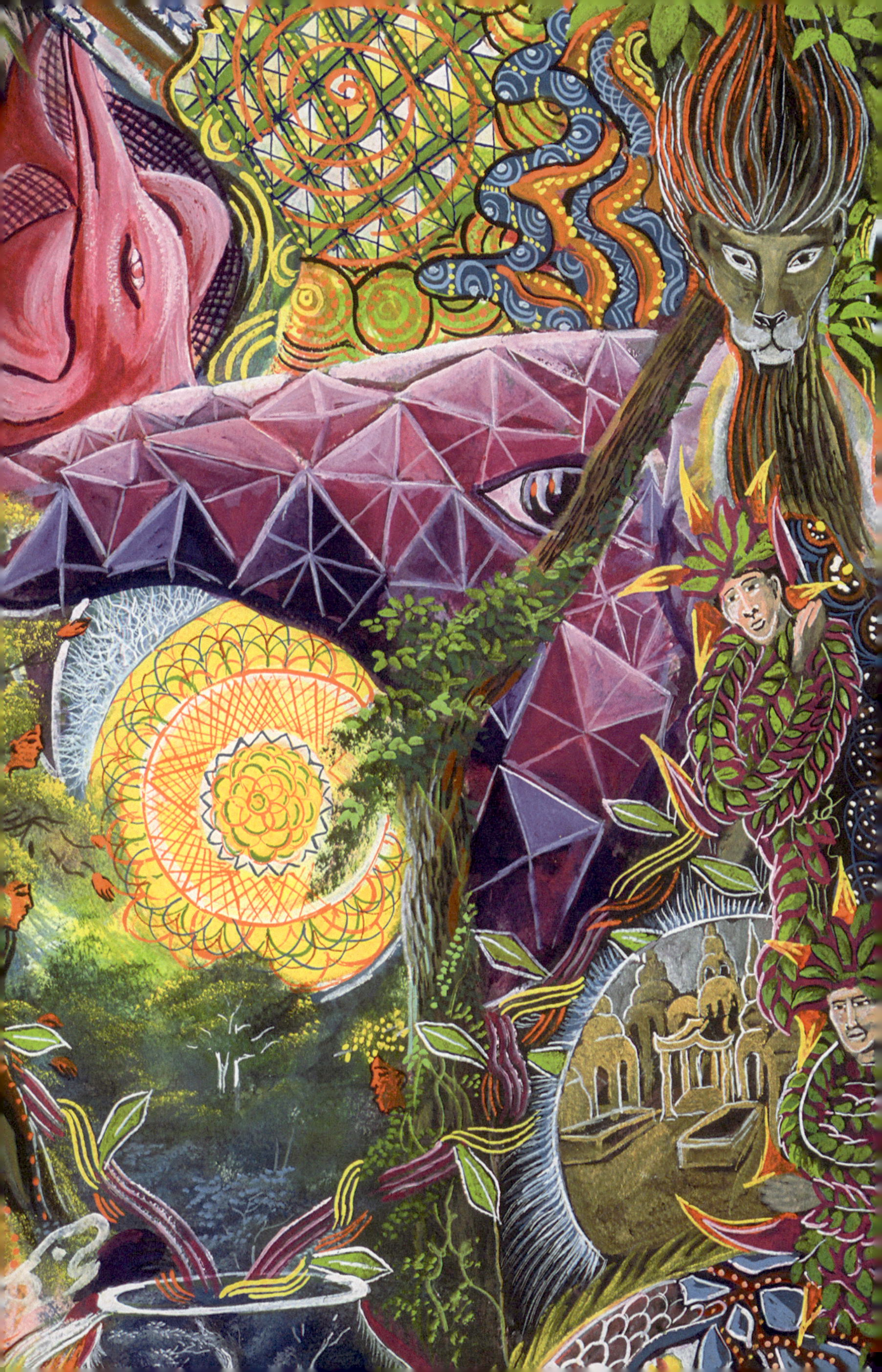

3

Your Brain on Psychedelics

MANOJ K. DOSS

IF YOU WERE TO ASK 10 SCIENTISTS how psychedelics work in the brain, chances are you would get 10 different answers. Our answers would vary based on a) our definition of a psychedelic, b) our models for brain function, and c) whether our theoretical framework focuses on brain activity at smaller or larger levels of analysis. Several proposed theories exist, but a lot of information remains unknown.

The "classic psychedelics" include drugs such as psilocybin (found in "magic mushrooms"), lysergic acid diethylamide (LSD), mescaline (found in certain cacti), and dimethyltryptamine (DMT). A common feature of all these drugs (as well as of lesser-known psychedelics like 2,5-dimethoxy-bromo-phenethylamine, or 2C-B) is their activation of various serotonin receptor subtypes, particularly the 5-HT_{2A} receptor. Receptors are proteins found on the billions of neurons that make up the brain and can be thought of as "locks" designed to be opened by a particular chemical "key" in order to allow neurons to communicate with each other (Figure 1). Typically, serotonin is the key that opens up 5-HT_{2A} receptors, which are most densely distributed in the cortex,[1] the outer layer of the brain that is particularly developed in humans. However, many psychedelics are structurally similar enough to serotonin such that they can fit into 5-HT_{2A} receptors but activate them in a way that clearly diverges from serotonin, as well as from certain medications that also activate these receptors but are not psychedelic (such as the Parkinson's medication lisuride). This idiosyncratic activation produces chemical exchanges between neurons that give rise to prototypical psychedelic effects such as visual distortions and seemingly profound insights. A psychedelic's affinity for 5-HT_{2A} receptors is directly related to its potency,[2] and blocking these receptors can prevent the subjective effects of psychedelics.[3]

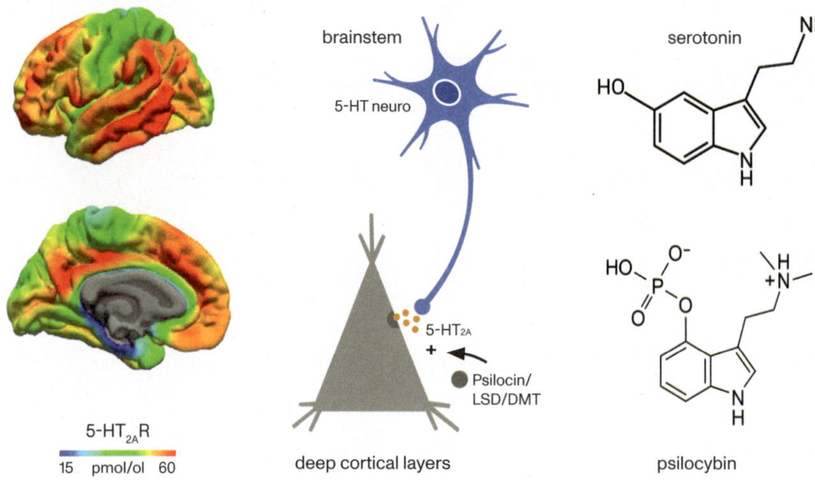

Figure 1
A 5-HT_{2A} receptor density map of the human brain; a serotonin neuron from the brain stem projecting to cortical neurons containing 5-HT_{2A} receptors; the similarity of these molecules to each other.

Other hallucinogens that bind to receptors other than the 5-HT_{2A} receptor are also sometimes referred to as "psychedelics." These drugs include "dissociatives" (drugs that block N-methyl-D-aspartate, or NMDA, receptors, like ketamine; phencyclidine, or PCP; dextromethorphan; and nitrous oxide) and "oneirogens" (drugs that activate κ-opioid receptors, like salvinorin A from *Salvia divinorum* and noribogaine, a metabolite of ibogaine, which is found in *Tabernanthe iboga*). The drug ±3,4-methylenedioxymethamphetamine (MDMA) also weakly binds to 5-HT_{2A} receptors, giving it a light psychedelic effect. However, MDMA's primary effects appear to come from releasing serotonin, dopamine, and norepinephrine, giving it stimulant effects shared with drugs like amphetamine and unique "entactogenic" effects, which involve particularly heightened emotional openness and feelings of empathy. Although the receptor targets of these drugs differ from those of drugs like psilocybin and LSD, the subjective effects can be somewhat similar, and as will be discussed, they may even share some downstream neural mechanisms. Here, "psychedelic" will refer only to hallucinogenic drugs that activate 5-HT_{2A} receptors.

The Changeable Brain

Recent work analyzing changes to synapses (the area where two neurons meet) under psychedelics suggests that psychedelics increase neural plasticity, or the brain's capacity to change. A single dose of a psychedelic (and also of ketamine and noribogaine) has been found to increase the number of dendrites (the branches that emanate from a neuron's body) and the number of spines on these dendrites (the bumps where another neuron can create a synapse). These changes happen within 24 hours and persist up to a month,[4] thereby potentially allowing for new learning even after the immediate intoxicating effects of the psychedelic wear off. Rampant plasticity, however, can be harmful, such as in addiction, and stimulants (for example, cocaine, amphetamine) also induce this type of plasticity.[5] One possibility is that stimulants drive plasticity over time across the brain, especially in the striatum, a region involved in habitual behaviours and addiction, whereas psychedelics may rapidly and preferentially drive plasticity in the cortex.

A related but different idea is that psychedelics enhance "metaplasticity," the regulation of plasticity that can make neural changes more sensitive to other factors such as the environment. Psychedelics may "reopen" critical periods that, when provided with the right input, can potentially allow one to rapidly learn certain types of information as if one were a child again. For example, a critical period for language learning occurs during childhood, after which it can be difficult to master a language. Although psychedelics have not been found to enhance language learning in adult humans, they have been found to facilitate what is known as "social reward learning" in adult mice.[6] Whereas juvenile mice learn to prefer hanging around spaces containing cues that remind them of their friends, adult mice can no longer learn such a preference. Two days after being administered psychedelics, however, adult mice preferentially learned to spend time in portions of an environment containing social cues. Moreover, when looking at the brains of these mice, scientists observed changes in the activation of neurons in the striatum (a form of plasticity) only in the presence of oxytocin, a neurohormone released from social bonding. Thus, psychedelics alone did not alter plasticity of the striatum, but rather, psychedelics coupled with environmental social cues did. Because ketamine, ibogaine, and MDMA also opened this critical period and produced similar changes in downstream gene expression as those of psychedelics, some scientists suggest that all these drugs should be considered "psychedelic" despite their activation of different receptors to begin the process.

The Thalamic Gating Model

More recent work has zoomed out from receptors and synapses and used a "systems level" analysis of the brain that looks at the activity of multiple neurons forming circuits. This research has been enabled by methods that can non-invasively measure activity across the whole brain—namely, functional magnetic resonance imaging (fMRI), a technology not available to researchers during the first wave of psychedelic research in the 1950s and 1960s (see chapter 2). fMRI measures blood flow, which correlates with neural activity (a region that is more active requires more blood). In addition to measuring how different brain areas activate and deactivate, researchers use the common fMRI measure of functional connectivity, the strength of coupling between two or more regions over time. If two brain areas tend to activate and deactivate together, these regions are likely communicating with each other (via direct anatomical connections or a third region that modulates the activity of these other regions), and researchers can look at how communication patterns change under different conditions (for example, under the effects of psychedelics).

The first systems-level model of psychedelic drug action was the thalamic gating model (Figure 2).[7] The thalamus is the structure in the brain through which all sensory information except smell passes before it is transmitted to the cortex. The thalamus is thought to act like a filter or gate for sorting out relevant sensory information, such as listening to a friend at a loud party. Gating of sensory information from the thalamus to the cortex is controlled by a circuit that also involves two subcortical structures, the globus pallidus and the striatum, in addition to the cortex and thalamus. Typically, the thalamus is under the control of the globus pallidus, which partially inhibits the thalamus, and the globus pallidus is under the control of the striatum, which partially inhibits the globus pallidus. When psychedelics activate 5-HT_{2A} receptors in the cortex, however, the cortex activates the striatum, which then inhibits the globus pallidus further, resulting in disinhibition of the thalamus. This disinhibition is thought to allow more sensory information to pass through the thalamus, thereby flooding the cortex with sensory information and producing greater distractibility and perceptual distortions.

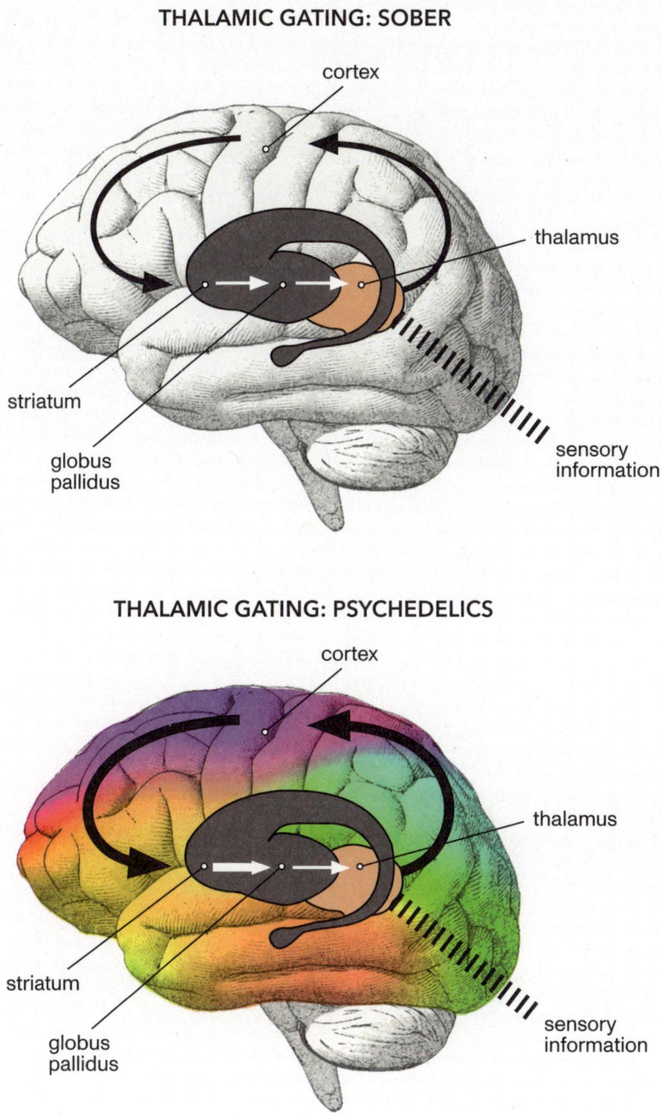

Figure 2
Thalamic Gating Model of Psychedelic Drug Action. Black arrows represent activation, and white arrows represent inhibition. Typically, the thalamus receives sensory information and transmits only a portion of this information to the cortex because it is inhibited by the globus pallidus. Under psychedelics, however, 5-HT_{2A} receptors in the cortex are activated, resulting in an increase in activation of the striatum (thicker black arrow), which increases its inhibition of the globus pallidus (thicker white arrow). This inhibition of the cortex results in disinhibition of the thalamus (thinner white arrow), which then increases its transmission of sensory information to the cortex (thicker black arrow).

Support for the thalamic gating model comes from multiple independent studies in humans that have found that psychedelics increase functional connectivity between the thalamus and the cortex.[8] Moreover, animal work has also found increased cortical activation under psychedelics mediated by the thalamus.[9] Nonetheless, a challenge to the thalamic gating model is that disinhibition of the thalamus should increase its activity, but various studies have had different results: psychedelics increase, decrease, or do not impact thalamic activity.[10]

Studies on prepulse inhibition provide an example of the mixed support for the thalamic gating model. One of the model's predictions is that psychedelics should impair one's ability to filter out sensory information. Prepulse inhibition is a measure of sensory filtering in which a response to a stimulus is smaller when preceded by a similar but weaker stimulus. For example, if a loud tone is played, a person will reflexively blink their eyes, but this response will be smaller if a softer tone is played just before it. Although animal studies have found psychedelics to decrease prepulse inhibition (a response to a loud tone is not decreased by a smaller preceding tone),[11] human studies have found mixed evidence. When the timing between the softer tone and louder tone is short, psychedelics decrease prepulse inhibition.[12] However, when the timing between the tones is longer, psychedelics have no effect on or even enhance prepulse inhibition.[13]

REBUS

More recently, some scientists have proposed a model known as RElaxed Beliefs Under pSychedelics (REBUS),[14] which is based on the predictive coding framework for brain function. Under this framework, the brain is always trying to predict the causes of sensory information and update its model to minimize prediction error, the difference between what it expects and what it actually receives from the senses. The brain is organized hierarchically from "low-level" areas, which are driven by individual senses, such as vision, to "high-level" areas, which integrate multiple senses and represent more abstract information, such as beliefs and one's sense of self. When a difference appears between incoming sensory information and a prediction, this prediction error is passed up to the next level of the brain's hierarchy in an effort to update the brain's model. If this information still cannot be explained, another prediction error occurs and is passed up the hierarchy until it can be explained away. Typically, most information is explained at lower levels, and only prediction errors that reach the highest level of the brain's hierarchy are those for which we have conscious awareness.

Here is an example that will make REBUS concrete and relevant to psychedelics. Typically, we might believe that walls do not breathe. This belief might be so strongly assumed by our brain that even with our imperfect visual system and under changing light conditions (conditions that produce low-level prediction errors), we still do not see motion in a wall. We might even miss the motion on a wall, such as from a colony of ants walking on it. However, under psychedelics, REBUS proposes that this belief about the world, that walls do not breathe, is now relaxed, and low-level prediction errors driven by imperfect visual information must be interpreted by the brain, resulting in illusory motion. Whereas other theories have proposed that illusory motion may simply come from activating 5-HT_{2A} receptors in visual regions of the brain[15] (where 5-HT_{2A} receptors are densely distributed[16]), REBUS requires an attenuation of the high-level brain.

REBUS adherents posit that at the top of the brain's hierarchy is the default mode network (DMN), a set of high-level brain areas that densely express 5-HT_{2A} receptors and support internal states such as episodic memory and mind wandering—and are affected by psychedelics. According to REBUS, the DMN represents the sense of self and heavily constrains the interpretation of sensory information. Several studies have found that psychedelics disrupt functional connectivity within the DMN,[17] a finding that has been interpreted as "ego dissolution," the loss of one's sense of self that is sometimes evoked by psychedelics. A consequence of disrupting the DMN's constraints on information processing is that high-level regions representing beliefs about the world and one's sense of self become more sensitive to sensory information, allowing for their revision. Such revision could be beneficial if, for example, a person has a negative view of who they are.

This hypersensitivity to environmental input also results in a larger number of states that the brain can go through and thus experiences we can have. This diversity in brain states has been measured by entropy. Entropy can be thought of as how evenly distributed the states of a system are. For example, a coin has two sides (heads or tails), and it is perfectly entropic because its affinity for both sides is equal. In contrast, the distribution of how tall people are is less entropic because certain heights are more common and others are rare. Psychedelics may drive the brain into more frequently experiencing rare states (Figure 3), and such variability may at least partially persist into the weeks after having a psychedelic experience, thereby enhancing cognitive flexibility (adaptively shifting between different cognitive states due to the demands of a changing environment). Although psychedelics can impair cognitive flexibility during their immediate effects,[18] when entropy would be expected to be highest, psychedelics have been found to enhance cognitive flexibility and neural variability one week after psychedelic therapy in patients with depression.[19]

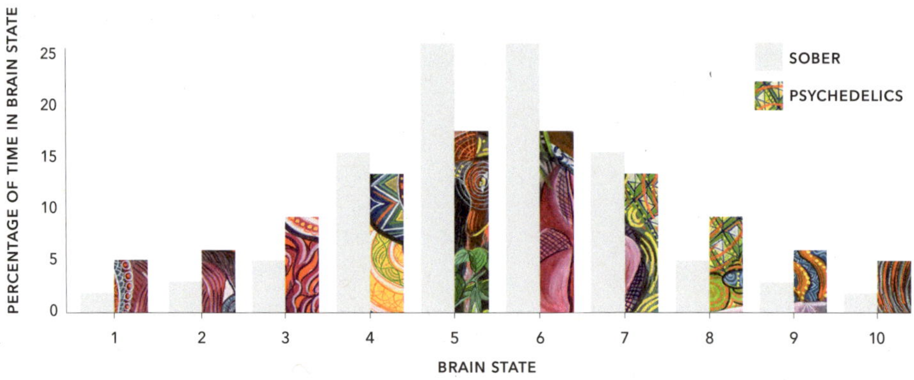

Figure 3
Distribution of Brain States. Example of how the brain can become more entropic under psychedelics. Here, the brain has 10 possible states. Under sober conditions, the brain spends most of its time in states 5 and 6 (for example, brain states associated with being attentive and planning for tomorrow) and rarely finds itself in states 1 and 10 (for example, brain states associated with being playful and in awe). Under psychedelics, the brain now spends less time in states 5 and 6 and more often finds itself in the rarer brain states.

REBUS is not without its flaws, however. One issue is its focus on the DMN, a network involved with not only self-referential processing but also non-self-related functions such as semantic memory (general knowledge about the world, such as what a pizza is) and theory of mind (the ability to understand the mental states of others). Moreover, drugs such as Δ9-tetrahydrocannabinol (THC from cannabis),[20] alcohol,[21] amphetamine,[22] and caffeine[23] can also decrease DMN functional connectivity. Ironically, ketamine, a drug often compared to psychedelics, has been found to decrease,[24] have no effect on,[25] or even increase[26] DMN functional connectivity. Complicating matters further is that larger effects of psychedelics are found outside of the DMN, including sensory areas[27] where REBUS predicts psychedelic effects should be smallest.

The REBUS model has other drawbacks. Another challenge to REBUS is that ego dissolution has been found to correlate with brain areas not within the DMN.[28] Although one study found that disrupted DMN functional connectivity was associated with reports of ego dissolution,[29] a direct attempt to replicate this result found no such association despite containing a larger sample of participants who moved less in the scanner[30] (motion can cause problems in fMRI data). Finally, increased entropy may be an artifact from scanning the brain under "resting-state" conditions in which no task is involved and participants can mentally engage however they please. Under non-drug resting-state conditions, more than 40 percent of participants report falling asleep in the scanner,[31] whereas psychedelics prevent sleep. Thus, it should not be surprising that participants cycle through more brain states and cognitive operations under a drug that keeps them awake compared with a placebo condition in which people may actually rest (but have the capacity to cycle through multiple brain or cognitive states if cued to do so). Indeed, caffeine has also been found to increase neural entropy.[32]

CCC

Other proposed models of psychedelic drug action are still in their infancy and integrate knowledge across different levels of analysis. The cortico-claustro-cortical (CCC) model, for example, focuses on the "claustrum," a tiny strip in the brain that densely expresses 5-HT_{2A} receptors and κ-opioid receptors and is highly connected to the rest of the brain.[33] Because the claustrum is so small, only recently have methods been developed to query its function. Typically, when exerting control over the rest of the brain, the prefrontal cortex is thought to send a signal to the claustrum, which may then coordinate activity into distinct brain states. However, CCC posits that under psychedelics a "misfire" occurs between the claustrum and cortex that produces less differentiated brain states typical of sobriety. Such diminished capacity to instantiate brain states could inhibit a person's ability to adapt to a changing environment, resulting in the experience of a loss of control reported under psychedelics.

FLUX

A model that I have recently been working on called "FLUency eXaggeration (FLUX)" aims to reconcile how psychedelics paradoxically produce experiences of heightened novelty and familiarity. This model proposes that psychedelics may enhance processing fluency, or the ease with which information is processed. The re-experience of a recent stimulus will be more easily processed than a novel stimulus, as measured by less brain activity and faster reactions to the familiar stimulus. Moreover, the fluency of a stimulus can also be enhanced by seeing related stimuli. For example, seeing the word "sweet" increases the fluency of the word "sour," and seeing the word "sour" increases the fluency of the word "lemon." Under psychedelics, however, seeing "sweet" enhanced fluency for the word "lemon," suggesting a more promiscuous fluency.[34]

Typically, the brain is thought to like familiar stimuli, as their fluency means that it expends fewer resources to process these stimuli. For example, the mere exposure effect is when one finds a face as more likeable simply after seeing it more than once, and the illusory truth effect is when one finds a statement to feel truer simply after reading or hearing it more than once. These "cognitive illusions" produced by fluency may even be heightened under psychedelics. People report becoming better friends after taking psychedelics together (even if they just laid on couches all day), and they report an undeniable sense of knowledge known as the "noetic quality" (for example, understanding consciousness and the universe despite not winning Nobel prizes for these supposed insights). Such misattributions may be especially likely when the source of fluency cannot be remembered. For example, if you keep hearing that all polar bears are left-handed, you might eventually believe this statement (due to increased fluency), but if you can explicitly remember that you heard this statement from a trickster friend, you may be less likely to misattribute the fluency to the plausibility of the statement.

Psychedelics operate differently on memories formed by recollection versus on those formed by fluency/familiarity. Psychedelics impair the formation of recollection memories that can explicitly localize a source (such as recognizing a face on the bus because the face belongs to the barista who made your coffee that morning). Yet psychedelics surprisingly spare or even enhance the formation of memories based on familiarity, in which one recognizes a previously seen stimulus simply based on a feeling of knowing (such as recognizing someone but not recalling where or when you met that individual; memory researchers have coincidentally referred to such feelings of familiarity as "noetic consciousness").[35] This is striking because drugs such as alcohol, ketamine, and THC impair the formation of memories based on both recollection and familiarity, and when recollection fails and familiarity is high, bizarre phenomena sometimes experienced under psychedelics can occur such as *déjà vu*, *presque vu* (the feeling of insight), and premonition.[36]

Psychedelics may produce these disparate effects on these two types of memories due to the expression of 5-HT_{2A} receptors on different types of neurons in different brain regions. As discussed, 5-HT_{2A} receptors are most densely distributed in the cortex on neurons that increase cortical activity, and the cortex supports feelings of familiarity, insight, and fluency. In contrast, 5-HT_{2A} receptors in the hippocampus, a region that supports recollection, are on inhibitory neurons that decrease hippocampal activity. Whereas REBUS predicts that the hippocampus should drive activity in the cortex (because it considers the hippocampus to be "low-level"), data show that psychedelics decrease functional connectivity between the hippocampus and cortex[37] (as would be predicted by activation of the cortex and inhibition of the hippocampus).

Recall that greater familiarity/fluency is associated with less brain activity. Thus, activating the cortex under psychedelics may produce a heightened sense of novelty when first perceiving a stimulus or thinking of an idea, but such enhanced processing will come with greater fluency on subsequent instances of processing. Because hippocampal function is disrupted, this heightened sense of fluency cannot be localized in memory and can be misattributed, resulting in a heightened sense of noeticism. Interestingly, if a stimulus becomes overly fluent (for example, writing a sentence a hundred times like Bart Simpson), a phenomenon known as *jamais vu* can occur in which the stimulus feels novel and foreign. This back-and-forth between a heightened experience of novelty and familiarity produced by fluency captures the dynamicity of specific brain and cognitive states under psychedelics (hence the name "FLUX").

The Future of Psychedelic Research

Although all of these models have their issues, they each have their own explanatory power in accounting for different psychedelic effects. Activating the 5-HT_{2A} receptor is necessary for subjective effects, while enhanced plasticity and metaplasticity may allow for long-lasting changes in mental function. Disrupted thalamic gating may underlie the overwhelming sensations one has under psychedelics, and disrupting the brain's hierarchy may allow one to diversify one's experience. Impaired coordination between the claustrum and cortex may reduce one's control over cognitive states. Finally, enhancing fluency may produce the paradoxical experience of both heightened novelty and familiarity under psychedelics. As psychedelic research progresses across levels of analysis, each of these models will need to be revised and unified for an overarching idea of how psychedelics work.

1 Beliveau, V., Ganz, M., Feng, L., Ozenne, B., Højgaard, L., Fisher, P. M., Svarer, C., Greve, D. N., & Knudsen, G. M. (2017). A high-resolution *in vivo* atlas of the human brain's serotonin system. *Journal of Neuroscience, 37*(1), 120–128. https://doi.org/10.1523/JNEUROSCI.2830-16.2016.

2 Glennon, R. A., Titeler, M., & McKenney, J. D. (1984). Evidence for 5-HT_2 involvement in the mechanism of action of hallucinogenic agents. *Life Sciences, 35*(25), 2505–2511. https://doi.org/10.1016/0024-3205(84)90436-3.

3 Vollenweider, F. X., Vollenweider-Scherpenhuyzen, M. F. I., Bäbler, A., Vogel, H., & Hell, D. (1998). Psilocybin induces schizophrenia-like psychosis in humans via a serotonin-2 agonist action. *NeuroReport, 9*(17), 3897–3902. https://doi.org/10.1097/00001756-199812010-00024.

4 Ly, C., Greb, A. C., Cameron, L. P., Wong, J. M., Barragan, E. V., Wilson, P. C., Burbach, K. F., Soltanzadeh Zarandi, S., Sood, A., Paddy, M. R., Duim, W. C., Dennis, M. Y., McAllister, K. A., Ori-McKenney, K. M., Gray, J. A., & Olson, D. E. (2018). Psychedelics promote structural and functional neural plasticity. *Cell Reports, 23*(11), 3170–3182. https://doi.org/10.1016/j.celrep.2018.05.022; and Shao, L.-X., Liao, C., Gregg, I., Davoudian, P. A., Savalia, N. K., Delagarza, K., & Kwan, A. C. (2021). Psilocybin induces rapid and persistent growth of dendritic spines in frontal cortex in vivo. *Neuron, 109*(16), 2535–2544.e4. https://doi.org/10.1016/j.neuron.2021.06.008.

5 Russo, S. J., Dietz, D. M., Dumitriu, D., Morrison, J. H., Malenka, R. C., & Nestler, E. J. (2010). The addicted synapse: Mechanisms of synaptic and structural plasticity in nucleus accumbens. *Trends in Neurosciences, 33*(6), 267–276. https://doi.org/10.1016/j.tins.2010.02.002.

6 Nardou, R., Sawyer, E., Song, Y. J., Wilkinson, M., Padovan-Hernandez, Y., De Deus, J. L., Wright, N., Lama, C., Faltin, S., Goff, L. A., Stein-O'Brien, G. L., & Dölen, G. (2023). Psychedelics reopen the social reward learning critical period. *Nature, 618*, 790–798. https://doi.org/10.1038/s41586-023-06204-3.

7 Vollenweider, F. X., & Geyer, M. A. (2001). A systems model of altered consciousness: Integrating natural and drug-induced psychoses. *Brain Research Bulletin, 56*(5), 495–507. https://doi.org/10.1016/S0361-9230(01)00646-3; and Doss, M. K., Madden, M. B., Gaddis, A., Nebel, M. B., Griffiths, R. R., Mathur, B. N., & Barrett, F. S. (2022). Models of psychedelic drug action: Modulation of cortical-subcortical circuits. *Brain, 145*(2), 441–456. https://doi.org/10.1093/brain/awab406.

8 Avram, M., Müller, F., Preller, K. H., Razi, A., Rogg, H., Korda, A., Holze, F., Vizeli, P., Ley, L., Liechti, M. E., & Borgwardt, S. (2024). Effective connectivity of thalamocortical interactions following d-amphetamine, LSD, and MDMA administration. *Biological Psychiatry: Cognitive Neuroscience and Neuroimaging, 9*(5), 522–532. https://doi.org/10.1016/j.bpsc.2023.07.010; Müller, F., Lenz, C., Dolder, P., Lang, U., Schmidt, A., Liechti, M., & Borgwardt, S. (2017). Increased thalamic resting-state connectivity as a core driver of LSD-induced hallucinations. *Acta Psychiatrica Scandinavica, 136*(6), 648–657. https://doi.org/10.1111/acps.12818; Tagliazucchi, E., Roseman, L., Kaelen, M., Orban, C., Muthukumaraswamy, S. D., Murphy, K., Laufs, H., Leech, R., McGonigle, J., Crossley, N., Bullmore, E., Williams, T., Bolstridge, M., Feilding, A., Nutt, D. J., & Carhart-Harris, R. (2016). Increased global functional connectivity correlates with LSD-induced ego dissolution. *Current Biology, 26*(8), 1043–1050. https://doi.org/10.1016/j.cub.2016.02.010; and Preller, K. H., Razi, A., Zeidman, P., Stämpfli, P., Friston, K. J., & Vollenweider, F. X. (2019). Effective connectivity changes in LSD-induced altered states of consciousness in humans. *Proceedings of the National Academy of Sciences, 116*(7), 2743–2748. https://doi.org/10.1073/pnas.1815129116.

9 Barre, A., Berthoux, C., De Bundel, D., Valjent, E., Bockaert, J., Marin, P., & Bécamel, C. (2016). Presynaptic serotonin 2A receptors modulate thalamocortical plasticity and associative learning. *PNAS, 113*(10), E1382–E1391. https://doi.org/10.1073/pnas.1525586113; and Inserra, A., De Gregorio, D., Rezai, T., Lopez-Canul, M. G., Comai, S., & Gobbi, G. (2021). Lysergic acid diethylamide differentially modulates the reticular thalamus, mediodorsal thalamus, and infralimbic prefrontal cortex: An in vivo electrophysiology study in male mice. *Journal of Psychopharmacology, 35*(4), 469–482. https://doi.org/10.1177/0269881121991569.

10 Carhart-Harris, R. L., Erritzoe, D., Williams, T., Stone, J. M., Reed, L. J., Colasanti, A., Tyacke, R. J., Leech, R., Malizia, A. L., Murphy, K., Hobden, P., Evans, J., Feilding, A., Wise, R. G., & Nutt, D. J. (2012). Neural correlates of the psychedelic state as determined by fMRI studies with psilocybin. *PNAS, 109*(6), 2138–2143. https://doi.org/10.1073/pnas.1119598109; Gouzoulis-Mayfrank, E., Schreckenberger, M., Sabri, O., Arning, C., Thelen, B., Spitzer, M., Kovar, K.-A., Hermle, L., Büll, U., & Sass, H. (1999). Neurometabolic effects of psilocybin, 3,4-methylenedioxyethylamphetamine (MDE) and d-methamphetamine in healthy volunteers a double-blind, placebo-controlled PET study with [18F]FDG. *Neuropsychopharmacology, 20*, 565–581. https://doi.org/10.1016/S0893-133X(98)00089-X; Hermle, L., Fünfgeld, M., Oepen, G., Botsch, H., Borchardt, D., Gouzoulis, E., Fehrenbach, R. A., & Spitzer, M. (1992). Mescaline-induced psychopathological,

neuropsychological, and neurometabolic effects in normal subjects: Experimental psychosis as a tool for psychiatric research. *Biological Psychiatry, 32*(11), 976–991. https://doi.org/10.1016/0006-3223(92)90059-9; Vollenweider, F. X., Leenders, K. L., Scharfetter, C., Maguire, P., Stadelmann, O., & Angst, J. (1997). Positron emission tomography and fluorodeoxyglucose studies of metabolic hyperfrontality and psychopathology in the psilocybin model of psychosis. *Neuropsychopharmacology, 16*, 357–372. https://doi.org/10.1016/S0893-133X(96)00246-1; Riba, J., Romero, S., Grasa, E., Mena, E., Carrió, I., & Barbanoj, M. J. (2006). Increased frontal and paralimbic activation following ayahuasca, the pan-Amazonian inebriant. *Psychopharmacology, 186*, 93–98. https://doi.org/10.1007/s00213-006-0358-7; and Lewis, C. R., Preller, K. H., Kraehenmann, R., Michels, L., Staempfli, P., & Vollenweider, F. X. (2017). Two dose investigation of the 5-HT-agonist psilocybin on relative and global cerebral blood flow. *NeuroImage, 159*(1), 70–78. https://doi.org/10.1016/j.neuroimage.2017.07.020.

11 Geyer, M. A., Krebs-Thomson, K., Braff, D. L., & Swerdlow, N. R. (2001). Pharmacological studies of prepulse inhibition models of sensorimotor gating deficits in schizophrenia: A decade in review. *Psychopharmacology, 156*, 117–154. https://doi.org/10.1007/s002130100811.

12 Vollenweider, F. X., Csomor, P. A., Knappe, B., Geyer, M. A., & Quednow, B. B. (2007). The effects of the preferential 5-HT2A agonist psilocybin on prepulse inhibition of startle in healthy human volunteers depend on interstimulus interval. *Neuropsychopharmacology, 32*, 1876–1887. https://doi.org/10.1038/sj.npp.1301324.

13 Heekeren, K., Neukirch, A., Daumann, J., Stoll, M., Obradovic, M., Kovar, K.-A., Geyer, M. A., & GouzouLis-Mayfrank, E. (2007). Prepulse inhibition of the startle reflex and its attentional modulation in the human S-ketamine and N,N-dimethyltryptamine (DMT) models of psychosis. *Journal of Psychopharmacology, 21*(3), 312–320. https://doi.org/10.1177/0269881107077734; and Gouzoulis-Mayfrank, E., Heekeren, K., Thelen, B., Lindenblatt, H., Kovar, K.-A., Sass, H., & Geyer, M. A. (1998). Effects of the hallucinogen psilocybin on habituation and prepulse inhibition of the startle reflex in humans. *Behavioural Pharmacology, 9*(7), 561–566. https://doi.org/10.1097/00008877-199811000-00011.

14 Doss et al. Models of psychedelic drug action; and Carhart-Harris, R. L., & Friston, K. J. (2019). REBUS and the anarchic brain: Toward a unified model of the brain action of psychedelics. *Pharmacological Reviews, 71*(3), 316–344. https://doi.org/10.1124/pr.118.017160.

15 Aqil, M., & Roseman, L. (2023). More than meets the eye: The role of sensory dimensions in psychedelic brain dynamics, experience, and therapeutics. *Neuropharmacology, 223*, Article 109300. https://doi.org/10.1016/j.neuropharm.2022.109300; and Cowan, J. D. (2015). Geometric visual hallucinations and the structure of the visual cortex. In D. Collerton, U. P. Mosimann, and E. Perry (Eds.), *The neuroscience of visual hallucinations* (pp. 217–253). Wiley. https://doi.org/10.1002/9781118892794.ch10.

16 Beliveau et al. High-resolution *in vivo* atlas.

17 Carhart-Harris et al. Neural correlates of the psychedelic experience; Carhart-Harris, R. L., Muthukumaraswamy, S., Roseman, L., Kaelen, M., Droog, W., Murphy, K., Tagliazucchi, E., Schenberg, E. E., Nest, T., Orban, C., Leech, R., Williams, L. T., Williams, T. M., Bolstridge, M., Sessa, B., McGonigle, J., Sereno, M. I., Nichols, D., Hellyer, P. J., … Nutt, D. J. (2016). Neural correlates of the LSD experience revealed by multimodal neuroimaging. *PNAS, 113*(17), 4853–4858. https://doi.org/10.1073/pnas.1518377113; Palhano-Fontes, F., Andrade, K. C., Tofoli, L. F., Santos, A. C., Crippa, J. A. S., Hallak, J. E. C., Ribeiro, S., & de Araujo, D. B. (2015). The psychedelic state induced by ayahuasca modulates the activity and connectivity of the default mode network. *PLOS ONE, 10*(2), Article e0118143. https://doi.org/10.1371/journal.pone.0118143; Müller, F., Dolder, P. C., Schmidt, A., Liechti, M. E., & Borgwardt, S. (2018). Altered network hub connectivity after acute LSD administration. *NeuroImage: Clinical, 18*, 694–701. https://doi.org/10.1016/j.nicl.2018.03.005; and Mason, N. L., Kuypers, K. P. C., Müller, F., Reckweg, J., Tse, D. H. Y., Toennes, S. W., Hutten, N. R. P. W., Jansen, J. F. A., Stiers, P., Feilding, A., & Ramaekers, J. G. (2020). Me, myself, bye: Regional alterations in glutamate and the experience of ego dissolution with psilocybin. *Neuropsychopharmacology, 45*, 2003–2011. https://doi.org/10.1038/s41386-020-0718-8.

18 Pokorny, T., Duerler, P., Seifritz, E., Vollenweider, F. X., & Preller, K. H. (2019). LSD acutely impairs working memory, executive functions, and cognitive flexibility, but not risk-based decision-making. *Psychological Medicine*, *50*(13), 2255–2265. https://doi.org/10.1017/S0033291719002393.

19 Doss, M. K., Považan, M., Rosenberg, M. D., Sepeda, N. D., Davis, A. K., Finan, P. H., Smith, G. S., Pekar, J. J., Barker, P. B., Griffiths, R. R., & Barrett, F. S. (2021). Psilocybin therapy increases cognitive

and neural flexibility in patients with major depressive disorder. *Translational Psychiatry, 11*, Article 574. https://doi.org/10.1038/s41398-021-01706-y.

20 Wall, M. B., Pope, R., Freeman, T. P., Kowalczyk, O. S., Demetriou, L., Mokrysz, C., Hindocha, C., Lawn, W., Bloomfield, M. A., Freeman, A. M., Feilding, A., Nutt, D., & Curran, H. V. (2019). Dissociable effects of cannabis with and without cannabidiol on the human brain's resting-state functional connectivity. *Journal of Psychopharmacology, 33*(7), 822–830. https://doi.org/10.1177/0269881119841568.

21 Weber, A. M., Soreni, N., & Noseworthy, M. D. (2014). A preliminary study on the effects of acute ethanol ingestion on default mode network and temporal fractal properties of the brain. *Magnetic Resonance Materials in Physics, Biology and Medicine, 27*, 291–301. https://doi.org/10.1007/s10334-013-0420-5.

22 Schrantee, A., Ferguson, B., Stoffers, D., Booij, J., Rombouts, S., & Reneman, L. (2016). Effects of dexamphetamine-induced dopamine release on resting-state network connectivity in recreational amphetamine users and healthy controls. *Brain Imaging and Behavior, 10*, 548–558. https://doi.org/10.1007/s11682-015-9419-z.

23 Picó-Pérez, M., Magalhães, R., Esteves, M., Vieira, R., Castanho, T. C., Amorim, L., Sousa, M., Coelho, A., Moreira, P. S., Cunha, R. A., & Sousa, N. (2023). Coffee consumption decreases the connectivity of the posterior Default Mode Network (DMN) at rest. *Frontiers in Behavioral Neuroscience, 17*, Article 1176382. https://doi.org/10.3389/fnbeh.2023.1176382.

24 Bonhomme, V., Vanhaudenhuyse, A., Demertzi, A., Bruno, M.-A., Jaquet, O., Bahri, M. A., Plenevaux, A., Boly, M., Boveroux, P., Soddu, A., Brichant, J. F., Maquet, P., & Laureys, S. (2016). Resting-state network-specific breakdown of functional connectivity during ketamine alteration of consciousness in volunteers. *Anesthesiology, 125*(5), 873–888. https://doi.org/10.1097/ALN.0000000000001275; and Zacharias, N., Musso, F., Müller, F., Lammers, F., Saleh, A., London, M., Boer, P., & Winterer, G. (2020). Ketamine effects on default mode network activity and vigilance: A randomized, placebo-controlled crossover simultaneous fMRI/EEG study. *Human Brain Mapping, 41*(1), 107–119. https://doi.org/10.1002/hbm.24791.

25 Mueller, F., Musso, F., London, M., de Boer, P., Zacharias, N., & Winterer, G. (2018). Pharmacological fMRI: Effects of subanesthetic ketamine on resting-state functional connectivity in the default mode network, salience network, dorsal attention network and executive control network. *NeuroImage: Clinical, 19*, 745–757. https://doi.org/10.1016/j.nicl.2018.05.037; and Niesters, M., Khalili-Mahani, N., Martini, C., Aarts, L., van Gerven, J., van Buchem, M. A., Dahan, A., & Rombouts, S. (2012). Effect of subanesthetic ketamine on intrinsic functional brain connectivity: A placebo-controlled functional magnetic resonance imaging study in healthy male volunteers. *Anesthesiology, 117*(4), 868–877. https://doi.org/10.1097/ALN.0b013e31826a0db3.

26 Fleming, L. M., Javitt, D. C., Carter, C. S., Kantrowitz, J. T., Girgis, R. R., Kegeles, L. S., Ragland, J. D., Maddock, R. J., Lesh, T. A., Tanase, C., Robinson, J., Potter, W. Z., Carlson, M., Wall, M. M., Choo, T.-H., Grinband, J., Lieberman, J., Krystal, J. H., & Corlett, P. R. (2019). A multicenter study of ketamine effects on functional connectivity: Large scale network relationships, hubs and symptom mechanisms. *NeuroImage: Clinical, 22*, Article 101739. https://doi.org/10.1016/j.nicl.2019.101739.

27 Carhart-Harris et al. Neural correlates of the LSD experience; Müller et al. Altered network hub connectivity; Mason et al. Me, myself, bye; Preller, K. H., Burt, J. B., Ji, J. L., Schleifer, C. H., Adkinson, B. D., Stämpfli, P., Seifritz, E., Repovs, G., Krystal, J. H., Murray, J. D., Vollenweider, F. X., & Anticevic, A. (2018). Changes in global and thalamic brain connectivity in LSD-induced altered states of consciousness are attributable to the 5-HT2A receptor. *eLife, 7*, Article e35082. https://doi.org/10.7554/eLife.35082; Preller, K. H., Duerler, P., Burt, J. B., Ji, J. L., Adkinson, B., Stämpfli, P., Seifritz, E., Repovš, G., Krystal, J. H., Murray, J. D., Anticevic, A., & Vollenweider, F. X. (2020). Psilocybin induces time-dependent changes in global functional connectivity. *Biological Psychiatry, 88*(2), 197–207. https://doi.org/10.1016/j.biopsych.2019.12.027; and Lebedev, A. V., Kaelen, M., Lövdén, M., Nilsson, J., Feilding, A., Nutt, D. J., & Carhart-Harris, R. L. (2016). LSD-induced entropic brain activity predicts subsequent personality change. *Human Brain Mapping, 37*(9), 3203–3213. https://doi.org/10.1002/hbm.23234.

28 Millière, R., Carhart-Harris, R. L., Roseman, L., Trautwein, F.-M., & Berkovich-Ohana, A. (2018). Psychedelics, meditation, and self-consciousness. *Frontiers in Psychology, 9*. https://doi.org/10.3389/fpsyg.2018.01475.

29 Carhart-Harris et al. Neural correlates of the LSD experience.

30 Müller et al. Altered network hub connectivity.

31 Soehner, A. M., Chase, H. W., Bertocci, M. A., Greenberg, T., Stiffler, R., Lockovich, J. C., Aslam, H.

A., Graur, S., Bebko, G., & Phillips, M. L. (2019). Unstable wakefulness during resting-state fMRI and its associations with network connectivity and affective psychopathology in young adults. *Journal of Affective Disorders, 258*, 125–132. https://doi.org/10.1016/j.jad.2019.07.066.

32 Chang, D., Song, D., Zhang, J., Shang, Y., Ge, Q., & Wang, Z. (2018). Caffeine caused a widespread increase of resting brain entropy. *Scientific Reports, 8*, Article 2700. https://doi.org/10.1038/s41598-018-21008-6.

33 Doss et al. Models of psychedelic drug action.

34 Spitzer, M., Thimm, M., Hermle, L., Holzmann, P., Kovar, K.-A., Heimann, H., Gouzoulis-Mayfrank, E., Kischka, U., & Schneider, F. (1996). Increased activation of indirect semantic associations under psilocybin. *Biological Psychiatry, 39*(12), 1055–1057. https://doi.org/10.1016/0006-3223(95)00418-1.

35 Doss, M. K., Samaha, J., Barrett, F. S., Griffiths, R. R., de Wit, H., Gallo, D. A., & Koen, J. D. (2024). Unique effects of sedatives, dissociatives, psychedelics, stimulants, and cannabinoids on episodic memory: A review and reanalysis of acute drug effects on recollection, familiarity, and metamemory. *Psychological Review, 131*(2), 523–562. https://doi.org/10.1037/rev0000455.

36 Cleary, A. M., & Claxton, A. B. (2018). Déjà vu: An illusion of prediction. *Psychological Science, 29*(4), 635–644. https://doi.org/10.1177/0956797617743018; Cleary, A. M., Brown, A. S., Sawyer, B. D., Nomi, J. S., Ajoku, A. C., & Ryals, A. J. (2012). Familiarity from the configuration of objects in 3-dimensional space and its relation to déjà vu: A virtual reality investigation. *Consciousness and Cognition, 21*(2), 969–975. https://doi.org/10.1016/j.concog.2011.12.010; and Kostic, B., Booth, S. E., & Cleary, A. M. (2015). The role of analogy in reports of presque vu: Does reporting the presque vu state signal the near retrieval of a source analogy? *Journal of Cognitive Psychology, 27*(6), 739–754. https://doi.org/10.1080/20445911.2015.1031792.

37 Carhart-Harris, R. L., Leech, R., Hellyer, P. J., Shanahan, M., Feilding, A., Tagliazucchi, E., Chialvo, D. R., & Nutt, D. (2014). The entropic brain: A theory of conscious states informed by neuroimaging research with psychedelic drugs. *Frontiers in Human Neuroscience, 8*. https://doi.org/10.3389/fnhum.2014.00020.

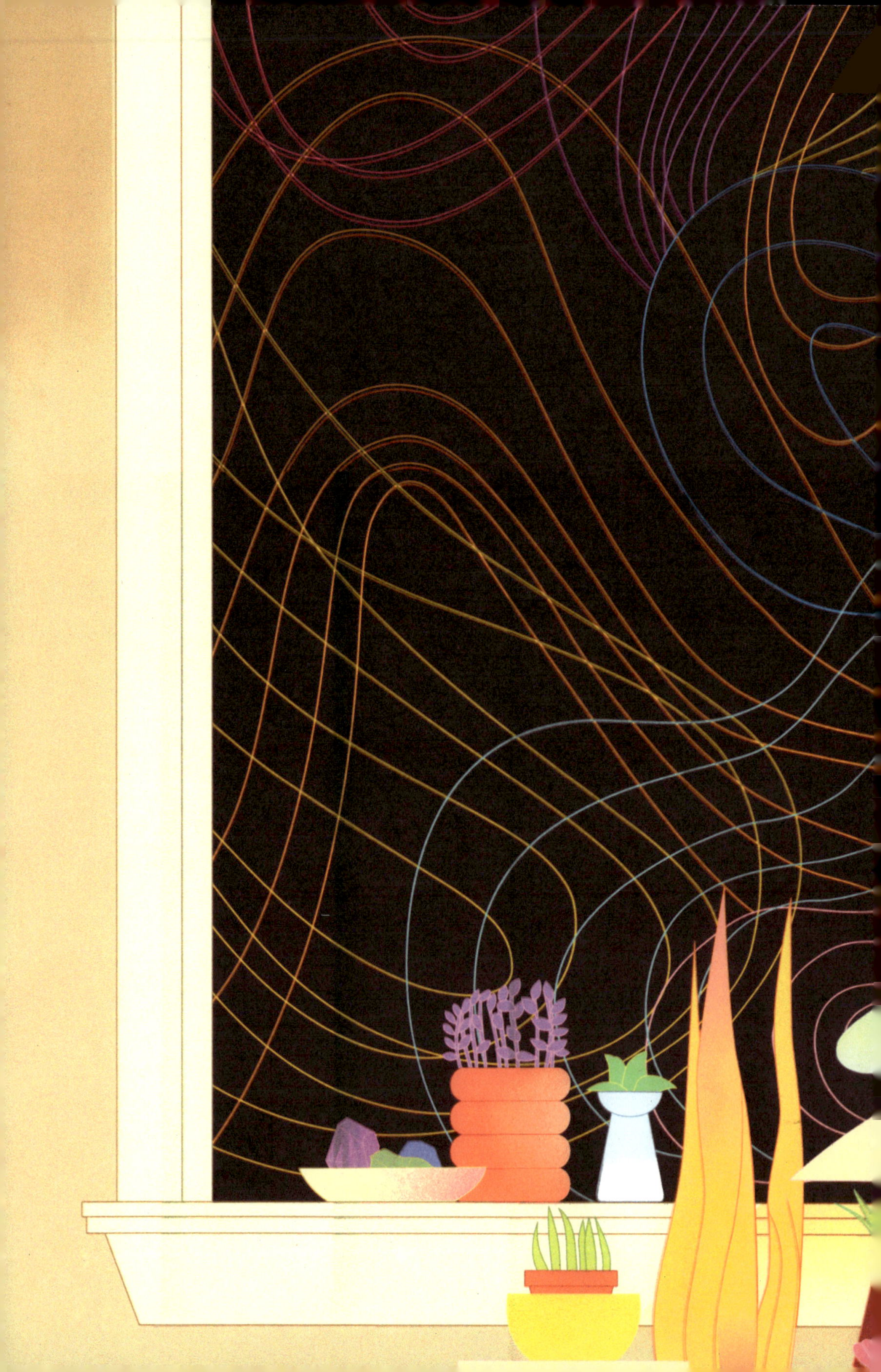

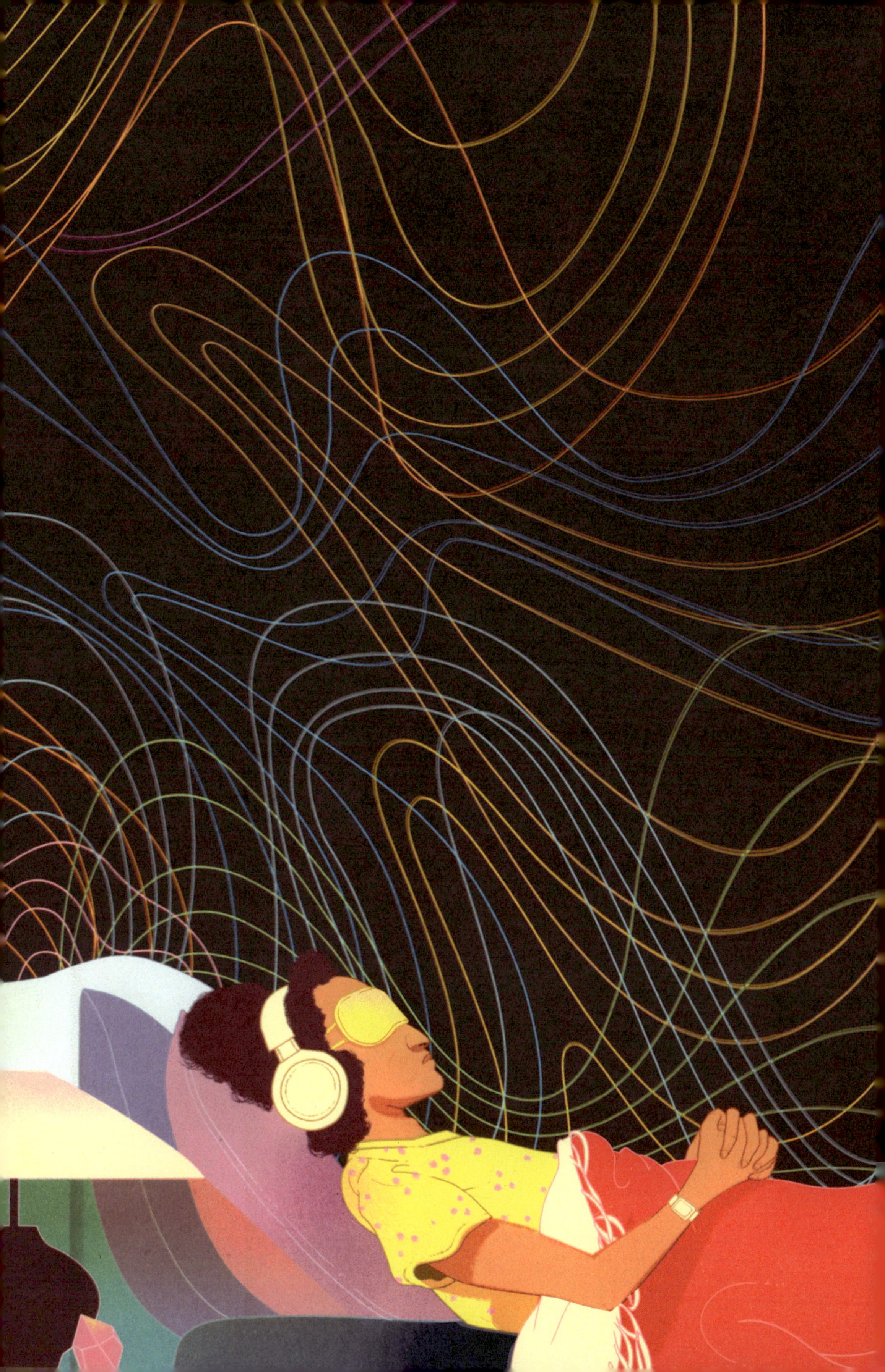

4

Psychedelic Therapy

ALEXANDRIA S. COLES
M. ISHRAT HUSAIN

MR. E (ANONYMIZED TO PROTECT PATIENT CONFIDENTIALITY) is a 46-year-old male who had been struggling with depression for more than a decade. He was experiencing chronic symptoms, including low mood, loss of interest in people and activities that he once enjoyed, fatigue, and insomnia. Mr. E had tried several different treatments for his depression, including antidepressant medications, repetitive transcranial magnetic stimulation, and cognitive behavioural therapy, with no relief. Upon consulting with a psychiatrist, Mr. E was deemed eligible to participate in an ongoing clinical trial of psilocybin therapy for treatment-resistant depression (TRD) at the Centre for Addiction and Mental Health (CAMH) in Toronto. During the study, he received a single dose of 25 milligrams of psilocybin (a dose large enough to produce hallucinations and other drug effects) combined with psychological support before, during, and after psilocybin administration. Beginning the day after psilocybin dosing, Mr. E experienced a rapid and large reduction in symptoms of depression. These improvements were sustained for several weeks after his involvement in the study such that he was considered in

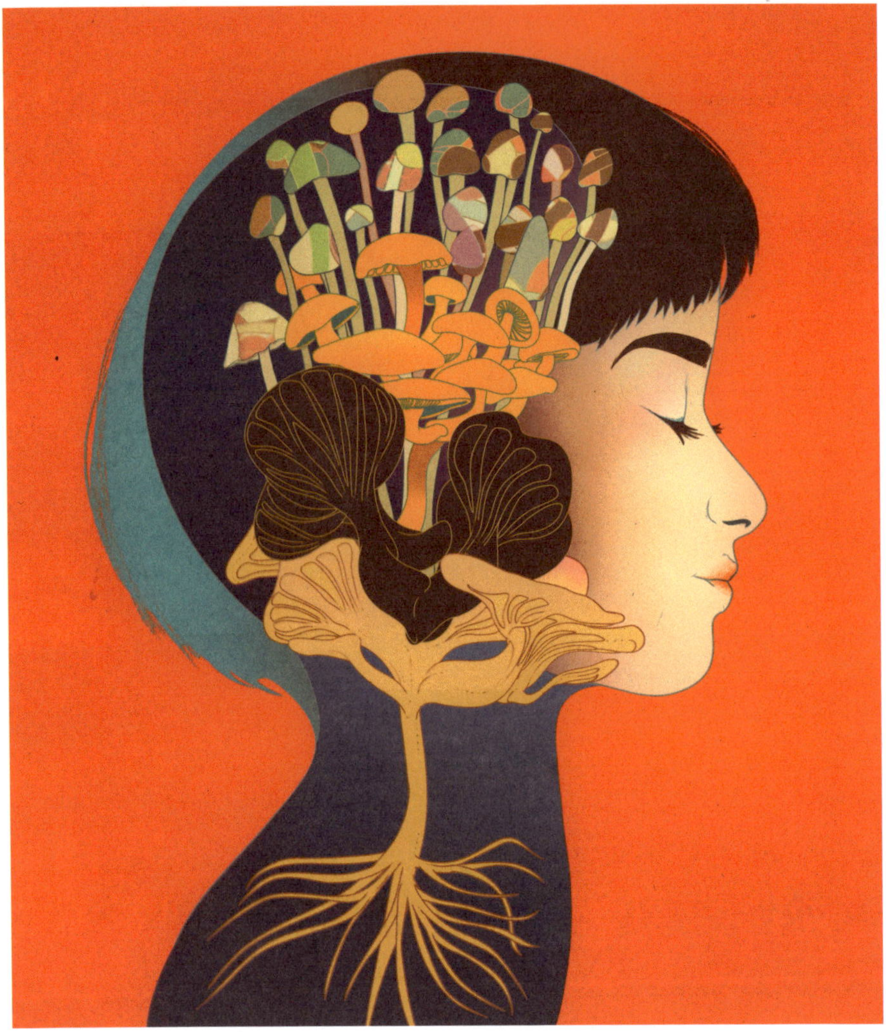

Figure 1
Illustration for *UCSF* Magazine by Marcos Chin.
Photo: Courtesy of the artist.

remission from his depression. Mr. E described his experience during the study as "the single most meaningful experience of my life," reporting that he felt lighter, able to feel emotions he hadn't felt in years, and excited to reconnect with his children. Research staff who dealt directly with Mr. E also noted a palpable change in his demeanour when he came in for follow-up visits, reporting that he was laughing, smiling, and engaging with staff.

Mr. E is one of thousands of patients who have received psychedelic therapy (PT) by way of clinical research trials. Like him, many patients have reported rapid and sustained symptom improvement in their mental health with PT, while others who have gone through the same clinical trials have experienced little to no improvement in symptoms. The reason some people feel better after PT while others do not is not yet fully understood. Although PT shows promise, more research is needed to understand how it works and to determine who can benefit from it safely and effectively.

Psychedelic Therapy

PT is the supervised administration of a psychedelic agent (such as psilocybin) combined with psychological support (therapy). PT is delivered by one or more trained therapists and involves at least one drug administration session, as well as non-drug preparation and integration sessions that occur before and after.[1] In this chapter, we will provide an overview of PT, including detailed descriptions of PT sessions (preparation, dose administration, integration) and of the risks and benefits of PT compared with traditional treatments and a discussion of specific psychedelic drug effects and their respective evidence for clinical use.

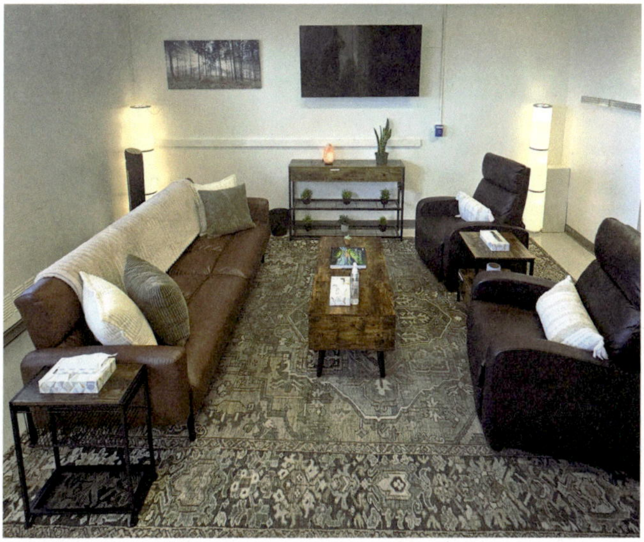

Figure 2
The physical environment for a psychedelic trip can have a profound impact on the patient's experience, which is why dosing rooms are designed to be calming. Psychedelic-assisted therapy room at Toronto Western Hospital.

Photo: Courtesy of Toronto Western Hospital.

Drug Administration Sessions

Drug administration sessions involve the ingestion of a psychedelic drug supervised by a licensed physician, combined with psychological support from one or more trained therapists. Therapists provide emotional support, safety monitoring, and guidance throughout the patient's entire psychedelic experience or trip. Therapists also often use coping skills such as deep breathing and imagery to guide participants during the dose administration session, particularly during periods of distress or emotional intensity.[2] With consent, therapists may also employ therapeutic touch–boundaried physical contact between therapists and patients to provide comfort and support.[3]

Drug administration sessions have several key features. They last several hours and are limited in number (typically one to three sessions lasting 4–12 hours each, depending on the drug).[4] Patients are continuously monitored by therapists and are never left alone during their psychedelic experience.

Another key aspect of the drug administration session is the setting, or physical environment, in which it takes place. Ideally, drug administration occurs in a private, comfortable, and aesthetically pleasing environment to reduce the likelihood of psychological distress and enhance the therapeutic experience.[5]

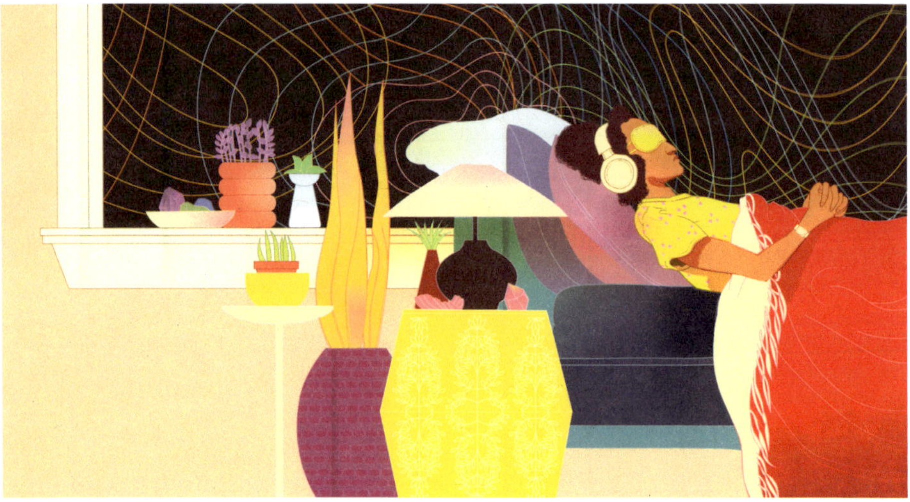

Figure 3
Illustration for *UCSF* Magazine by Marcos Chin.
Photo: Courtesy of the artist.

This includes factors such as comfortable furniture (a bed or couch), neutral artwork (such as nature scenes or abstract images), art and journalling supplies, adjustable lighting, textured materials, and plants, all of which aim to enhance the probability of a positive psychedelic experience. In some cases, patients are encouraged to bring in personal items such as photos or mementos to provide comfort during the experience. Eye shades and noise-cancelling headphones that play a pre-selected psychedelic-inspired playlist are also commonly provided to allow the individual to turn inward and focus on the psychedelic experience without distraction.[6] Notably, studies that do not address the physical environment (those taking place in clinical or hospital settings) have recorded much higher rates of anxiety and negative experiences, emphasizing the importance of setting for drug administration sessions.[7]

Once the effects of the drug have worn off, patients are discharged by a physician into the care of a pre-specified caregiver (family member or friend) with instructions on what to expect and how to care for the patient post-trip.

Preparation Session and Integration Sessions

Both preparation and integration sessions are considered critical aspects of PT. Preparation sessions, which can last several hours, are led by trained therapists and typically occur within one week prior to the drug administration session. Sometimes, multiple sessions in the weeks leading up to the dosing sessions are needed to adequately prepare patients for their upcoming experience. The purpose of preparation sessions is for the patient to set expectations and intentions for their upcoming psychedelic experience and establish a therapeutic rapport with the therapists who will be guiding them through it.[8] Assigned therapists work to provide psychoeducation regarding the specific psychedelic drug that will be used and its possible effects, as well as a breakdown of what the dose administration day may look like (from dosing to discharge at the end of the day). A patient's potential concerns or fears related to the psychedelic experience, their relevant psychiatric history, and their current life circumstances are also often discussed. Preparation sessions are critical for fostering an individual's positive and open mindset prior to psychedelic dose administration, which reduces anxieties and the likelihood of a "bad trip" or need for psychiatric intervention.[9]

In the days following the drug administration session, one to two integration sessions (1–2 hours each in length) are held with the individual and led by the same therapists who were present for the preparation and dose administration sessions. This is done to ensure continuity of care and maintenance of therapeutic rapport. The purpose of integration sessions is to review the psychedelic experience in detail from both the patient's and the therapists' points of view. Therapists often employ various tenets of psychotherapy during these integration sessions to help patients reflect on and work through any emotional or psychologically distressing aspects of their psychedelic experience, as well as work to integrate what they have learned into their daily lives.[10]

Psychedelic Therapies versus Traditional Treatments

The gold standard treatment for mental disorders, including major depressive disorder (MDD) and post-traumatic stress disorder (PTSD), typically involves the daily administration of psychiatric medications (such as antidepressants) and regular structured psychotherapy (such as cognitive behavioural therapy).[11] While these treatments are considered effective for some, many individuals do not achieve a meaningful reduction in symptoms. Research comparing PT with current first-line treatments, including antidepressant medications, is limited. However, preliminary evidence suggests that PT may be equally as effective as certain antidepressants for the treatment of depressive symptoms.[12] While this is promising, it is important to note that research on the therapeutic use of psychedelics for mental disorders remains in its early stages. Further disorder-specific studies are needed to determine the comparative safety and effectiveness of PT versus traditional treatment options.

Compared with traditional treatment options, PT may offer several advantages. For instance, antidepressant medications require daily administration, can take several weeks to begin working, and are effective only as long as the medication is adhered to. Alternatively, the beneficial effects of psychedelic therapies are rapid, with some people experiencing improvements in symptoms after a single dose, with positive effects lasting between one month and one year.[13] Traditional psychiatric medications are also often accompanied by adverse effects, such as decreased libido and weight gain, that may not improve with continued use and are not well tolerated by many individuals.[14] Psychedelics have been reported to show mild and transient adverse effects that typically last only as long as the drug administration session.[15] As a result, PT may allow for improved treatment compliance and reduced burden of adverse effects, offering a potentially viable alternative to traditional treatments.

A noteworthy disadvantage of PT is the significant resources (therapists, physicians, clinical space for drug administration) and time required for proper administration and monitoring. Psychedelic drugs remain classified as Schedule I substances, limiting their use to research settings and, in very rare circumstances, in specialized clinics following regulatory approval.[16]

Risks of Psychedelic Therapies

Overall, psychedelics have a well-established safety profile, with a low probability of physiological toxicity and addiction potential.[17] Despite this, PT may not be suitable for all individuals and carries some noteworthy but expected risks, including psychological and physiological effects, which will be discussed in detail later in the chapter.

Psychedelic use can also involve unexpected risks. A bad trip, characterized by anxiety, paranoia, fear, and dysphoria due to acute drug effects, is always possible. Adequate preparation and integration therapy sessions are necessary to reduce the possibility of this occurrence. In rare cases, individuals may develop what is known as "hallucinogen-induced persistent perpetual disorder," where effects of the psychedelic drug last longer than anticipated, though this disorder has never been reported in clinical settings.[18]

Psychedelic use may also increase an individual's risk for psychosis, specifically in those with a family history of psychotic illness. The incidence of these adverse reactions is low, and reactions have historically affected individuals with pre-existing mental illness or family history of related conditions.[19] Additionally, some case reports have suggested that psychedelic use may increase an individual's suicidal ideation when taken in unsafe and unmonitored situations, though evidence for this is limited.[20] These risks can be mitigated through rigorous patient screening protocols, and patients with a history of psychosis should not consume psychedelic drugs.

Finally, psychedelic drugs may interact with certain types of prescribed medications, including certain antidepressants (monoamine oxidase inhibitors) and lithium.[21] Tapering off these medications for sufficient time prior to psychedelic use can prevent these interactions.

Despite these risks, research continues to suggest that compared with alcohol and other controlled substances, psychedelics are safe for use in humans.[22] Specific psychedelic drugs and their risks, as well as a summary of the current evidence for use of these drugs in the treatment of disorders, are listed below.

PSILOCYBIN

Psilocybin, the naturally occurring psychoactive compound found in over 200 varieties of hallucinogenic ("magic") mushroom species, is currently the most widely researched psychedelic. High doses are associated with a variety of psychological effects, including changes to, or slowed perception of, time; visual disturbances; and euphoria. Physiological side effects have been reported as transient and may include dizziness, nausea, vomiting, stomach pain, changes in blood pressure, and pupillary dilation. Acute effects of psilocybin administration last between 5 and 8 hours, with symptoms lasting only while the drug remains in the individual's system.[23]

Outside of research settings, the recent rise in popularity of psilocybin has led to an increase in "microdosing" within the general population, involving daily self-administration of small doses (less than 1 gram) that results in little to no disruption in functioning but has been reported to induce subtle enhancements to mood, concentration, and creativity. While microdosing of psilocybin has been anecdotally associated with these benefits, limited research has been conducted in this area, and microdosing's effects on mental health have not been well documented.[24]

In the past decade, clinical research in psilocybin has accelerated, with studies being conducted to investigate the drug's effects on disorders such as MDD, TRD, end of life distress, and substance use disorders (tobacco and alcohol). Depressive disorders have received the most attention in psilocybin research thus far. Several studies have investigated the effects of one to three administrations of high dose psilocybin in MDD,[25] TRD,[26] bipolar depression,[27] and depression associated with diagnosis of life-threatening illness.[28] Results indicate that psilocybin administration paired with psychological support is associated with rapid, robust, and sustained reductions in depressive symptoms across participants, with beneficial effects lasting between 1 and 12 months.[29] Studies comparing different doses of psilocybin indicate that larger doses (25–30 milligrams) may be more effective than lower doses for treatment of depressive symptoms.[30]

One small study has examined the effects of psilocybin on symptoms of obsessive-compulsive disorder (OCD). Participants received up to four separate doses, ranging from sub-hallucinogenic amounts (25 micrograms per kilogram) to high doses (300 micrograms per kilogram) of psilocybin. Significant reductions in OCD symptoms were observed across participants in at least one of the follow-up testing sessions.[31]

Finally, two studies have been conducted investigating the effects of psilocybin on tobacco and alcohol use disorders. Participants in both studies saw significant increases in abstinence rates and decreased craving (for both substances) following psilocybin administration.[32]

LSD

Lysergic acid diethylamide (LSD), also known as "acid," is a partially synthetic psychoactive compound created from lysergic acid, a naturally occurring compound found in the parasitic rye fungus *Claviceps purpurea*. Synthesized by accident in 1943 by Swiss chemist Albert Hofmann, LSD is known for its hallucinogenic properties.[33] Like other psychedelics, LSD has a variety of psychological and physiological effects. The psychological symptoms of LSD at moderate to high doses (more than 100 micrograms) include synesthesia, enhanced sensory perception, and visual hallucinations, resulting in the broadening of thought processes, dissolution of ego, enhanced empathy, and feelings of closeness to others. Physiological symptoms of LSD include increased heart rate, blood pressure changes, nausea, and dizziness.[34]

Recently, LSD has been studied for its potential beneficial effects in the treatment of anxiety disorders. A study compared two doses of 200 micrograms of LSD to placebo in adult patients with anxiety disorders, with the doses of LSD resulting in rapid and significant reductions in anxiety-related symptoms, as well as depressive and general psychiatric symptoms. These effects were maintained at follow-up assessments conducted at 16 weeks post-LSD administration.[35] A second study saw similar results in patients with anxiety due to life-threatening disease diagnoses. After two dosing sessions of 200 micrograms of LSD, participants saw a clinically significant reduction in anxiety symptoms, with improvements maintained up to 1-year post-administration.[36]

LSD has also been studied for its effects on alcohol misuse. Six studies investigating the effects of LSD on alcohol use disorder were conducted between 1966 and 1970 with promising results. One-time administration of LSD, with doses ranging between 450 and 800 micrograms, resulted in significant reductions in problematic alcohol use at 3 and 6 months follow up, though results were not maintained when participants were re-evaluated at 1-year post-administration.[37] Notably, these studies were poorly described, and modern trials investigating the effects of LSD on substance use outcomes are lacking.

MDMA

MDMA (3,4-methylenedioxymethamphetamine) is a synthetic combination of psychedelic and amphetamine compounds that provide the basis of the recreational drug known as "ecstasy."[38] A single, low to moderate dose of MDMA can produce psychological effects such as elevated mood, arousal, and a feeling of closeness with others as well as physiological effects such as increased energy, elevated blood pressure, faintness, jaw clenching, sweating, and nausea.[39] Additionally, high doses of MDMA may lead to acute toxicity, resulting in symptoms that include hyperthermia (abnormally high body temperature), hyponatremia (low blood sodium levels), and cardiovascular events, though probability is low and MDMA is considered safe and tolerable when administered at moderate doses in a controlled environment. Due to its amphetamine properties, MDMA has the highest abuse potential of all psychedelic drugs, but likelihood of dependence is still considered low.[40]

Several studies have investigated the therapeutic potential of MDMA in the treatment of PTSD, a disorder characterized by symptoms such as hypervigilance, avoidance, and the re-experiencing of traumatic events by way of flashbacks.[41] Study results indicate that two to three sessions of MDMA-assisted psychotherapy may lead to pronounced and sustained improvements in PTSD symptoms for up to 12 months following dose administration, as well as reductions in nightmares and improvements in anxiety, sleep quality, and general well-being.[42]

DMT AND AYAHUASCA

DMT (N, N-dimethyltryptamine) is a naturally occurring psychedelic compound found in the seeds, bark, and leaves of several different plants, as well as the venom of the *Incilius alvarius* toad, all of which can be found in the Amazonian forest.[43] DMT molecules are also naturally produced in the pineal gland of the human brain, for reasons not yet understood. This psychedelic compound is a short-lasting psychedelic (10–20 minutes) known to produce visual and auditory distortions, memory impairment, and "peak" mystical-type experiences which may result in feeling a oneness with the universe, reduced boundaries between self and the world, and ego dissolution.[44] When taken orally, DMT is metabolized before any psychedelic effects can be experienced; consequently, the route of administration for DMT is inhalation, which allows for direct access to the bloodstream via the lungs and results in rapid onset of effects.[45]

A related psychedelic is ayahuasca. DMT is the main psychedelic component found in this South American brewed beverage used for religious ceremonies and healing rituals by the Indigenous peoples of the Amazon forest. It is created by boiling two plants, *Banisteriopsis caapi* and *Psychotria viridis*, to create a drink for oral consumption. This combination of plants contains three important ingredients, along with DMT: harmine, harmaline, and tetrahydroharmine (monoamine oxidase inhibitors), which serve to inhibit the breakdown of DMT that typically occurs when consumed orally, allowing for the user to experience its psychedelic effects.[46] When ayahuasca is consumed, its effects are similar to those of DMT but are less intense and longer-lasting (6–8 hours). Furthermore, ayahuasca is known for its physiological effects, known as "the purge," involving intense vomiting, shaking, and diarrhea, which is considered an integral part of the ayahuasca ceremony. Nonetheless, DMT and ayahuasca are considered safe and tolerable for patients, with the exception of individuals with a personal or family history of psychosis, as ayahuasca consumption may increase the risk of a psychotic episode.[47]

Currently, five open-label studies[48] and one randomized clinical trial[49] have been conducted to investigate the effects of DMT (both traditionally prepared ayahuasca and synthetic-inhaled or IV-administered versions) on symptoms of depression. These studies reported significant and lasting reductions in participants' depressive symptoms, with improvements beginning within hours of dose administration (20–24). In most studies, effects were maintained up to 4 weeks post-dose, though long-term efficacy studies are required.

The Future of Psychedelic Therapies

Preliminary evidence suggests that PT may offer a promising treatment for mental disorders, including depression, anxiety, and PTSD. PT may offer several advantages over current treatment modalities, including shorter treatment. Yet while preliminary studies suggest that PT is safe and tolerable, psychedelic use involves several risks and may not be suitable for all individuals.

Though promising, current research on PT for the treatment of mental disorders is preliminary, and more research is required. Further controlled trials are necessary to better understand the effects of psychedelics on each disorder, the specific doses required for each drug, and the number of treatment sessions needed. Moreover, the long-term effects of psychedelic use are not known, warranting long-term follow-up studies. As such, PT is not yet ready for clinical use, and its use should be restricted to clinical trials or regulator-approved specialized clinics.

1 Greenway, K. T., Garel, N., Jerome, L., & Feduccia, A. A. (2020). Integrating psychotherapy and psychopharmacology: Psychedelic-assisted psychotherapy and other combined treatments. *Expert Review of Clinical Pharmacology, 13*(6), 655–670. https://doi.org/10.1080/17512433.2020.1772054

2 Greenway et al. Integrating psychotherapy and psychopharmacology.; and Cavarra, M., Falzone, A., Ramaekers, J. G., Kuypers, K. P. C., & Mento, C. (2022). Psychedelic-assisted psychotherapy—A systematic review of associated psychological interventions. *Frontiers in Psychology, 13*, Article 887255. https://doi.org/10.3389/fpsyg.2022.887255

3 Cavarra et al. Psychedelic-assisted psychotherapy.

4 Greenway et al. Integrating psychotherapy and psychopharmacology.

5 Okano, L., Jones, G., Deyo, B., Brandenburg, A., & Hale, W. (2022). Therapeutic setting as an essential component of psychedelic research methodology: Reporting recommendations emerging from clinical trials of 3,4-methylenedioxymethamphetamine for post-traumatic stress disorder. *Frontiers in Psychiatry, 13*, Article 965641. https://doi.org/10.3389/fpsyt.2022.965641; and Johnson, M. W., Richards, W. A., & Griffiths, R. R. (2008). Human hallucinogen research: Guidelines for safety. *Journal of Psychopharmacology, 22*(6), 603–620. https://doi.org/10.1177/0269881108093587

6 Okano et al. Therapeutic setting.

7 Johnson et al. Human hallucinogen research.

8 Greenway et al. Integrating psychotherapy and psychopharmacology.

9 Greenway et al. Integrating psychotherapy and psychopharmacology.; and Cavarra et al. Psychedelic-assisted psychotherapy.

10 Greenway et al. Integrating psychotherapy and psychopharmacology.

11 Leichsenring, F., Steinert, C., Rabung, S., & Ioannidis, J. P. A. (2022). The efficacy of psychotherapies and pharmacotherapies for mental disorders in adults: An umbrella review and meta-analytic evaluation of recent meta-analyses. *World Psychiatry, 21*(1), 133–145. https://doi.org/10.1002/wps.20941

12 da Costa, S. C., Oesterle, T., Rummans, T. A., Richelson, E., & Gold, M. (2022). Psychedelic drugs for psychiatric disorders. *Journal of the Neurological Sciences, 440*, Article 120332. https://doi.org/10.1016/j.jns.2022.120332; and Carhart-Harris, R., Giribaldi, B., Watts, R., Baker-Jones, M., Murphy-Beiner, A., Murphy, R., Martell, J., Blemings, A., Erritzoe, D., & Nutt, D. J. (2021). Trial of psilocybin versus escitalopram for depression. *New England Journal of Medicine, 384*(15), 1402–1411. https://doi.org/10.1056/NEJMoa2032994

13 da Costa et al. Psychedelic drugs for psychiatric disorders.

14 Muttoni, S., Ardissino, M., & John, C. (2019). Classical psychedelics for the treatment of depression and anxiety: A systematic review. *Journal of Affective Disorders, 258*, 11–24. https://doi.org/10.1016/j.jad.2019.07.076; and Rucker, J. J., Jelen, L. A., Flynn, S., Frowde, K. D., & Young, A. H. (2016). Psychedelics in the treatment of unipolar mood disorders: A systematic review. *Journal of Psychopharmacology, 30*(12), 1220–1229. https://doi.org/10.1177/0269881116679368

15 da Costa et al. Psychedelic drugs for psychiatric disorders.

16 Greenway et al. Integrating psychotherapy and psychopharmacology.

17 Johnson et al. Human hallucinogen research.

18 Johnson et al. Human hallucinogen research.; and Schlag, A. K., Aday, J., Salam, I., Neill, J. C., & Nutt, D. J. (2022). Adverse effects of psychedelics: From anecdotes and misinformation to systematic science. *Journal of Psychopharmacology, 36*(3), 258–272. https://doi.org/10.1177/02698811211069100

19 Johnson et al. Human hallucinogen research.; and Schlag et al. Adverse effects of psychedelics.

20 Schlag et al. Adverse effects of psychedelics.

21 Johnson et al. Human hallucinogen research.; and Schlag et al. Adverse effects of psychedelics.

22 Schlag et al. Adverse effects of psychedelics.

23 Sharma, P., Nguyen, Q. A., Matthews, S. J., Carpenter, E., Mathews, D. B., Patten, C. A., & Hammond, C. J. (2023). Psilocybin history, action and reaction: A narrative clinical review. *Journal of Psychopharmacology, 37*(9), 849–865. https://doi.org/10.1177/02698811231190858; and Madras, B. K. (2022). Psilocybin in treatment-resistant depression. *New England Journal of Medicine, 387*(18), 1708–1709. https://doi.org/10.1056/NEJMe2210975

24 Sharma et al. Psilocybin history, action and reaction.; and Kuypers, K. P., Ng, L., Erritzoe, D., Knudsen, G. M., Nichols, C. D., Nichols, D. E., Pani, L., Soula, A., & Nutt, D. (2019). Microdosing psychedelics: More questions than answers? An overview and suggestions for future research. *Journal of Psychopharmacology, 33*(9), 1039–1057. https://doi.org/10.1177/0269881119857204

25 Carhart-Harris et al. Trial of psilocybin versus escitalopram.; and Davis, A. K., Barrett, F. S., May,

D. G., Cosimano, M. P., Sepeda, N. D., Johnson, M. W., Finan, P. H., & Griffiths, R. R. (2021). Effects of psilocybin-assisted therapy on major depressive disorder: A randomized clinical trial. *JAMA Psychiatry, 78*(5), 481–489. https://doi.org/10.1001/jamapsychiatry.2020.3285; and Raison, C. L., Sanacora, G., Woolley, J., Heinzerling, K., Dunlop, B. W., Brown, R. T., Kakar, R., Hassman, M., Trivedi, R. P., Robison, R., Gukasyan, N., Nayak, S. M., Hu, X., O'Donnell, K. C., Kelmendi, B., Sloshower, J., Johnson, A. D., Gazzaley, A., Griffiths, R. R., & Hilton, J. W. (2023). Single-dose psilocybin treatment for major depressive disorder: A randomized clinical trial. *JAMA, 330*(9), 843–853. https://doi.org/10.1001/jama.2023.14530; and Sloshower, J., Skosnik, P. D., Safi-Aghdam, H., Pathania, S., Syed, S., Pittman, B., & D'Souza, D. C. (2023). Psilocybin-assisted therapy for major depressive disorder: An exploratory placebo-controlled, fixed-order trial. *Journal of Psychopharmacology, 37*(7), 698–706. https://doi.org/10.1177/02698811231154852; and von Rotz, R., Schindowski, E. M., Jungwirth, J., Schuldt, A., Rieser, N. M., Zahoranszky, K., Seifritz, E., Nowak, A., Nowak, P., Jaencke, L., Preller, K. H., & Vollenweider, F. X. (2023). Single-dose psilocybin-assisted therapy in major depressive disorder: A placebo-controlled, double-blind, randomised clinical trial. *eClinicalMedicine, 56*, Article 101809. https://doi.org/10.1016/j.eclinm.2022.101809

26 Goodwin, G. M., Aaronson, S. T., Alvarez, O., Arden, P. C., Baker, A., Bennett, J. C., Bird, C., Blom, R. E., Brennan, C., Brusch, D., Burke, L., Campbell-Coker, K., Carhart-Harris, R., Cattell, J., Daniel, A., DeBattista, C., Dunlop, B. W., Eisen, K., Feifel, D., … Malievskaia, E. (2022). Single-dose psilocybin for a treatment-resistant episode of major depression. *New England Journal of Medicine, 387*(18), 1637–1648. https://doi.org/10.1056/NEJMoa2206443; and Carhart-Harris, R. L., Bolstridge, M., Rucker, J., Day, C. M. J., Erritzoe, D., Kaelen, M., Bloomfield, M., Rickard, J. A., Forbes, B., Feilding, A., Taylor, D., Pilling, S., Curran, V. H., & Nutt, D. J. (2016). Psilocybin with psychological support for treatment-resistant depression: An open-label feasibility study. *The Lancet Psychiatry, 3*(7), 619–627. https://doi.org/10.1016/S2215-0366(16)30065-7; and Carhart-Harris, R. L., Bolstridge, M., Day, C. M. J., Rucker, J., Watts, R., Erritzoe, D. E., Kaelen, M., Giribaldi, B., Bloomfield, M., Pilling, S., Rickard, J. A., Forbes, B., Feilding, A., Taylor, D., Curran, H. V., & Nutt, D. J. (2018). Psilocybin with psychological support for treatment-resistant depression: Six-month follow-up. *Psychopharmacology, 235*(2), 399–408. https://doi.org/10.1007/s00213-017-4771-x; and Goodwin, G. M., Croal, M., Feifel, D., Kelly, J. R., Marwood, L., Mistry, S., O'Keane, V., Peck, S. K., Simmons, H., Sisa, C., Stansfield, S. C., Tsai, J., Williams, S., & Malievskaia, E. (2023). Psilocybin for treatment resistant depression in patients taking a concomitant SSRI medication. *Neuropsychopharmacology, 48*(10), 1492–1499. https://doi.org/10.1038/s41386-023-01648-7

27 Aaronson, S. T., van der Vaart, A., Miller, T., LaPratt, J., Swartz, K., Shoultz, A., Lauterbach, M., Sackeim, H. A., & Suppes, T. (2024). Single-dose synthetic psilocybin with psychotherapy for treatment-resistant bipolar type II major depressive episodes: A nonrandomized open-label trial. *JAMA Psychiatry, 81*(6), 555–562. https://doi.org/10.1001/jamapsychiatry.2023.4685; and Rosenblat, J. (2024, April). *Psilocybin-assisted psychotherapy for treatment-resistant depression: A randomized phase II clinical trial comparing one versus two psychedelic doses of psilocybin (PSI-1V2)* (Clinical trial registration No. NCT06341426). ClinicalTrials.gov. https://clinicaltrials.gov/study/NCT06341426

28 Agrawal, M., Emanuel, E., Richards, B., Richards, W., Roddy, K., & Thambi, P. (2023). Assessment of psilocybin therapy for patients with cancer and major depression disorder. *JAMA Oncology, 9*(6), 864–866. https://doi.org/10.1001/jamaoncol.2023.0351; and Griffiths, R. R., Johnson, M. W., Carducci, M. A., Umbricht, A., Richards, W. A., Richards, B. D., Cosimano, M. P., & Klinedinst, M. A. (2016). Psilocybin produces substantial and sustained decreases in depression and anxiety in patients with life-threatening cancer: A randomized double-blind trial. *Journal of Psychopharmacology, 30*(12), 1181–1197. https://doi.org/10.1177/0269881116675513; and Lewis, B. R., Garland, E. L., Byrne, K., Durns, T., Hendrick, J., Beck, A., & Thielking, P. (2023). HOPE: A pilot study of psilocybin enhanced group psychotherapy in patients with cancer. *Journal of Pain and Symptom Management, 66*(3), 258–269. https://doi.org/10.1016/j.jpainsymman.2023.06.006; and Shnayder, S., Ameli, R., Sinaii, N., Berger, A., & Agrawal, M. (2023). Psilocybin-assisted therapy improves psycho-social-spiritual well-being in cancer patients. *Journal of Affective Disorders, 323*, 592–597. https://doi.org/10.1016/j.jad.2022.11.046; and Ross, S., Bossis, A., Guss, J., Agin-Liebes, G., Malone, T., Cohen, B., Mennenga, S. E., Belser, A., Kalliontzi, K., Babb, J., Su, Z., Corby, P., & Schmidt, B. L. (2016). Rapid and sustained symptom reduction following psilocybin treatment for anxiety and depression in patients with life-threatening cancer: A randomized controlled trial. *Journal of Psychopharmacology, 30*(12), 1165–1180. https://doi.org/10.1177/0269881116675512

29 Davis et al. Effects of psilocybin-assisted therapy on major depressive disorder.; and Raison et al. Single-dose psilocybin treatment for major depressive disorder.; and von Rotz et al. Single-dose psilocybin-assisted therapy in major depressive disorder.; and Carhart-Harris et al. Psilocybin with psychological support for treatment-resistant depression: An open-label feasibility study.; and Gukasyan, N., Davis, A. K., Barrett, F. S., Cosimano, M. P., Sepeda, N. D., Johnson, M. W., & Griffiths, R. R. (2022). Efficacy and safety of psilocybin-assisted treatment for major depressive disorder: Prospective 12-month follow-up. *Journal of Psychopharmacology, 36*(2), 151–158. https://doi.org/10.1177/02698811211073759

30 Carhart-Harris et al. Psilocybin with psychological support for treatment-resistant depression: An open-label feasibility study.; and Griffiths et al. Psilocybin produces substantial and sustained decreases in depression and anxiety.

31 Moreno, F. A., Wiegand, C. B., Taitano, E. K., & Delgado, P. L. (2006). Safety, tolerability, and efficacy of psilocybin in 9 patients with obsessive-compulsive disorder. *Journal of Clinical Psychiatry, 67*(11), 1735–1740. https://doi.org/10.4088/JCP.v67n1110

32 Bogenschutz, M. P., Forcehimes, A. A., Pommy, J. A., Wilcox, C. E., Barbosa, P., & Strassman, R. J. (2015). Psilocybin-assisted treatment for alcohol dependence: A proof-of-concept study. *Journal of Psychopharmacology, 29*(3), 289–299. https://doi.org/10.1177/0269881114565144; and Johnson, M. W., Garcia-Romeu, A., & Griffiths, R. R. (2017). Long-term follow-up of psilocybin-facilitated smoking cessation. *American Journal of Drug and Alcohol Abuse, 43*(1), 55–60. https://doi.org/10.3109/00952990.2016.1170135

33 Reiff, C. M., Richman, E. E., Nemeroff, C. B., Carpenter, L. L., Widge, A. S., Rodriguez, C. I., Kalin, N. H., & McDonald, W. M. (2020). Psychedelics and psychedelic-assisted psychotherapy. *Focus, 19*(1), 95–115. https://doi.org/10.1176/appi.focus.19104

34 Reiff et al. Psychedelics and psychedelic-assisted psychotherapy.

35 Holze, F., Gasser, P., Müller, F., Strebel, M., & Liechti, M. E. (2024). LSD-assisted therapy in patients with anxiety: Open-label prospective 12-month follow-up. *British Journal of Psychiatry, 225*(3), 362–370. https://doi.org/10.1192/bjp.2024.99

36 Gasser, P., Kirchner, K., & Passie, T. (2015). LSD-assisted psychotherapy for anxiety associated with a life-threatening disease: A qualitative study of acute and sustained subjective effects. *Journal of Psychopharmacology, 29*(1), 57–68. https://doi.org/10.1177/0269881114555249

37 Krebs, T. S., & Johansen, P. Ø. (2012). Lysergic acid diethylamide (LSD) for alcoholism: Meta-analysis of randomized controlled trials. *Journal of Psychopharmacology, 26*(7), 994–1002. https://doi.org/10.1177/0269881112439253

38 Varker, T., Watson, L., Gibson, K., Forbes, D., & O'Donnell, M. L. (2021). Efficacy of psychoactive drugs for the treatment of posttraumatic stress disorder: A systematic review of MDMA, ketamine, LSD and psilocybin. *Journal of Psychoactive Drugs, 53*(1), 85–95. https://doi.org/10.1080/02791072.2020.1817639

39 Costa, G., & Gołembiowska, K. (2022). Neurotoxicity of MDMA: Main effects and mechanisms. *Experimental Neurology, 347*, Article 113894. https://doi.org/10.1016/j.expneurol.2021.113894

40 Johnson et al. Human hallucinogen research.

41 Smith, K. W., Sicignano, D. J., Hernandez, A. V., & White, C. M. (2022). MDMA-assisted psychotherapy for treatment of posttraumatic stress disorder: A systematic review with meta-analysis. *Journal of Clinical Pharmacology, 62*(4), 463–471. https://doi.org/10.1002/jcph.1995

42 Smith et al. MDMA-assisted psychotherapy for treatment of posttraumatic stress disorder.; and Ot'alora G., M., Grigsby, J., Poulter, B., Van Derveer, J. W., III, Giron, S. G., Jerome, L., Feduccia, A. A., Hamilton, S., Yazar-Klosinski, B., Emerson, A., Mithoefer, M. C., & Doblin, R. (2018). 3,4-Methylenedioxymethamphetamine-assisted psychotherapy for treatment of chronic posttraumatic stress disorder: A randomized phase 2 controlled trial. *Journal of Psychopharmacology, 32*(12), 1295–1307. https://doi.org/10.1177/0269881118806297; and Mitchell, J. M., Bogenschutz, M., Lilienstein, A., Harrison, C., Kleiman, S., Parker-Guilbert, K., Ot'alora G., M., Garas, W., Paleos, C., Gorman, I., Nicholas, C., Mithoefer, M., Carlin, S., Poulter, B., Mithoefer, A., Quevedo, S., Wells, G., Klaire, S. S., van der Kolk, B., … Doblin, R. (2021). MDMA-assisted therapy for severe PTSD: A randomized, double-blind, placebo-controlled phase 3 study. *Nature Medicine, 27*(6), 1025–1033. https://doi.org/10.1038/s41591-021-01336-3; and Mithoefer, M. C., Mithoefer, A. T., Feduccia, A. A., Jerome, L., Wagner, M., Wymer, J., Holland, J., Hamilton, S., Yazar-Klosinski, B., Emerson, A., & Doblin, R. (2018). 3,4-Methylenedioxymethamphetamine (MDMA)-assisted psychotherapy for post-traumatic stress disorder in military veterans, firefighters, and police officers: A randomised, double-blind, dose-response, phase 2 clinical trial. *The Lancet Psychiatry, 5*(6), 486–497. https://doi.org/10.1016/

S2215-0366(18)30135-4; and Mithoefer, M. C., Wagner, M. T., Mithoefer, A. T., Jerome, L., Martin, S. F., Yazar-Klosinski, B., Michel, Y., Brewerton, T. D., & Doblin, R. (2013). Durability of improvement in post-traumatic stress disorder symptoms and absence of harmful effects or drug dependency after 3,4-methylenedioxymethamphetamine-assisted psychotherapy: A prospective long-term follow-up study. *Journal of Psychopharmacology, 27*(1), 28–39. https://doi.org/10.1177/0269881112456611; and Mithoefer, M. C., Wagner, M. T., Mithoefer, A. T., Jerome, L., & Doblin, R. (2011). The safety and efficacy of ±3,4-methylenedioxymethamphetamine-assisted psychotherapy in subjects with chronic, treatment-resistant posttraumatic stress disorder: The first randomized controlled pilot study. *Journal of Psychopharmacology, 25*(4), 439–452. https://doi.org/10.1177/0269881110378371; and Sessa, B. (2017). MDMA and PTSD treatment: "PTSD: From novel pathophysiology to innovative therapeutics." *Neuroscience Letters, 649*, 176–180. https://doi.org/10.1016/j.neulet.2016.07.004; and Oehen, P., Traber, R., Widmer, V., & Schnyder, U. (2013). A randomized, controlled pilot study of MDMA (± 3,4-methylenedioxymethamphetamine)-assisted psychotherapy for treatment of resistant, chronic post-traumatic stress disorder (PTSD). *Journal of Psychopharmacology, 27*(1), 40–52. https://doi.org/10.1177/0269881112464827; and Emerson, A., Ponté, L., Jerome, L., & Doblin, R. (2014). History and future of the Multidisciplinary Association for Psychedelic Studies (MAPS). *Journal of Psychoactive Drugs, 46*(1), 27–36. https://doi.org/10.1080/02791072.2014.877321

43 Reckweg, J. T., Uthaug, M. V., Szabo, A., Davis, A. K., Lancelotta, R., Mason, N. L., & Ramaekers, J. G. (2022). The clinical pharmacology and potential therapeutic applications of 5-methoxy-N,N-dimethyltryptamine (5-MeO-DMT). *Journal of Neurochemistry, 162*(1), 128–146. https://doi.org/10.1111/jnc.15587

44 Reckweg et al. The clinical pharmacology and potential therapeutic applications of 5-MeO-DMT.; and Barker, S. A. (2018). N, N-Dimethyltryptamine (DMT), an endogenous hallucinogen: Past, present, and future research to determine its role and function. *Frontiers in Neuroscience, 12*, Article 536. https://doi.org/10.3389/fnins.2018.00536

45 Barker. N, N-Dimethyltryptamine (DMT), an endogenous hallucinogen.

46 Reckweg et al. The clinical pharmacology and potential therapeutic applications of 5-MeO-DMT.

47 Reiff et al. Psychedelics and psychedelic-assisted psychotherapy.

48 D'Souza, D. C., Syed, S. A., Flynn, L. T., Safi-Aghdam, H., Cozzi, N. V., & Ranganathan, M. (2022). Exploratory study of the dose-related safety, tolerability, and efficacy of dimethyltryptamine (DMT) in healthy volunteers and major depressive disorder. *Neuropsychopharmacology, 47*(10), 1854–1862. https://doi.org/10.1038/s41386-022-01344-y; and Falchi-Carvalho, M., Palhano-Fontes, F., Wießner, I., Barros, H., Bolcont, R., Laborde, S., Palhano-Fontes, F., Alchieri, J. C., Araújo, D. B., & Galvão-Coelho, N. L. (2025). Rapid and sustained antidepressant effects of vaporized N,N-dimethyltryptamine: A phase 2a clinical trial in treatment-resistant depression. *Neuropsychopharmacology, 50*(6), 895–903. https://doi.org/10.1038/s41386-025-02091-6; and Osório, F. de L., Sanches, R. F., Macedo, L. R., dos Santos, R. G., Maia-de-Oliveira, J. P., Wichert-Ana, L., de Araujo, D. B., Riba, J., Crippa, J. A. S., & Hallak, J. E. C. (2015). Antidepressant effects of a single dose of ayahuasca in patients with recurrent depression: A preliminary report. *Revista Brasileira de Psiquiatria, 37*(1), 13–20. https://doi.org/10.1590/1516-4446-2014-1496; and Reckweg, J. T., van Leeuwen, C. J., Henquet, C., van Amelsvoort, T., Theunissen, E. L., Mason, N. L., Paci, R., Terwey, T. H., & Ramaekers, J. G. (2023). A phase 1/2 trial to assess safety and efficacy of a vaporized 5-methoxy-N,N-dimethyltryptamine formulation (GH001) in patients with treatment-resistant depression. *Frontiers in Psychiatry, 14*, Article 1133414. https://doi.org/10.3389/fpsyt.2023.1133414; and Sanches, R. F., Osório, F. de L., dos Santos, R. G., Macedo, L. R. H., Maia-de-Oliveira, J. P., Wichert-Ana, L., de Araujo, D. B., Riba, J., Crippa, J. A. S., & Hallak, J. E. C. (2016). Antidepressant effects of a single dose of ayahuasca in patients with recurrent depression: A SPECT study. *Journal of Clinical Psychopharmacology, 36*(1), 77–81. https://doi.org/10.1097/JCP.0000000000000436

49 Palhano-Fontes, F., Barreto, D., Onias, H., Andrade, K. C., Novaes, M. M., Pessoa, J. A., Mota-Rolim, S. A., Osório, F. L., Sanches, R., dos Santos, R. G., Tofoli, L. F., de Oliveira Silveira, G., Yonamine, M., Riba, J., Santos, F. R., Silva-Junior, A. A., Alchieri, J. C., Galvão-Coelho, N. L., Lobao-Soares, B., … Araújo, D. B. (2019). Rapid antidepressant effects of the psychedelic ayahuasca in treatment-resistant depression: A randomized placebo-controlled trial. *Psychological Medicine, 49*(4), 655–663. https://doi.org/10.1017/S0033291718001356

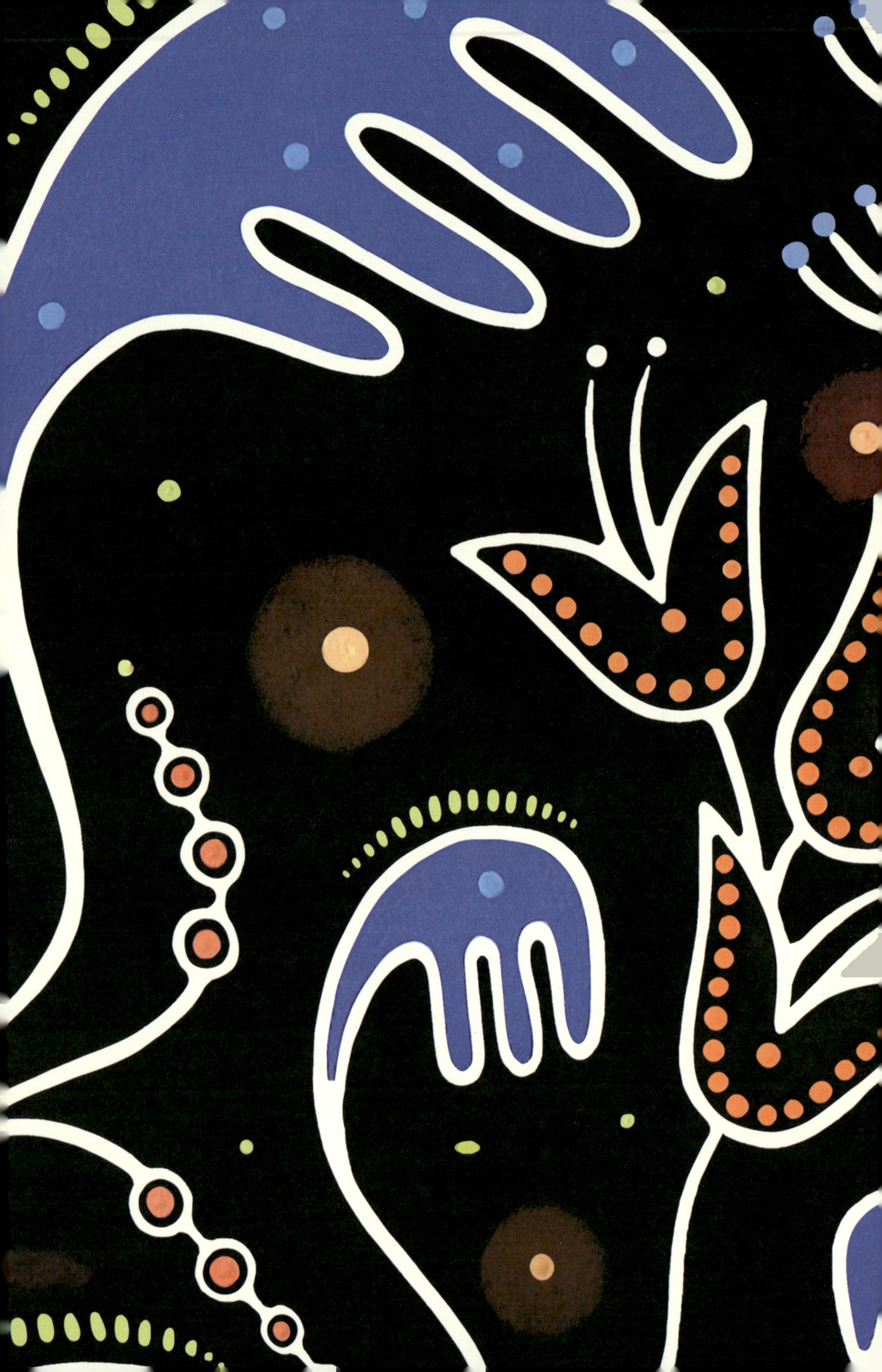

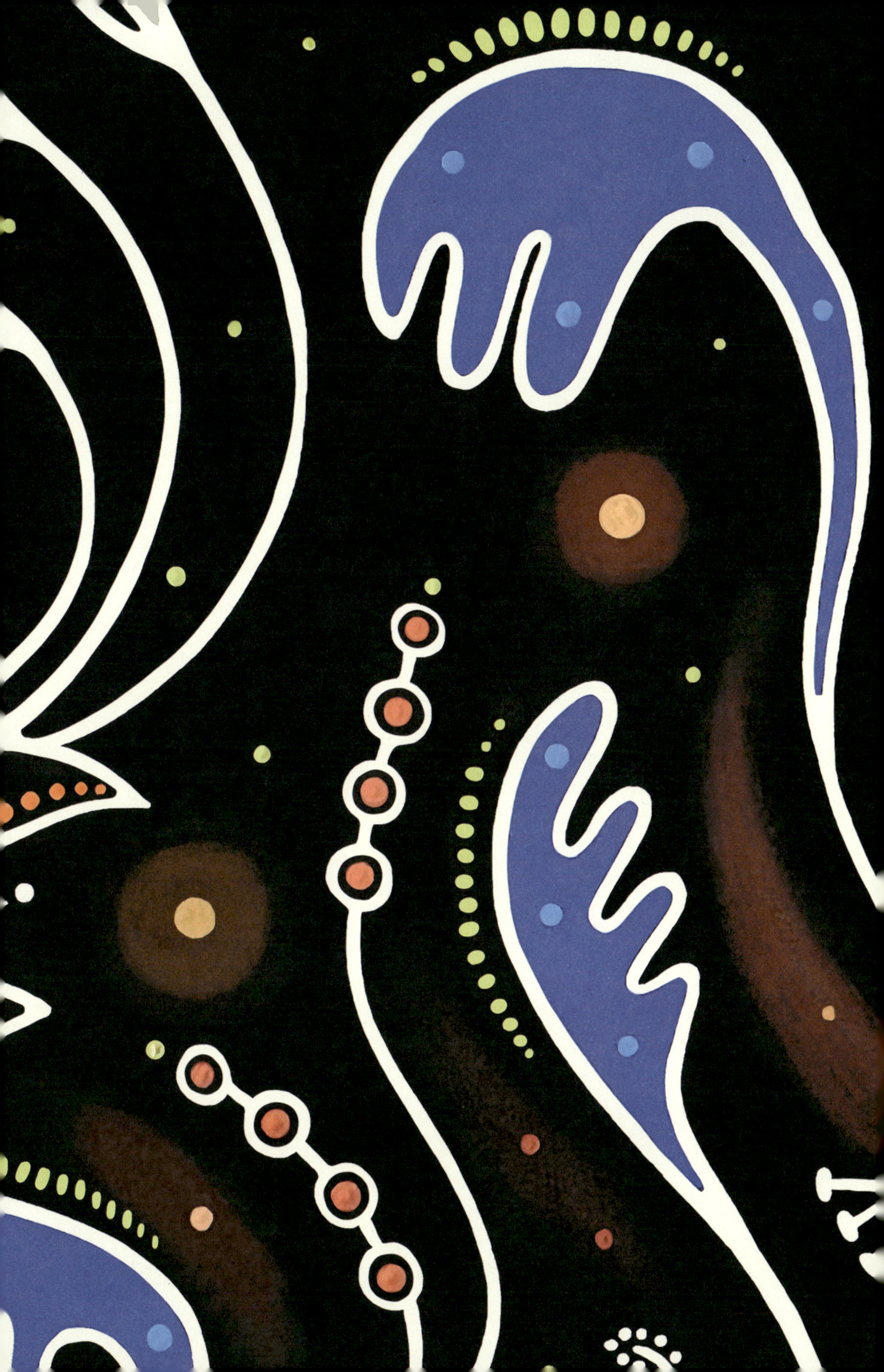

5

Indigenous Perspectives on Plant Medicines

KELLY BOUTSALIS

THERE ARE AN INCREDIBLE NUMBER OF ISSUES that complicate Indigenous people's relationships to psychedelics, despite being the first stewards for many of them. There are many variations on what people feel comfortable calling them–in North America, some use the term "plant medicine" to encompass all types, even fungi. If defaulting to another umbrella term, others call them just "medicine" or "Spirit medicine."

"Something I was taught very early on [is] that we don't call plant medicine 'psychedelics,'" says Sutton King, the Menominee and Oneida Co-Founder, President, and Executive Director of the Urban Indigenous Collective (UIC), an organization that provides culturally tailored public health and community care in New York City. "It's disrespectful to call them that. These are our relatives, our grandmas, our grandpas, and they have living memory."

With those teachings, King is one of several voices focusing on bringing plant medicines like psilocybin, peyote, and ayahuasca to Indigenous people, navigating the complicated issues around them, from commodification and extraction to criminalization and tokenization.

While Indigenous peoples, the original stewards of many plant medicines, face roadblocks to using them, there remains a promising future in some communities.

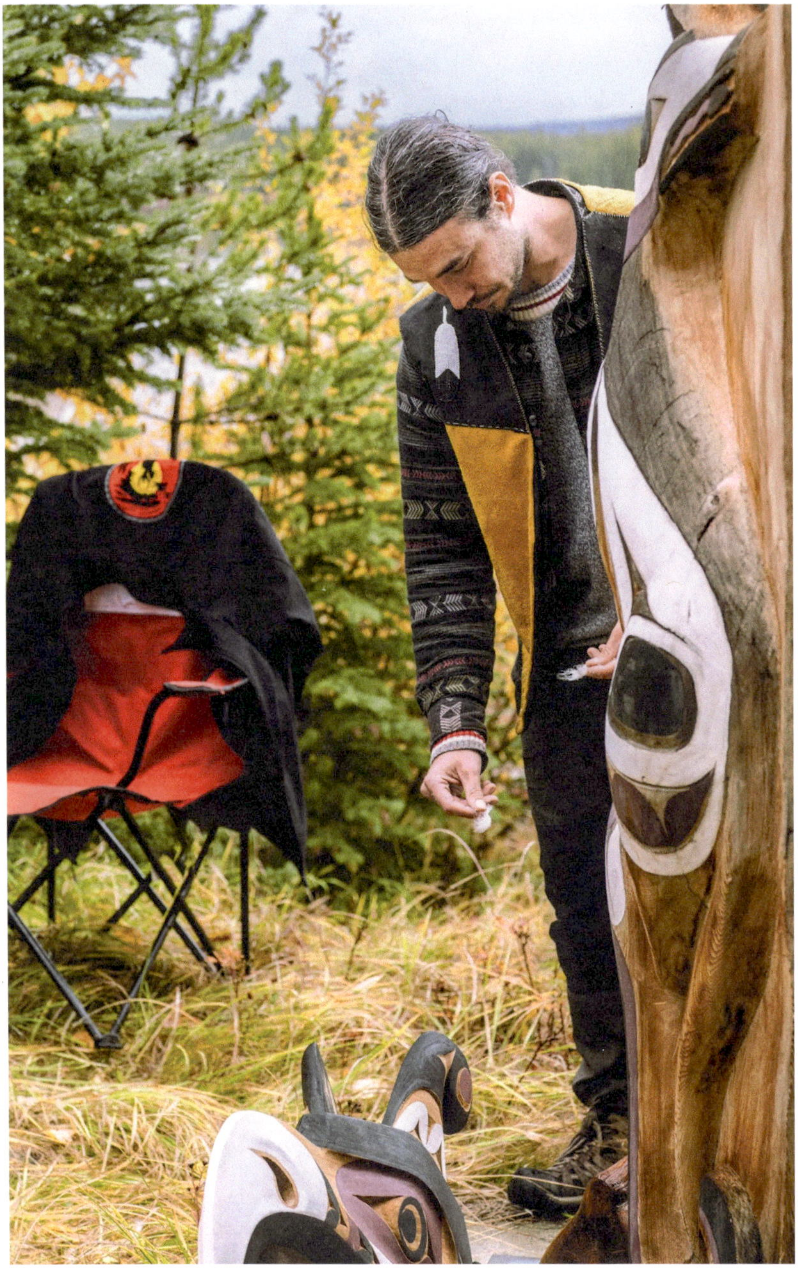

Figure 1
Trevor Mack, co-founder of the non-profit cultural and educational organization Nenqayni, leaves an eagle down offering by the totem pole.

Photo: Courtesy of Nolan Guichón.

Trevor Mack, from the Tsilhqot'in Nation, is a filmmaker and the co-founder of non-profit cultural and educational organization Nenqayni. He believes that plant medicines are being shared among Indigenous communities across Canada, which will lead to "true nation-to-nation familial relationships and connections."

"Indigenous people have spatial identity, and I consider myself as Tsilhqot'in before Canadian. It means 'people of the Glacier Rock River,' which is an actual river that you can taste, touch, smell, see," he says. "The foundation of the identity comes from gratitude and humility, whereas, if it's a temporal identity, that's the opposite, because it's been made in our own mind. The spatial identity found [from] plant medicines, and ceremonies over tens of thousands of years, [has] tried to keep that expanded awareness experience alive in generation after generation."

Mack's life-changing journey into plant medicines began with research. He didn't know who to go to or where to go and landed on growing his own mushrooms. After all, "the West Coast is the most highly saturated place for psilocybin mushrooms on the whole planet," says Mack.

While Western science says that Indigenous people in Canada didn't use plant medicines for mind-altering effects, Mack and the Elders he learned from believe differently.[1]

Plant medicines have been used since time immemorial, and a long history of the Western way of science perceiving Indigenous people incorrectly may be the reason why this use isn't found in scientific texts.[2] There is also the matter of oral histories, Knowledge Keepers, and Elders not being considered authorities on the subject and, on the flip side, a level of distrust by Indigenous people in extractive scientific studies.

Mack sees First Nations communities in Canada using these types of medicines as another way to deepen the integral relationship between the land, plants, and humans. They are communal experiences, which he says are more in line with Indigenous societies.

"What's specific about plant medicines is it's an actual tangible alive thing from the planet. It has messages for us," says Mack. "When you really experience your body dissolving into the lake or morphing into a tree, [when] the plant beings actually communicate to you, it's only then when you can begin to truly understand what the ancestors were really talking about, [and] the strength of that is how the Indigenous societies are still here."

Indigenous worldviews that interweave language, songs, and ceremonies all come back to the land, and plant medicines are part of that. Many Indigenous communities sing to the seeds and spores as they are planted and nurtured, as Mack did for his mushrooms.[3]

"They open your eyes to a greater panoramic view of reality," says Mack. "Nearly all of the Indigenous societies were based off of this higher state of reality, whether it was with plant medicines, meditation, or fasting–different techniques, different speed, and different accelerations–but they get to the same place.

"Indigenous communities in Canada already have a framework to hold these experiences. Whether it's big house ceremonies on the West Coast or the Long House ceremonies on the East Coast, they have always been the safe space," he adds.

Currently, Mack says that some Indigenous communities are incrementally structuring language and society around these ways of healing. "It's being implemented within the cultural framework that goes hand in hand with helping whoever brought the medicines, their families, their community, whether that's monetarily, culturally, or generationally."

Beyond Canada

In the U.S., the focus of Native Americans is on conservation. This is due to the different legal landscape in America, versus that in Canada, and the influence of the Native American Church, a large religious movement that incorporates peyote into its ceremonies.

Christine Diindiisi McCleave, PhD, Turtle Mountain Anishinaabe, was the project manager for the Report of the Federally Recognized American Tribes & Indigenous Community Working Group, and through her work, she has seen first-hand how the U.S. is the centre of the global extraction and commodification of these medicines.[4]

Iboga derives from Africa, ayahuasca from the Amazon, and mescaline from Peru, for instance, so protecting global medicines becomes complicated legally.

On top of that, the psychedelic movement's relationship with Indigenous people is twisted. In many communities, a healer is born into, or chosen for, this special honour. That person has special gifts. In sharp contrast to this is the Western model, where training happens before a certification, or the New Age model, where someone goes to live amongst the Indigenous people in the Amazon for a couple of years and comes back as a shaman.

"There's this romanticization, tokenization, and cultural misappropriation," says McCleave. "They're just fascinated with the Indigenous peoples who have this sacred, spiritual ceremonial knowledge, without acknowledging the fact that colonization nearly wiped it out in some cases and did wipe it out for a lot of people."

Many Indigenous peoples aren't practising sacred ceremonies, at the same time as there is a great need for healing of historical and intergenerational trauma.

The irony is not lost on McCleave, a generational survivor of Indian boarding schools (residential schools), that she has the option of quasi-New Age mushroom therapy to try and heal that trauma.

Further away, in Central Africa, there is unprecedented progress that McCleave is really encouraged by. Indigenous tribes in Gabon have entered an inter-tribal coalition to become party to the Nagoya Protocol (its full title is *The Nagoya Protocol on Access to Genetic Resources and the Fair and Equitable Sharing of Benefits Arising from Their Utilization*). They are the only Indigenous group that has given consent for people to use their medicine, sourced from Gabon.

"Instead of doing biopiracy, like stealing a plant and growing it somewhere else, they source it from Gabon so that it's ethically sourced, sustainable, and the tribes get part of the profit," she says.

While McCleave thinks the Nagoya Protocol's use of free and informed consent is the best model out there for plant medicine conservation, she doesn't think all the other Indigenous communities are ready yet for that type of structure.

"They have not organized themselves to a point where they can address their own issues in all of their various communities across different countries," she says. "The Amazon is huge, with different legislative structures and governments, and the Indigenous peoples have their own battles. Psychedelics is [on the] bottom of their list [of] issues to address; they're busy putting out other fires, literally."

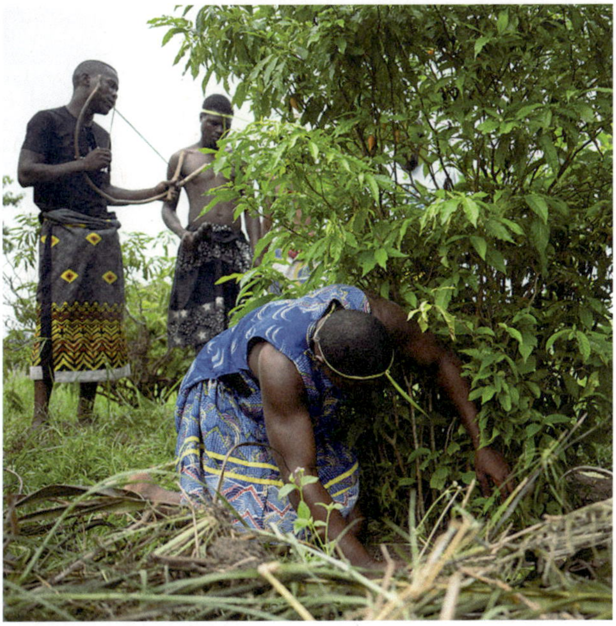

Figure 2
In Ndossa Village, Gabon, a Bwèté participant extracts iboga root–a powerful psychedelic, which is under threat because of poaching that serves a growing international market.
Photo: NAO MUKADI/AFP via Getty Images.

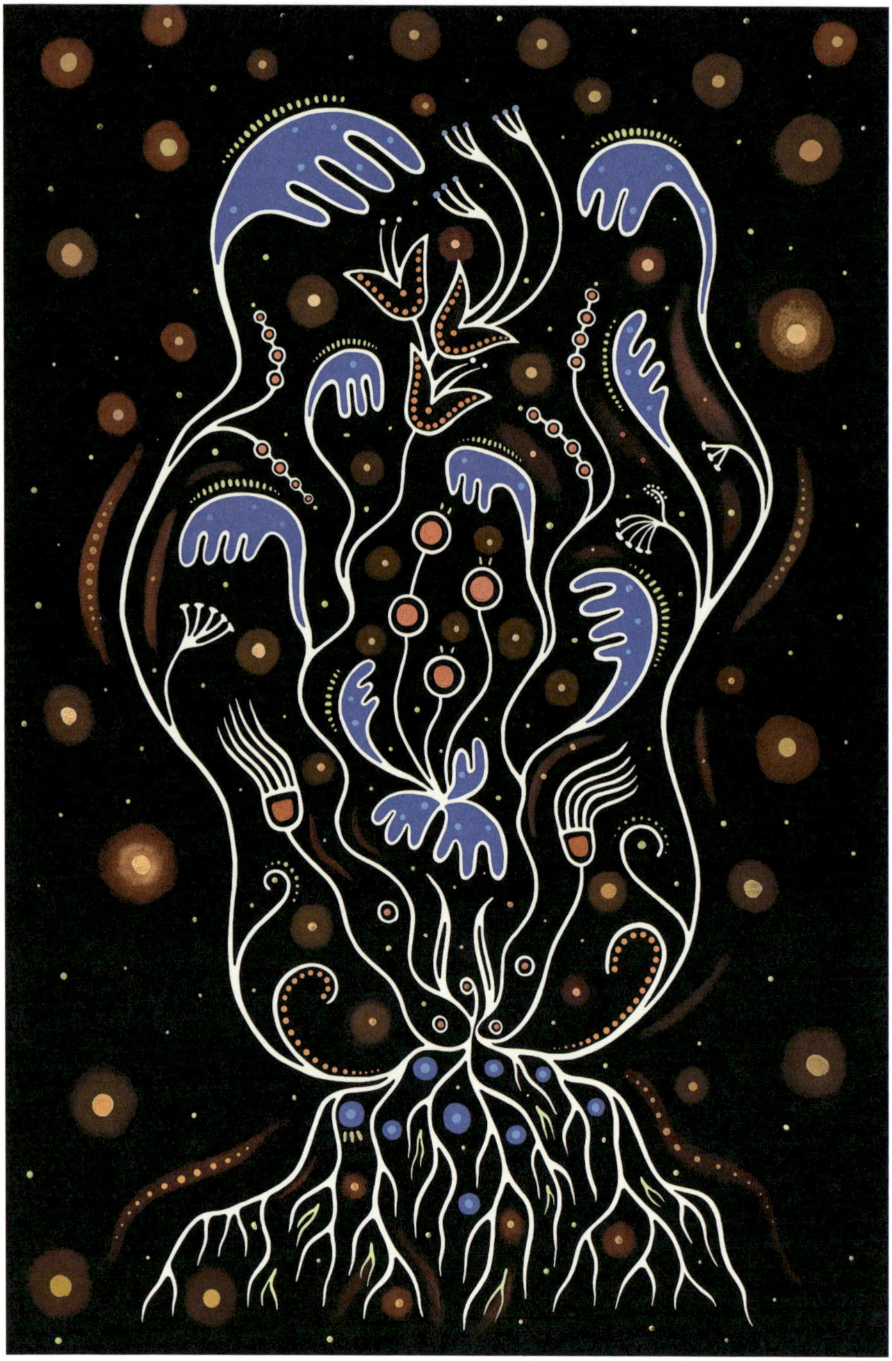

Figure 3
Plant Medicine by Christi Belcourt, 2022.

Photo: Courtesy of the artist.

Consultation Is Key

UIC's King is putting out smaller fires in Manhattan, bringing urban Indigenous peoples together in decolonized and safe spaces, with free, prior, and informed consent. Understanding deeply how mental health issues could be aided by plant medicine's use, she spent three years with the Indigenous Medicine Conservation (IMC) Fund, an Indigenous-led philanthropic vehicle that supports the conservation of ayahuasca, iboga, psilocybin mushrooms, and peyote. Once it was up and sustainable, she passed it along to the traditional keepers of those medicines to focus on her UIC, with aims to provide direct services of psychedelics and plant medicines to the urban Native community in New York City.

Beginning that work with consultation was key. UIC co-founder Ariel Richer uses the knowledge gained during her PhD studies to research that community's attitudes toward and understanding of those medicines, which has revealed an overall confusion from Indigenous clients.

"In the quantitative survey, we're asking folks to match different psychedelics or plant medicines based on what we're describing, and then in the conversations, we're asking what psychedelics and plant medicines means to you," says King.

"[We're learning] how we can be a safe space for our community, the education that is really necessary before one of our community members ends up in some psychedelic or plant medicine retreat, or steps into a ketamine clinic here in the city, making sure that these providers have education around how to protect our Indigenous community, versus further traumatizing them," she says.

It's a huge undertaking, considering that many people are trying to understand their own positions on plant medicine within their tribal councils or within the Native American Church.

"There's so much education necessary, and this psychedelic industry is moving on the time in which capitalism often does, very fast, and breaking things, whereas Indigenous peoples are intentional and moving in a good way," she says.

She has witnessed intentional work first-hand, at the Yaqui Intercultural Medicine Clinic in Sonora, Mexico, through her work with the IMC Fund.

"They are bringing different plant medicines together to support the healing of their community, those who have experienced sexual violence, substance misuse, and the way that they're reclaiming even medicines that were not traditionally part of their way of being and knowing really planted so many seeds for me in the Urban Indigenous Collective," she says.

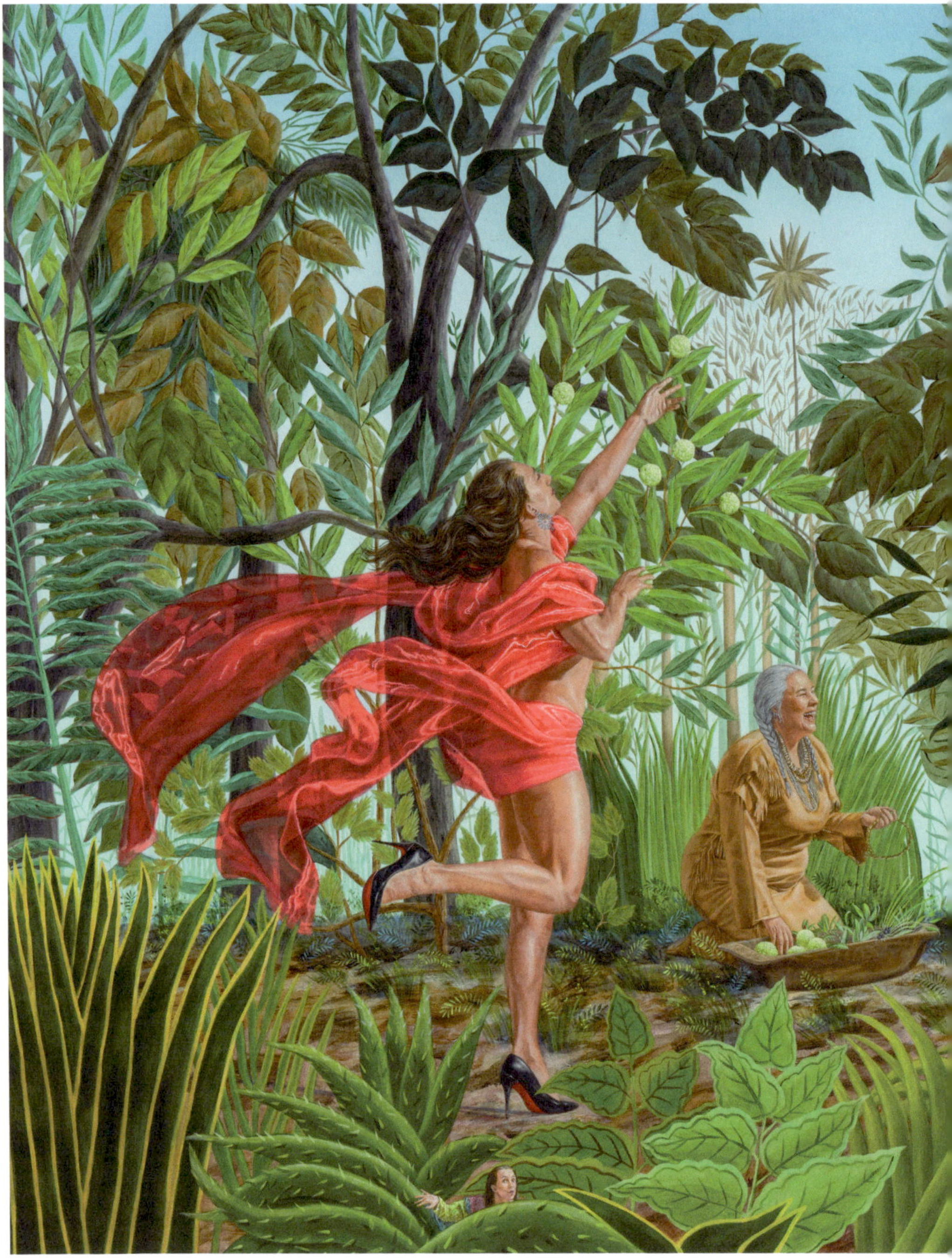

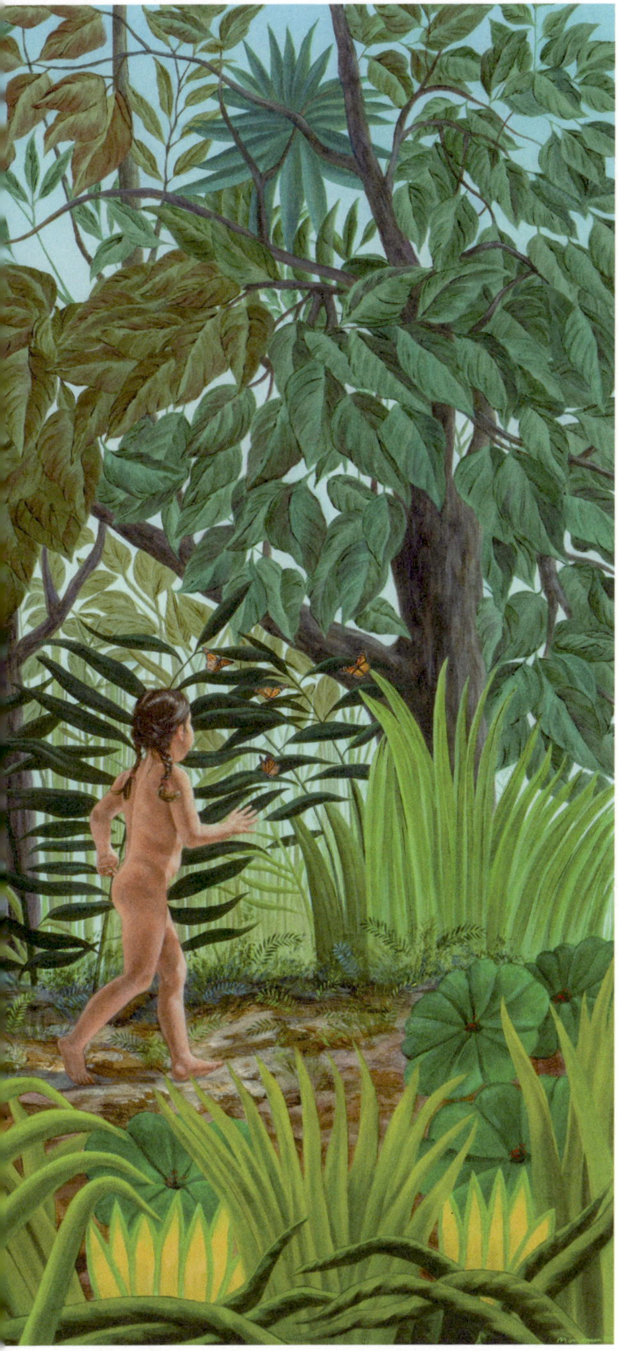

Figure 4
Kent Monkman, *Intermediary Study for Grandmother Knew All the Medicines*, 2022. Private collection.

Photo: Courtesy of the artist.

The Future of Plant Medicines

For everyone interviewed, and even those that declined to be interviewed, there was a prevailing sense of fatigue. Without even diving deeply into each of the fraught issues affecting their work in this space—whether that's on their own or within Indigenous communities—the biggest issue is being ignored by non-Indigenous people.

"Native people won't engage in the psychedelic sector, [because] the psychedelic sector has not acknowledged the historical context and the harms that they're doing," says McCleave. "This is triggering historical trauma and perpetuating colonial systems."

There is hope in the future for these medicines, however.

Looking forward, Mack believes that the reconnecting with plant medicines will lead to new ceremonies, which again goes back to a deepening of culture and well-being.

"More and more Indigenous communities have contextualized these experiences, of these psychedelic plant medicines within their culture, and then in 50 years, 600 different communities [across Canada] will coalesce into the creation of 200–400-year visions for their community, and then, it all becomes like a glowing spider web," says Mack. "If we're continually blaming outside and looking outside, then we're only going to focus on the extraction and on the bad stuff. But when it's coming from the inside, that's where the visions are. That's where the opportunities are, because it's transforming and changing."

1 Turner, Nancy J., & Cuerrier, A. (2022). "'Frog's umbrella' and 'ghost's face powder': The cultural roles of mushrooms and other fungi for Canadian Indigenous Peoples." *Botany*, *100*(2), 183–205. https://doi.org/10.1139/cjb-2021-0052.

2 Fotiou, E. (2020). The role of Indigenous knowledges in psychedelic science. *Journal of Psychedelic Science, 4*(1), 16–23. https://doi.org/10.1556/20 54.2019.031.

3 Gaughan, S. J., & James, J. E. (2025). Psychedelic exceptionalism, Indigeneity, and the war on drugs: Antiracism and decolonizing psychedelic plant medicine. *American Journal of Bioethics, 25*(1), 71–73. https://doi.org/10.1080/15265161.2024.2433442

4 McCleave, C. D. (2025). *More than peyote: Historical trauma and the politics of cultural survival in the age of psychedelic colonialism* [Doctoral dissertation, University of Alaska Fairbanks]. University of Alaska Fairbanks Institutional Repository.

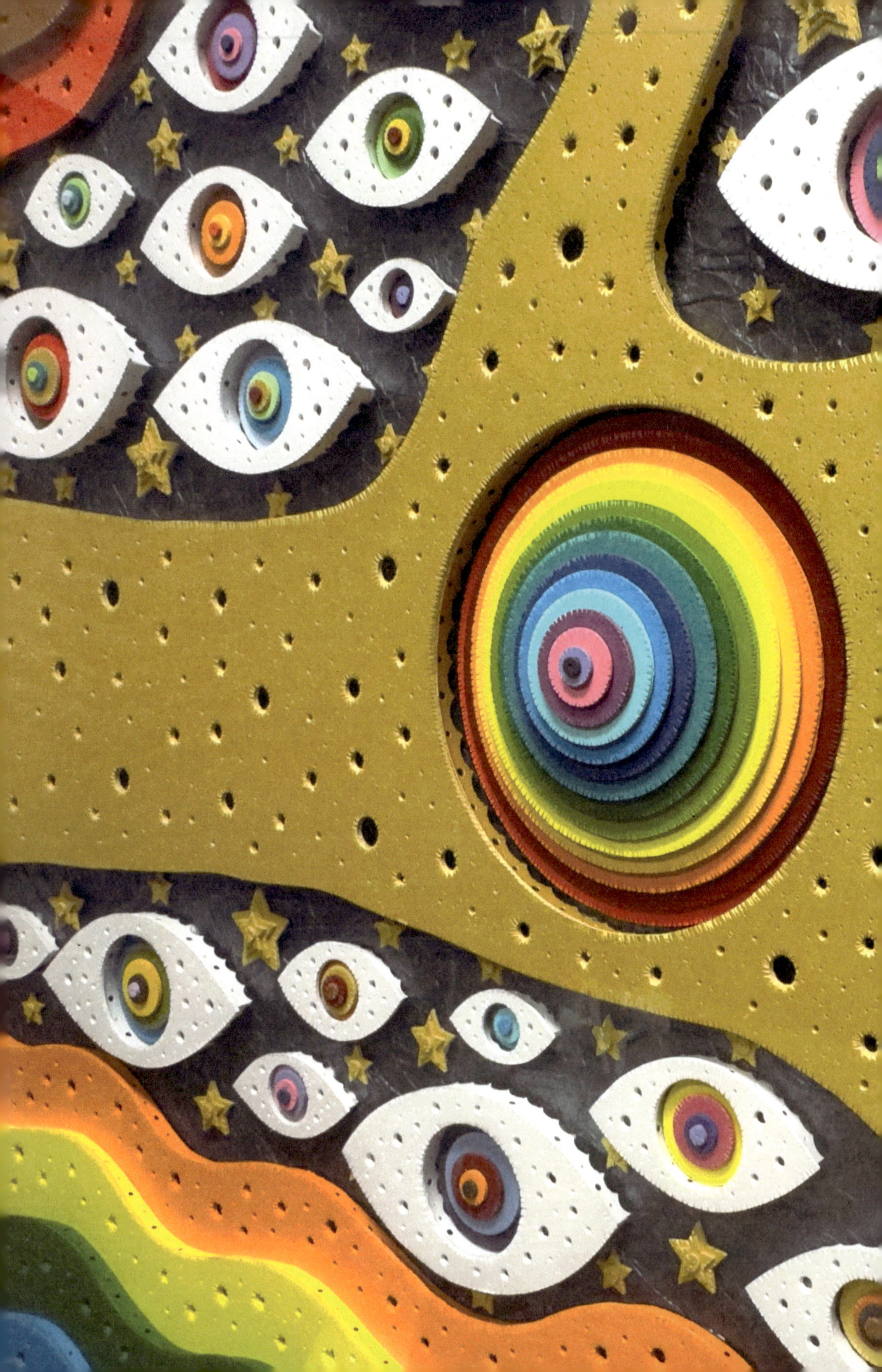

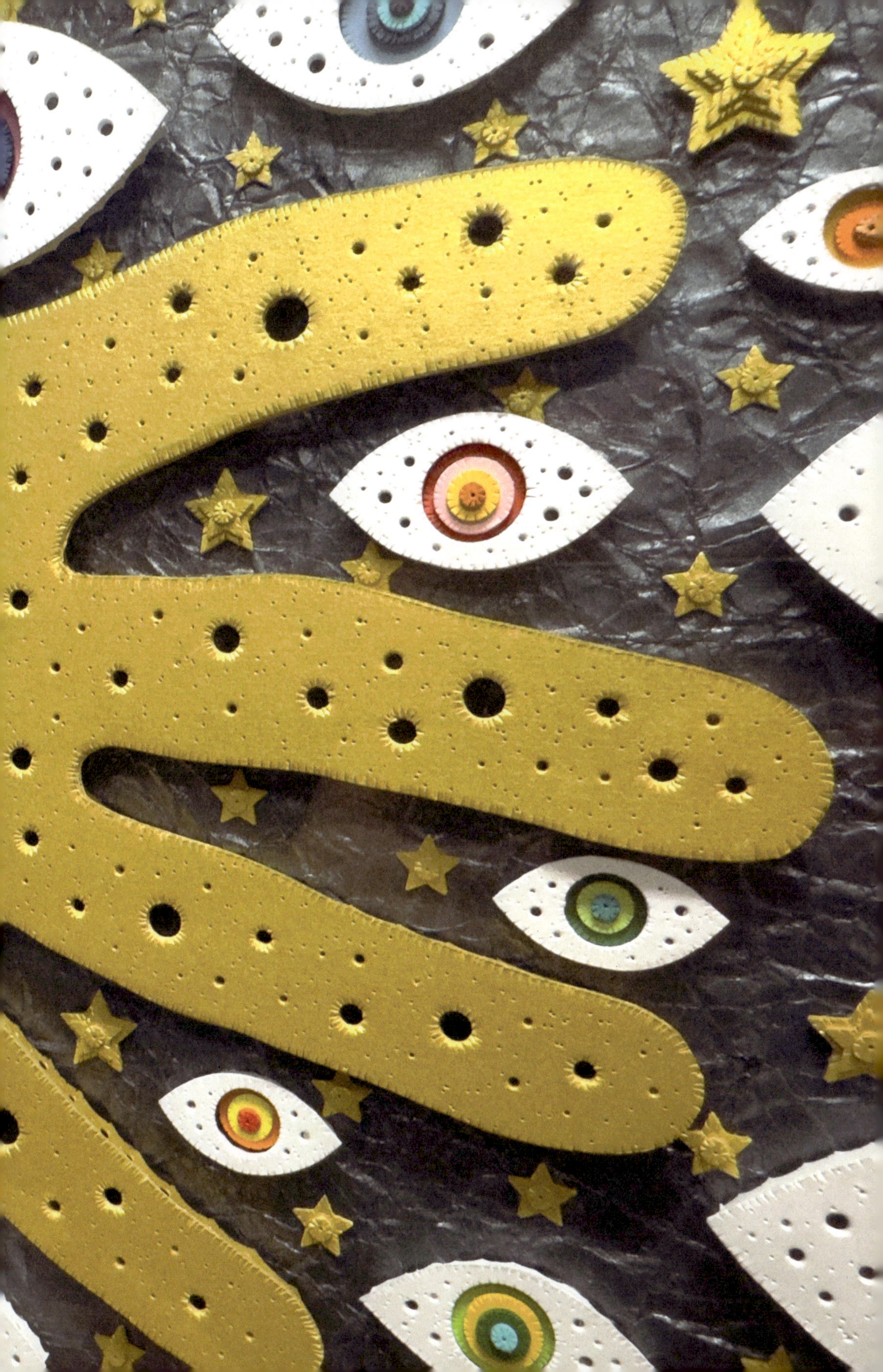

6

Our Psychedelic Future

COLIN J. FLEMING

IN THE EARLY DAYS OF THE SO-CALLED PSYCHEDELIC RENAISSANCE, it was easy to get swept up in the hype. LSD, MDMA, and magic mushrooms were somehow cool again. More than that, after decades underground, they had re-emerged as miracle cures at a time when countries like Canada were wrestling with the twin crises of opioid addiction and deteriorating mental health.

Exactly when this renaissance began is hard to pinpoint. Many researchers point to a 2006 study published in *Psychopharmacology* by four Johns Hopkins researchers, including the late famed psychopharmacologist Roland R. Griffiths, with the rather underwhelming academic title "Psilocybin Can Occasion Mystical-Type Experiences Having Substantial and Sustained Personal Meaning and Spiritual Significance."[1] As the *New Republic* reported, "From this key point of departure, Johns Hopkins commissioned a welter of important follow-up research,"[2] which eventually led to the establishment of the Johns Hopkins Center for Psychedelic and Consciousness Research.

But it probably wasn't until the publication of Michael Pollan's bestselling book, *How to Change Your Mind*, in 2019 that the newly emerging psychedelic research fully breached mainstream discourse. Like a 1960s-era Bob Dylan, Pollan somehow managed to both capture the zeitgeist and shape it, balancing his journalistic skepticism with boyish wonder. The result is a sweeping, elegantly written work of non-fiction, which deftly moves from Indigenous history to hippie counterculture to contemporary science. Although Pollan is measured in his approach, his excitement for psychedelics is palpable–a quality that proved infectious.

In the wake of *How to Change Your Mind*, more research emerged and, with it, a flurry of media attention. CBC described "how psychedelic drugs are changing lives and transforming psychiatry."[3] Vox published an explainer on the "extraordinary therapeutic potential of psychedelic drugs."[4] *New York* Magazine's Andrew Sullivan urged readers to say, "Yes to Drugs."[5] The hype was inescapable.

One of the biggest boosters was Rick Doblin, the founder of the Multidisciplinary Association of Psychedelic Studies (MAPS), whom Pollan described in *How to Change Your Mind* as a "great shaggy dog with a bone" who "had been lobbying to change the government's mind about psychedelics since shortly after graduating from New College, in Florida, in 1987."[6] In 2019, Doblin, who had long since graduated from fringe figure to thought leader, took the stage at a TED conference in Vancouver. "Humanity now is in a race between catastrophe and consciousness," he told the adoring audience. "The psychedelic renaissance is here to help consciousness triumph."[7]

But just a few years later, signs began to appear that the psychedelics bubble, if not quite bursting, was losing air. In 2022, *New York* Magazine released a video from a 2015 MAPS MDMA clinical trial of "two B.C. therapists cuddling, spooning, blindfolding and pinning down a distressed PTSD patient."[8] The footage, while disturbing, was only a facet of a season-long podcast exploring a pattern of "a culture that has historically swept both sexual and psychological abuses under the rug."[9]

That same year, three researchers from Johns Hopkins–including Roland R. Griffiths–published a paper in *JAMA Psychiatry* warning of the "hype bubble driven largely by media and industry interests."[10] "The potential for blowback is real," the authors explained. "Many people forget that there were years of glowing reviews in the 1950s and 1960s before the press turned alarmist and a government clampdown prevented research progress for decades."[11]

The researchers' predictions, while perhaps a little alarmist, have largely proven correct. As we noted in the introduction, the FDA's rejection of MDMA, Matthew Perry's ketamine overdose, and the fall of large psychedelics companies like Field Trip Health & Wellness have further deflated the psychedelics bubble.

That said, the news isn't all dire for psychedelic evangelists. On June 28, 2025, New Zealand became the latest country to approve psilocybin for medicinal use.[12]

That same month, "Texas' Republican governor, Greg Abbott, signed legislation … that will fund studies of the psychedelic drug ibogaine and, advocates hope, spur more states to follow."[13]

Still, the Johns Hopkins researchers were right about this: We need a clear-eyed, measured approach. One that acknowledges the therapeutic and spiritual power of psychedelic drugs, as well as their potential pitfalls. One informed by science, history, and Indigenous ways of knowing.

This book was an attempt to do just that. Here, I try to bring that same approach to the future of psychedelics and some of the many issues we must face to get it right.

Safety

I grew up in Canada in the '90s, a time of anti-psychedelic hysteria. Some variation of a rumour was always swirling around about a guy in a van hanging out near our elementary school, handing kids candy secretly dosed with LSD. (There was no such guy.) Just as alarming, we were told that psychedelics made you think you could fly so that you jumped off a rooftop, plunging to your death like a burnout hippie Icarus. Plus, as those egg-sizzling ads frequently told us, psychedelics fried your brain.

Much of this we know now is wrong. As a class of drugs, the so-called classical psychedelics (LSD, magic mushrooms, ayahuasca, etc.) that act on the 5-HT_{2A} receptors are mostly non-toxic and non-addictive.[14] And for many people suffering from PTSD, addiction, depression, or a host of other ailments, psychedelics can actually heal the brain.

All that said, too many of today's psychedelic evangelists dismiss genuine safety concerns as hysteria. But we have plenty to worry about.

First, psychedelics can indeed catalyze a schizophrenic break, although usually only for those prone to the disease. (That's why psychedelic clinical trials almost always exclude people with a family history of schizophrenia.) While a schizophrenic break is a rare occurrence, it's also a devastating one.

Second, psychedelic drugs, especially when taken at a high dose, can lead to accidents—even fatal ones. In March 2020, Will Nash, a Middlebury College student just months shy of graduating, took a half tab of LSD and, later, magic mushrooms with some friends. "What was a mellow and pleasant evening … turned scary and even violent," his mother, Kristin Nash, told the *Microdose*.[15] In his psychotic state, Will chugged a jar of protein powder, mistaking it for water. He died of asphyxiation before the ambulance came. In the summer of 2025, a

21-year-old man in Texas, while high on psilocybin, placed a pencil upright on his desk, then slammed his head down repeatedly. The pencil pierced both eyes, reaching his brain—and eventually killing him.[16] While cases like these may be rare, they do happen. So as psychedelics become increasingly normalized, more harm reduction strategies must be put in place. Even something as simple as encouraging trippers to have a sober, experienced guide could mitigate a lot of potential accidents.

Third, while classical psychedelics like LSD and psilocybin may be non-toxic, others can cause a lot of harm. According to the UC Berkeley Center for the Science of Psychedelics, "There are numerous reports in the scientific literature of people having fatal cardiac events after taking ibogaine."[17] In a feature-length story in the *New York Times* on at-home ketamine treatment, investigative reporter Chris Hamby reported that while ketamine was lifesaving for many, its drawbacks including "addiction and bladder damage ... have been largely played down by the drug's medical proponents."[18] Smoking the venom of the Sonoran Desert toad, perhaps unsurprisingly, can also be dangerous and, in very rare instances, fatal.

Finally, psychedelic trips can be downright terrifying, even for those who are well prepared (see chapter 4). In one clinical trial, "65% of individuals described one of their psilocybin experiences as one of the five most psychologically challenging experiences of their life and 25% of individuals described it as the single most psychologically challenging experience of their life."[19] Now, as many psychedelic advocates will point out, terror during a trip is often fleeting and can quickly be replaced by feelings of awe or joy. (Such was the case during Albert Hofmann's infamous LSD-fuelled bike ride.) Plus, even scary trips can yield therapeutic results. More interesting still, new research suggests that the "co-use of MDMA with psilocybin/LSD may buffer against challenging experiences."[20] But "may" is far from a guarantee. And if we want to have an honest conversation about the future of psychedelics, we need to admit that bad trips are a real risk.

Accessibility

Magic mushrooms may come cheap. But legal psychedelic-assisted therapy is expensive. In Oregon, which became the first state in America to legalize psilocybin in 2023, the first licensed facility charged $3,500 for a single trip—excluding the mushrooms themselves. [21]

While many accused the facility of price gouging, psychedelic-assisted therapy is also just inherently expensive. Imperial College's psilocybin trials—which, as a

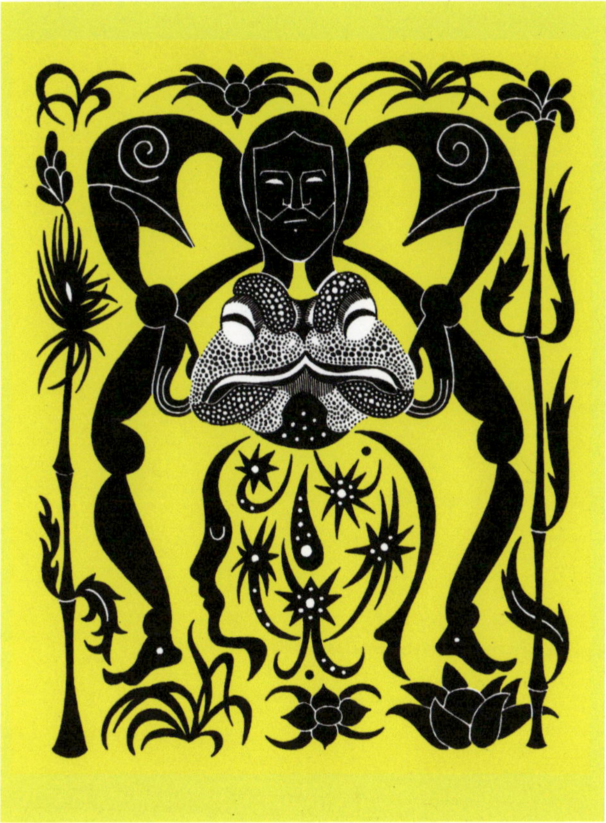

Figure 1
Sonoran Desert toad illustration by Boris Pramatarov.
Photo: Courtesy of the artist.

2019 story in the *Guardian* reported, took "multiple hours in clinical settings with expert guides"–cost "£2,000 each, including doctors and therapists, and many patients could need multiple treatments each year for continued benefits."[22] Even Robin Carhart-Harris, who runs Imperial College's Centre for Psychedelic Research and is one of the most bullish scientific figures in the field, admitted that "psilocybin therapy would be significantly more expensive than antidepressants and potentially more than counselling."[23]

One of the issues with psilocybin is that the trips can last as long as 8 hours, and generally the longer the trip, the greater the cost of supervision. But the cost issue also arises with ketamine–a Health Canada- and FDA-approved approved anaesthetic used off-label for psychedelic therapy–which occasions psychedelic effects that last as little as an hour. In 2021, when I enlisted in ketamine-assisted therapy at a private clinic in Toronto, it cost me more than $5,000 for six rounds of treatment. That may be cheaper than psilocybin-assisted therapy, but it's still prohibitively expensive for most.

All that said, some people are more optimistic about the cost of psychedelic-assisted therapy. In fact, a 2023 study in *Psychological Medicine* found that psilocybin-assisted therapy was actually more cost-effective than the combination of ongoing cognitive behavioural therapy and antidepressants, although not by much.[24]

Regardless, while psychedelics may be an important new treatment modality, they do little to solve the problem of access.

Conservation

If you want to understand the conservation crisis in psychedelics, start with peyote. A small, unassuming cactus often adorned with pink flowers, peyote grows throughout Mexico and southwestern Texas.[25] It also produces mescaline, a powerful hallucinogen that inspired Aldous Huxley's 1954 classic *The Doors of Perception*. But thousands of years before Huxley and his contemporaries began experimenting with mescaline, peyote was a sacred plant to dozens of Indigenous groups in the area, including the Huichol, whose spiritual peyote pilgrimages Dr. Jennings describes in chapter 1.

Today, the Huichol, Navajo, and other Indigenous groups across the U.S., Mexico, and even Canada continue to use peyote. While consuming peyote remains illegal for most in Canada and the U.S., Indigenous peoples are allowed to use peyote for religious purposes.

However, even with this important exemption, Indigenous access to peyote is under constant threat. Talking to the *Guardian* in 2022, Steven Van Heiden, president of the Cactus Conservation Institute, warned that the sacred cacti were threatened by everything from cattle grazing to wind turbines to oil and gas projects.[26] But with the surge in popularity of psychedelics in recent years, a new threat to peyote has emerged: overharvesting. "It's heartbreaking," Miriam Volat, executive director of the Indigenous Peyote Conservation Initiative told *DoubleBlind* magazine, adding that poaching had "increased dramatically" since she'd been working as an ecologist and facilitator.[27]

Because of the rise of overharvesting, Indigenous and environmental leaders like Volat argue that psychedelics legalization and decriminalization measures should exclude peyote to protect the plant. Some states and cities have heeded the call. For example, in 2021, two years after it decriminalized psychedelics, the Californian city of Santa Cruz "rolled back the law's provision on peyote, effectively recriminalizing the cactus."[28]

But other groups have taken a different tack. Decriminalize Nature, an organization whose mission is to "improve human health and well-being by decriminalizing and expanding access to entheogenic plants and fungi through political and community organizing, education and advocacy,"[29] argues that the decriminalization of peyote for all peoples is essential to the plant's conservation. Their position on peyote has put them at odds with organizations like the Indigenous Peyote Conservation Initiative, leading to some very public–and very ugly–spats.

While peyote seems to get the most press, many other psychedelics are also under threat. Of those, the strangest is probably the Sonoran Desert toad. The toad, whose scientific name is *Incilius alvarius*, is found in northwestern Mexico and southwestern U.S.[30] Its toxins, after being milked and dried, form a powerful crystallized psychedelic containing 5-MeO-DMT, which has been dubbed the "God Molecule" and occasions an incredibly potent psychedelic experience lasting between 20 and 30 minutes.[31] As the *New Yorker* reported in 2022, the popularity of smoking toad–thanks in no small part to public figures like Mike Tyson and Hunter Biden, who "credits toad for keeping him off cocaine for a year"–has exploded.[32] For the toad, this popularity has been disastrous. As the *New York Times* documented, "Scientists are warning that the scramble by users to obtain the toads – involving poaching, over-harvesting and illegal trafficking in arid expanses straddling the border with Mexico – could trigger a collapse in Sonoran desert toad populations."[33]

Similar concerns have arisen for iboga, a psychedelic tree shrub used by the Bwètè in spiritual rituals. In recent years, ibogaine (the psychedelic compound in iboga) has grown in popularity as a treatment for opioid addiction and PTSD. Although the drug is illegal in much of the world, including Canada and the U.S., it remains unregulated in places like Mexico and Costa Rica, where clinics have flourished. But as *National Geographic* reported, "Most iboga and ibogaine used by clinics around the world originates from plants poached from Gabon's forests and smuggled out of Cameroon."[34] To counteract this, a nascent fair-trade iboga industry has emerged in Gabon, but whether it will stick is unclear, especially because poached iboga is cheaper.

Another option, of course, is synthetics. Lab-made 5-MeO-DMT can be smoked without needing to milk a toad, for example. But this also raises the issue of who owns biological data and who profits. Cost also remains a problem. In 2018, *Quartz* reported that, pound-for-pound, synthetic psilocybin was "13 times the price of the drug as its [*sic*] sold on the street."[35] As companies scale up and processes get refined, production costs should come down. Should these drugs become legalized, costs should come down even further.

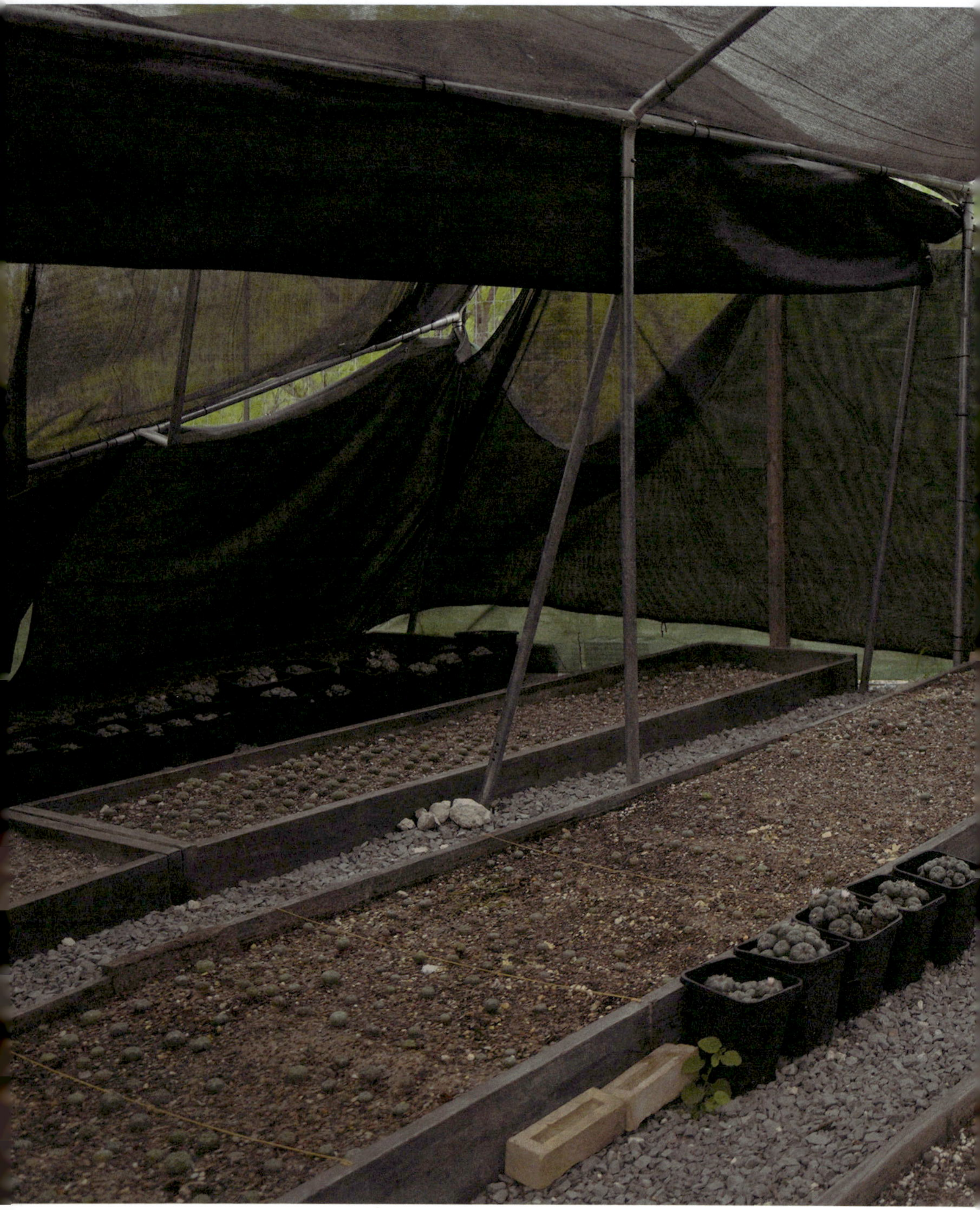

Figure 2 Adrian Primeaux, of the Yankton Sioux and Apache, stands in a peyote nursery.
Photo: AP Images / Jessie Wardarski.

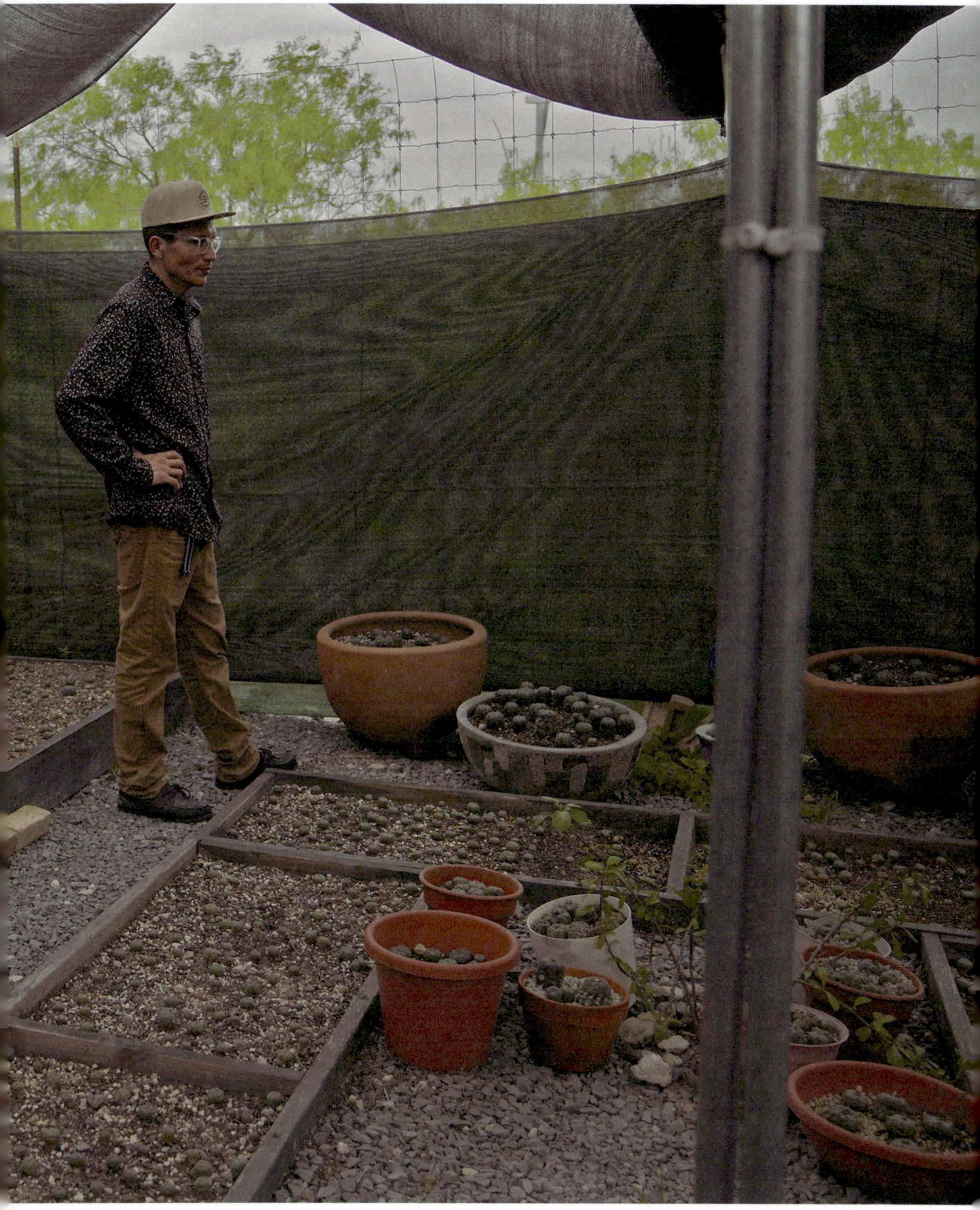

Patents, Nature, and Indigenous Knowledge

Writing in 2019, Michael Pollan wondered if there was any money to be made in psychedelics: "[T]his class of drugs offers [pharmaceutical companies] little if any intellectual property: psilocybin is a product of nature, and the patent on LSD expired years ago."[36] Therefore, he argued, there would be little incentive to spend the tens of millions of dollars needed to shepherd existing psychedelic drugs through costly and complex clinical trials.

But what he failed to anticipate was the emergence of so-called next-generation psychedelics: derivatives and analogues of existing molecules that, according to scientist and drug developer Dr. Jason Wallach, are tweaked to "create compounds with improved clinical profiles by optimizing the pharmacodynamics (effect of the drug on the body) and pharmacokinetics (effect of the body on the drug) to improve efficacy and tolerability."[37] Cybin, a publicly traded Canadian pharmaceutical company, is testing CYB003, a "psilocybin analog" with "fast onset and short duration of effect."[38] Translation: People get higher faster, and the trips don't last as long, which means that treatment time–and therefore costs–could be cut significantly. GH Research, "a clinical-stage biopharmaceutical company,"[39] is betting big on GH001, a form of 5-MeO-DMT designed for "administration via a proprietary inhalation approach."[40] (This, presumably, is more convenient than the old-school method of getting high on 5-MeO-DMT: smoking the dried venom of the Sonoran Desert toad.)

Developing next-generation psychedelics like these may sound niche, but it's a multibillion-dollar industry, and today, there are literally hundreds of patents on new psychedelic drugs. Why such excitement? Because if one of these companies can successfully bring a new drug to market, the upside is massive.

Consider the market for depression. In 2021, *Berkeley Political Review* reported that one in six Americans were on antidepressants–drugs that must be taken daily, are often ineffective, and can come with a bevy of side effects, including sexual dysfunction.[41] A new psilocybin-based drug, which works better than traditional antidepressants and has fewer unwanted side effects, for example, could rattle the entire industry–and make a ton of money.

While the prospect of handsome returns has many investors salivating, it has also caused a lot of controversy. In 2019, Compass Pathways patented its method of synthesizing psilocybin, which Peter Van der Heyden, the co-founder of psychedelics manufacturer Psygen Labs, called "unconscionable." Talking to *Wired*, the 70-year-old scientist said, "[Psilocybin is] something–I don't know how else to say it–a gift to mankind."[42]

That's a fair point. But psilocybin didn't arrive in America and the wider West as a bow-wrapped present from Mother Nature. It came via Gordon Wasson, who learned the secrets of the magic mushroom from Maria Sabina, a Mazatec shaman who suffered greatly for sharing said gift. The same can be said of many other psychedelic drugs, which have long been stewarded by Indigenous peoples across the world. Without the knowledge of Bwèté practitioners, for example, would companies be studying ibogaine as a potential treatment for opioid addiction? And, if not, what do these companies owe the Indigenous keepers of this knowledge?

Writing in *Double Blind* magazine, authors Alnoor Ladha and Rene Suša dubbed the psychedelic patent race just another form of colonialism:

> There have been attempts by a few Western pharmaceutical and biotechnical companies to partner with Indigenous peoples to modify the plants they have responsibly stewarded and/or offer them compensation, but this pales in comparison to the number of companies who have not and, while a step in the right direction, is negligible relative to the exploitive history of the modern pharmaceutical industry since its inception.[43]

That might be an overly cynical take. But if the nascent psychedelic drug industry truly wants to be a force for good in the world—as so many companies claim they are—they need to take a long, hard look at their business model.

Legalization

According to many of the scientists and scholars I talked to, it is not a matter of if psychedelics will be legalized but when. Between the multibillion-dollar psychedelic drug industry and increased activist pressure, it is almost impossible to fathom ongoing criminalization of psychedelics in Canada and the U.S., even with setbacks like the FDA's rejection of MDMA. Some of the dominoes, like psilocybin, are poised to fall soon, while others, such as 5-MeO-DMT and ibogaine, will likely take a little longer. If this happens, we will be forced to contend with a more nuanced question: How can we best legalize these drugs *responsibly*?

One approach might be to look to Australia, which became the first country to legalize MDMA and psilocybin for mental health treatment. Unsurprisingly, millions around the world applauded the move. But others, including Dr. Paul Liknaitzky, the head of the Clinical Psychedelic Lab at Monash University in Australia, were more apprehensive. Talking to the *Microdose* just weeks after the changes came into effect, Dr. Liknaitzky warned of a "scarcity of adequately trained and experienced clinicians that can responsibly support treatment."[44]

Other doctors in Australia were even more alarmed. Writing in the *Australian & New Zealand Journal of Psychiatry* in 2023, a quartet of researchers cautioned:

> Initial results have been promising by most standards, yet many questions remain. These include (but are not limited to): what are the best models of psychotherapeutic care to be delivered alongside the psychedelic dosing; what is the long-term safety profile, especially in terms of psychological recovery and relapse; and how might we differentiate those patients who will benefit from those for whom it could actually be detrimental. Until these questions have been addressed in empirical research, the decision to increase public access outside of clinical trials is questionable, if not concerning.[45]

These questions, while fundamental, represent only a fraction of the issues with legalization. Among the others are those I touched on in this very essay, including conservation, harm reduction, patents, and reciprocity. Plus, what about spiritual use? Recreational use? If doctors have a right to treat patients with psilocybin, shouldn't shamans? If private clinics are prohibitively expensive, should ordinary people be allowed to treat themselves? Or is that simply far too dangerous?

Time for Dialogue

These are complex, multi-layered questions that none of us can answer alone. They demand far more study, inquiry, and debate, with a special emphasis on including those voices that have long been marginalized and ignored. The hype of the early 1960s turned into the anti-drug hysteria of the 1970s because, at least in part, we stopped listening to each other. Both the promise and the pitfalls of psychedelic use are considerable, and much more work needs to be done to understand both how they work on the brain and the ways that they can be best administered. We won't ever have all the answers, yet if we can keep this conversation going, we can move closer to the thoughtful, nuanced engagement that psychedelics demand.

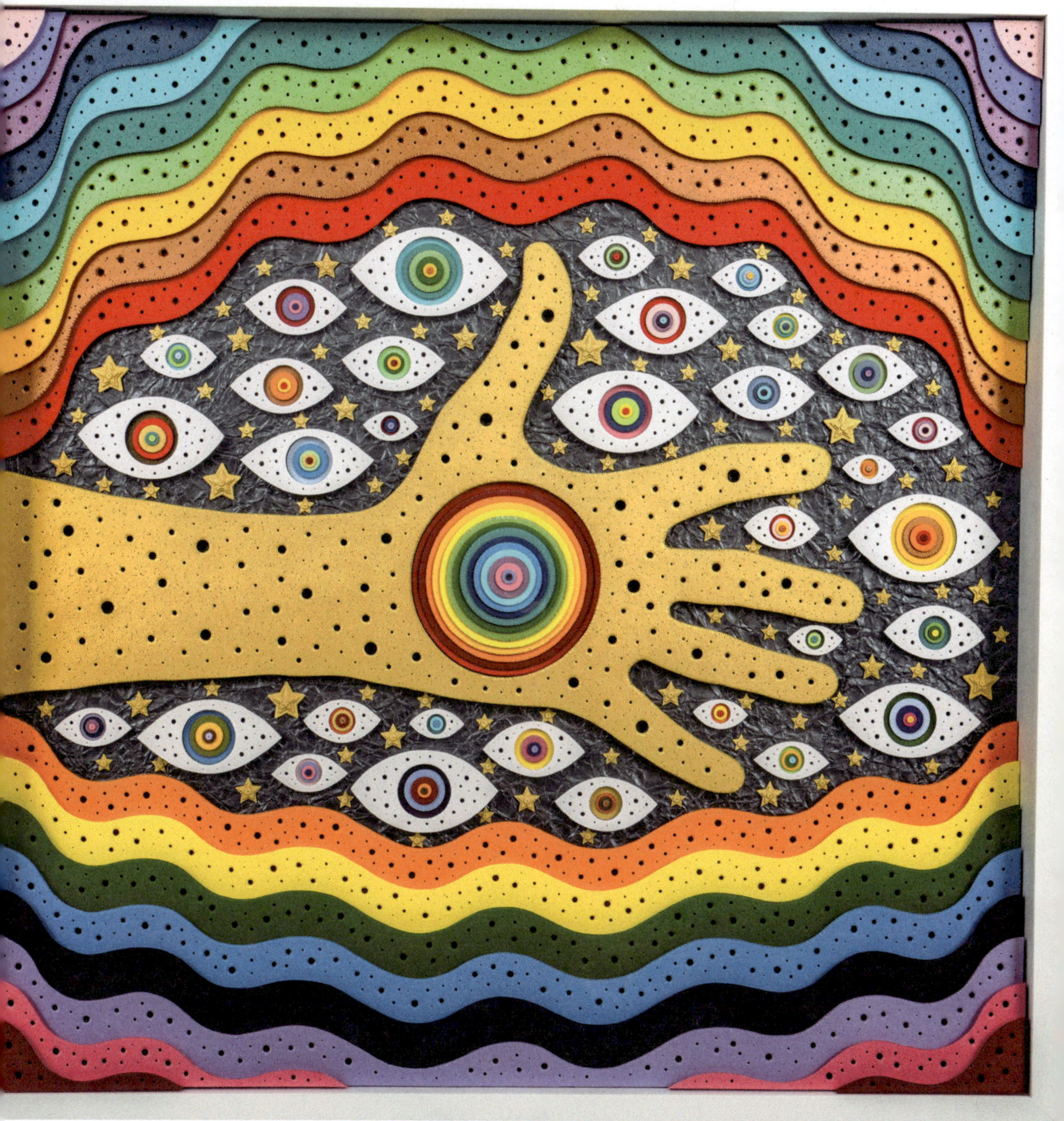

Figure 3
Breakthrough by Michael Velliquette, 2026. Artist Michael Velliquette describes his dimensional paper artwork as building portals to new worlds.

Photo: Courtesy of the artist.

1 Griffiths, R. R., Richards, W. A., Mccann, U., & Jesse, R. (2006). Psilocybin can occasion mystical-type experiences having substantial and sustained personal meaning and spiritual significance. *Psychopharmacology*, *187*, 268–283. https://doi.org/10.1007/s00213-006-0457-5.

2 Semley, J. (2020, April 27.) Turn on, tune in, cash in. *The New Republic*. https://newrepublic.com/article/157144/microdosing-magic-mushrooms-renaissance-psychedelic-drugs.

3 CBC Radio. (2018, December 28). *The big trip: How psychedelic drugs are changing lives and transforming psychiatry*. CBC. https://www.cbc.ca/radio/day6/the-big-trip-how-psychedelic-drugs-are-changing-lives-and-transforming-psychiatry-1.4955762.

4 Illing, S. (2019, January 10). *Psychedelic drugs and the future of mental health care*. Vox. https://www.vox.com/science-and-health/2019/1/10/18007558/denver-psilocybin-psychedelic-mushrooms-ayahuasca-depression-mental-health.

5 Sullivan, A. (2018, May 25). Andrew Sullivan: Why we should say yes to drugs. *New York* Magazine. https://nymag.com/intelligencer/2018/05/andrew-sullivan-why-we-should-say-yes-to-drugs.html.

6 Pollan, M. (2019). *How to change your mind*. Penguin.

7 Doblin, R. (2019, April). *The future of psychedelic-assisted psychotherapy* [Video]. TED Conferences. https://www.ted.com/talks/rick_doblin_the_future_of_psychedelic_assisted_psychotherapy.

8 Lindsay, B. (2022, April 9). *Footage of therapists spooning and pinning down patient in B.C. trial for MDMA therapy prompts review*. CBC. https://www.cbc.ca/news/canada/british-columbia/bc-mdma-therapy-videos-1.6400256.

9 *New York* Magazine Press Room. (2021, November 30). *New York* Magazine launches its first-ever investigative series podcast, cover story. *New York* Magazine. https://nymag.com/press/2021/11/new-york-launches-its-first-investigative-series-podcast.html.

10 Yaden, D. B., Potash, J. B., & Griffiths, R. R. (2022). Preparing for the bursting of the psychedelic hype bubble. *JAMA Psychiatry*, *79*(10), 943–944. https://doi.org/10.1001/jamapsychiatry.2022.2546.

11 Yaden et al. Preparing for the bursting.

12 Jerusalem Post staff. (2025, June 21). New Zealand approves medical use of psilocybin for depression treatment. *The Jerusalem Post*. https://www.jpost.com/health-and-wellness/article-858283.

13 Schumaker, E. (2025, June 11). New Texas law will fund research on psychedelic medicine. *POLITICO Pro*. https://subscriber.politicopro.com/article/2025/06/new-texas-law-will-fund-research-on-psychedelic-medicine-00401279.

14 UC Berkeley Center for the Science of Psychedelics. (n.d.). *Understanding risk in the use of psychedelics*. https://psychedelics.berkeley.edu/understanding-risk/; and Calleja-Conde, J., Morales-García, J. A., Echeverry-Alzate, V., Bühler, K. M., Giné, E., & López-Moreno, J. A. (2022). Classic psychedelics and alcohol use disorders: A systematic review of human and animal studies. *Addiction Biology*, *27*(6), Article e13229. https://doi.org/10.1111/adb.13229.

15 Hu, J. C. (2022, January 17). 5 questions for Kristin Nash. *The Microdose*. https://themicrodose.substack.com/p/5-questions-for-kristin-nash.

16 Blanton, A. M., Parikh, P., Zhou, S., Mohamed, M., Ufret-Vincenty, R. L., & Mancini, R. (2025). Self-inflicted transorbital intracranial foreign body following ingestion of hallucinogenic psilocybin mushrooms. *American Journal of Ophthalmology Case Reports*, *39*, Article 102359. https://doi.org/10.1016/j.ajoc.2025.102359.

17 UC Berkeley Center for the Science of Psychedelics. (n.d.). *Ibogaine*. https://psychedelics.berkeley.edu/substance/ibogaine/.

18 Hamby, C. (2023, February 20). "A fraught new frontier in telehealth: Ketamine." *The New York Times*. https://www.nytimes.com/2023/02/20/us/ketamine-telemedicine.html.

19 Zeifman, R. J., Kettner, H., Pagni, B. A., Mallard, A., Roberts, D. E., Erritzoe, D., Ross, S., & Carhart-Harris, R. (2023). Co-use of MDMA with psilocybin/LSD may buffer against challenging experiences and enhance positive experiences. *Scientific Reports, 13*, Article 13645. https://doi.org/10.1038/s41598-023-40856-5.

20 Zeifman et al. Co-use of MDMA with psilocybin/LSD.

21 Krishnan, M. (2023, May 9). *America's first legal shroom therapy center will charge $3,500 for "high dose" trips*. Vice. https://www.vice.com/en/article/wxjdan/oregon-legal-shroom-therapy-center-psilocybin.

22 Jacobs, J. (2019, July 15). "They broke my mental shackles": Could magic mushrooms be the answer to depression? *The Guardian*. https://www.theguardian.com/science/2019/jun/10/magic-mushrooms-treatment-depression-aztecs-psilocybin-mental-health-medicine.

23 Jacobs. "They broke my mental shackles."

24 McCrone, P., Fisher, H., Knight, C., Harding, R., Schlag, A. K., Nutt, D. J., & Neill, J. C. (2023). Cost-effectiveness of psilocybin-assisted therapy for severe depression: Exploratory findings from a decision analytic model. *Psychological Medicine, 53*(16), 7619–7626. https://doi.org/10.1017/S0033291723001411.

25 Peyote. (2022, January 25). In *Wikipedia*. https://www.en.wikipedia.org/wiki/Peyote.

26 Golden, H. (2022, December 9). Inside the battle to save the sacred peyote ceremony: "We're in dire straits." *The Guardian*. https://www.theguardian.com/us-news/2022/dec/09/peyote-native-americanmedicine-nacna-federal-protection.

27 Hendelman, A. D. (2022, August 3). The peyote plot: The Indigenous fight to conserve the sacred plant and the spiritual medicine it contains. *Double Blind*. https://www.doubleblindmag.com/the-peyote-plot/.

28 Adlin, B. (2021, October 2). *Santa Cruz removes peyote and other mescaline-containing cacti from psychedelics decriminalization law*. Marijuana Moment. https://www.marijuanamoment.net/santa-cruz-removes-peyote-and-other-mescaline-containing-cacti-from-psychedelicsdecriminalization-law/.

29 Decriminalize Nature. (n.d.). *Purpose statement*. https://www.decriminalizenature.org/about.

30 Colorado River toad. (2021, February 6). In *Wikipedia*. https://www.en.wikipedia.org/wiki/Colorado_River_toad.

31 UC Berkeley Center for the Science of Psychedelics. (n.d.). *5-MEo-DMT therapy information*. https://www.psychedelics.berkeley.edu/substance/5-meo-dmt/.

32 de Greef, K. (2022, March 17). The Pied Piper of psychedelic toads. *The New Yorker*. https://www.newyorker.com/magazine/2022/03/28/the-pied-piper-of-psychedelic-toads.

33 Romero, S. (2022, March 20). Demand for this toad's psychedelic toxin is booming. *The New York Times*. https://www.nytimes.com/2022/03/20/us/toad-venom-psychedelic.html#:~:text=But%20in%20a%20sign%20of,in%20Sonoran%20desert%20toad%20populations.

34 Nuwer, R. (2023, March 8). The psychoactive drug ibogaine could save lives—and everyone wants to cash in. *National Geographic*. https://www.nationalgeographic.com/animals/article/ibogainepschedelic-drug-root-fair-trade-gabon.

35 Goldhill, O. (2018, March 24). *Scientists who want to study psychedelic mushrooms have to pay $7,000 per gram*. Quartz. https://www.qz.com/1235963/scientists-who-want-to-study-psychedelicmushrooms-have-to-pay-7000-per-gram.

36 Pollan. *How to change your mind*.

37 Wallach, J. (2021, October 1). The Need for New Psychedelic Compounds. 2021. *Psychology Today*. https://www.psychologytoday.com/nz/blog/pathways-of-progress/202110/the-need-for-new-psychedelic-compounds.

38 Cybin. (n.d.). *CYB003*. https://www.cybin.com/cyb003/.

39 GH Research. (n.d.). *Company*. https://www.ghres.com/company.

40 GH Research. (n.d.). *Pipeline*. https://www.ghres.com/pipeline.

41 Pagaduan, M. (2021, November 7). America's epidemic of antidepressants. *Berkeley Political Review*. https://www.bpr.berkeley.edu/2021/11/07/americas-epidemic-of-antidepressants/.

42 Semley, J. (2022, July 26). The high-stakes race to engineer new psychedelic drugs. *Wired*. https://www.wired.com/story/race-to-engineer-new-psychedelic-drugs/.

43 Ladha, A., & Suša, R. (2022, November 29). Why the "psychedelic renaissance" is just colonialism by another name. *Double Blind*. https://www.doubleblindmag.com/colonialism-byanother-name/.

44 Hu, J. C. (2023, July 24). The view from Australia: 5 questions for psychedelics researcher Paul Liknaitzky. *The Microdose*. https://www.themicrodose.substack.com/p/the-view-from-australia-5-questions.

45 Rossell, S. L., Meikle, S. E., Williams, M. L., & Castle, D. J. (2023). Why didn't the TGA consult with Australian researchers and clinicians with experience in psilocybin-assisted psychotherapy for treatment-resistant major depressive disorder? *Australian & New Zealand Journal of Psychiatry, 57*(7), 935–936. https://doi.org/10.1177/00048674231172691.

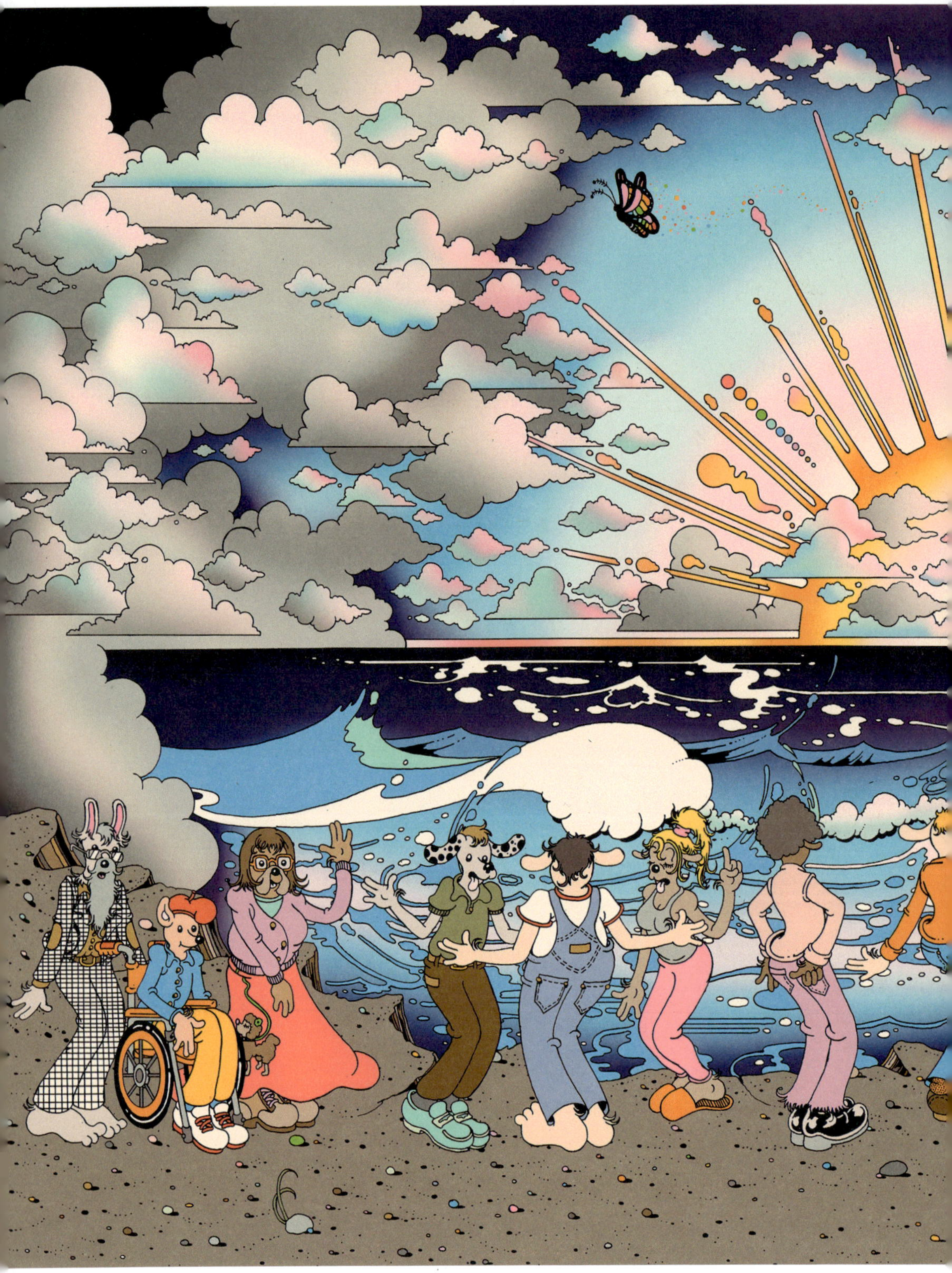

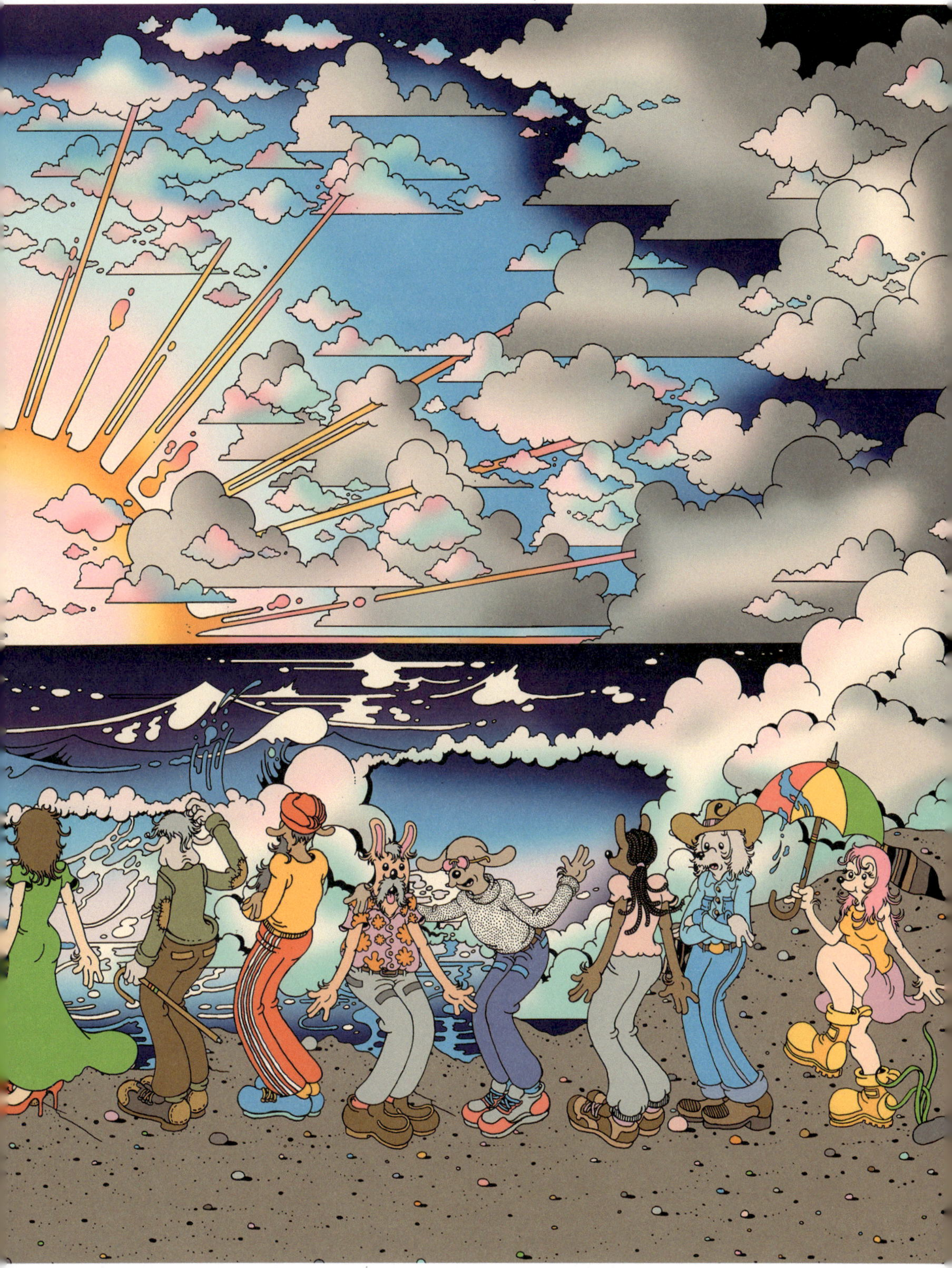

Published by the Royal Ontario Museum, with the generous support of the Louise Hawley Stone Charitable Trust.

ROM, 100 Queen's Park, Toronto, Ontario, M5S 2C6
rom.on.ca

Cover design: Tara Winterhalt

AVP, Publishing & Editorial Content: Sheeza Sarfraz
Senior Designer: Tara Winterhalt
Communications Coordinator: Monika Tragarz
Copyeditor: Marnie Lamb
Proofreader: Marnie Lamb

Artwork Details:
iii: Xiaojing Yan, *Magic Rabbit* (2026).
iv–v: Annie MacDonell, *Ego Death Trip* (2023).
vi: Fly agaric mushrooms by Paul Eekhoff © ROM.
viii–ix: José Benítez Sánchez, *The Deification of Tatéi Haitsi Kipiri, Our Mother Dew Soul* (1975).
xiv–xv: Martin Sharp, *Explosion, Jimi Hendrix* (1967).
12–13: Unrecorded Huichol artist, Harvest yarn painting (about 1950–75).
42–43: J. Cushing, *Grateful Dead, The Doors, U.F.O, Captain Speed* (1967).
64–65: Pablo Amaringo, *El Encanto de las Piedras*, as featured in the book *The Ayahuasca Visions of Pablo Amaringo* by Howard G. Charing and Peter Cloudsley.
82–83: Illustration for UCSF Magazine by Marcos Chin.
100–101: Christi Belcourt, *Plant Medicine*.
114–115: Michael Velliquette, *Breakthrough* (2026).
132–33: Illustration by Brian Blomerth © ROM (2026).

Library and Archives Canada Cataloguing in Publication
Title: Psychedelics: culture. crime. cure. / edited by Justin Jennings and Colin J. Fleming.
Other titles: Psychedelics (Toronto, Ont.)
Names: Jennings, Justin, editor. | Fleming, Colin J., editor.
Royal Ontario Museum, publisher, host institution.
Description: A companion to the Royal Ontario Museum exhibition, June 6, 2026 to December 6, 2026.
Identifiers: Canadiana 20260165042 | ISBN 9780888545374 (softcover)
Subjects: LCSH: Hallucinogenic drugs—Exhibitions.
LCGFT: Exhibition catalogs.
Classification: LCC RM324.8 .P79 2026 | DDC 615.7/883—dc23

Printed in Canada.
ROM is an agency of the Government of Ontario.

Contributors

Justin Jennings is Senior Curator of Latin American Archaeology at Royal Ontario Museum and Associate Professor of Anthropology at the University of Toronto. He has published 17 books, most recently *Rethinking Global Governance* (2023), *Understanding Early Large-Scale Collectives* (2025), and *Did the Ancient State Exist?* (2026).

Erika Dyck is a professor and a Canada Research Chair in the History of Health & Social Justice at the University of Saskatchewan. She has written several books, including *Psychedelic Psychiatry* (2008), *The Acid Room* (2022), and *Psychedelics: A Visual Odyssey* (2024).

Dr. Manoj K. Doss is a cognitive neuropsychopharmacologist at Dell Medical School at the University of Texas at Austin. His research aims to understand the neurocognitive mechanisms of psychoactive drugs, with a focus on how psychedelics impact learning and memory in humans.

Alexandria S. Coles is the Manager of Clinical Research at University Health Network, with experience in the conduct and management of psychedelic clinical trials for mental health disorders.

Dr. M. Ishrat Husain is an associate professor in the Department of Psychiatry and the Cameron Wilson Chair in Depression Studies at the University of Toronto. He also serves as the Department Head and Program Medical Director of the Centre for Mental Health, University Health Network.

Kelly Boutsalis is a Mohawk journalist from the Six Nations of the Grand River reserve. Currently living in Toronto, she devotes the bulk of her work to highlighting Indigenous stories. Her byline has appeared in *The New York Times*, *Toronto Star*, *Toronto Life*, and *The Walrus*.

Colin J. Fleming is a graduate of Columbia University who collaborates with experts at the Royal Ontario Museum to write everything from ad copy to magazine stories. His writing has appeared in *Toronto Life*, *The Daily Beast*, and on CBC Comedy, among others. He is also the co-creator of the *SickKids VS* podcast.